Ecovillage Living

Ecovillage Living

Restoring the Earth and Her People

Edited by Hildur Jackson and Karen Svensson

Would it be an exaggeration to claim that the emergence of the ecovillage movement is the most significant event in the 20th century? I don't think so.
Ted Trainer, University of New South Wales, Australia

Gaia Trust

Green Books

The 15 Elements of Ecovillage Living

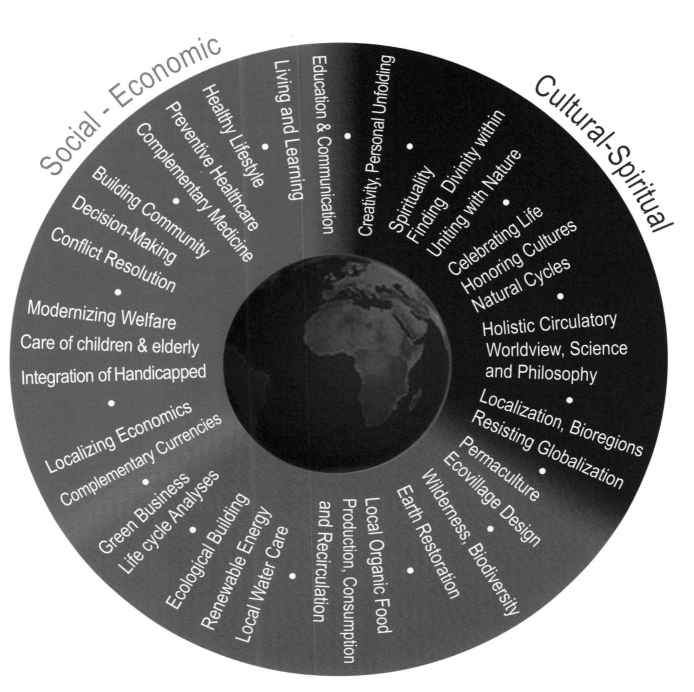

Social - Economic
- Healthy Lifestyle
- Preventive Healthcare
- Complementary Medicine
- Building Community
- Decision-Making
- Conflict Resolution
- Modernizing Welfare
- Care of children & elderly
- Integration of Handicapped
- Localizing Economics
- Complementary Currencies
- Green Business
- Life cycle Analyses

Ecological
- Ecological Building
- Renewable Energy
- Local Water Care
- Local Organic Food Production, Consumption and Recirculation
- Earth Restoration
- Wilderness, Biodiversity
- Ecovillage Design
- Permaculture

Cultural-Spiritual
- Living and Learning
- Education & Communication
- Creativity, Personal Unfolding
- Spirituality
- Finding Divinity within
- Uniting with Nature
- Celebrating Life
- Honoring Cultures
- Natural Cycles
- Holistic Circulatory Worldview, Science and Philosophy
- Localization, Bioregions
- Resisting Globalization

Concept: Hildur Jackson, Karen Svensson
Design: Kolja Hejgaard

The above elements constitute a broad definition of sustainability, including social and cultural/spiritual dimensions. A good way of restoring the Earth, ourselves and other living beings is to integrate the principles of Ecovillage Living in daily life.

Welcome Dear Reader!

Over the past decades, people around the world have experimented with alternatives to a society, which they consider destructive. The ecovillage vision was born out of these experiments, providing solutions both urban and rural; both in the northern and in the southern hemisphere; and on every scale, from the family nucleus to local communities and global organizations. Ecovillages are basically a matter of living on the Earth with respect for all beings and natural systems. They embody a mindful lifestyle, which can be continued indefinitely in the future. As such, they are shaping nothing less than a new culture, designed to restore the Earth and her people.

This book brings together the best of knowledge and experience from ecovillages around the planet, directly from the mouths of those who have pioneered the development to date. It is structured around the ecological, social and spiritual/cultural dimensions, which ecovillages integrate with varying emphasis according to the motivation of their initiators. It should be especially useful for those thousands of people who every year make the decision to take personal action, by integrating more sustainable practices and habits into their daily lives; starting up a new ecovillage project; joining an existing ecovillage; or by increasing the sustainability of their families, communities, neighborhoods, and organizations.

For the purposes of this publication, we have subdivided each of the three ecovillage dimensions (ecological, social and cultural-spiritual) into five elements – 15 in all, as shown in the ecovillage sustainability circle (opposite page). These elements make up the main building blocks of ecovillages. Each element is described in detail through articles and interviews, and illustrated with examples.

You will see that, though ecovillages build on a common vision, they differ greatly from each other according to the difference in focus placed on their ecological, social, and/or cultural-spiritual dimensions. They are also greatly influenced by different climatic conditions, their natural environment and prevalent local cultures. This book will present you with pictorial overviews of 15 different ecovillages (in the sections of the book where they have most to offer). It is also rich in examples and photos from other sustainable communities the world over, and may help you ask yourself if this is how you want to live, or whether you would like to implement some of the principles of ecovillage living in your current living environment.

The ecovillage vision can also be applied in the political sphere, offering an alternative to commercial globalization. In a recent revolutionary development, a number of countries in the Southern hemisphere are beginning to study the ecovillage concept as a possible basis for a new development model that addresses real local problems rather than the needs of foreign commercial interests.

We hope that this book will inspire you, providing a glimpse of the enormous potential for positive change that is available to us and can lead us into a more harmonious and satisfying future.

Hildur Jackson

Karen Svensson

Editors

From left: Hildur Jackson and Karen Svensson in front of the Gaia Villages/GEN offices with a representative of a Korean ecovillage group. Photo: courtesy Yeon-Hyun Cho.

Ecovillage Living:
Restoring the Earth and Her People

Contents

The Social Dimension · 75

The Cultural-Spiritual Dimension · 106

Ecovillages in the Southern Hemisphere 133

The Process of Creating an Ecovillage 143

Expanding the Ecovillage Concept 153

Resources 176

First published in the UK in 2002 by Green Books Ltd., Foxhole, Dartington, Totnes, Devon TQ9 6EB
www.greenbooks.co.uk

In association with Gaia Trust, www.gaia.org

Copyright © Gaia Trust 2002

Excerpts from this book may be reproduced strictly for non-profit educational purposes, and accompanied with a source reference.

Design by Karen Svensson, with thanks to Kolja Hejgaard for technical and DTP support.

Cover: straw roof over the community building in Tlholego ecovillage, South Africa (pages 141-142). Photo: Declan Kennedy.

Printed by Book Print, Barcelona, Spain.

A catalogue record for this book is available from the British Library.   ISBN 1 903998 16 6

With thanks to all contributors: content contributors to this book are from all over the world, mostly but not exclusively from ecovillages and other communities, and include local government officials, educators, environmental activists, as well as people from the business sector, international organizations, and NGOs. Most are members of GEN, the Global Ecovillage Network. For information about GEN, related literature, contact information to a wide range of ecovillages, and much more, visit www.gaia.org

GEN (The Global Ecovillage Network) is a grass roots non-profit organization that links together ecovillages and related projects worldwide. The Network supports models of sustainable living globally, in order to inspire and encourage the creation of more viable lifestyles on this planet.

Huehuecoyotl ecovillage in Mexico (page 124) © Art Ludwig

The Right to Realize a Dream

Preface by Hildur Jackson

Humans are a problem-solving species, capable of thinking, learning and manifesting thoughts and dreams. Often dreams are reactions to problems and are thus a problem solving mechanism. We dream and imagine how things can be better. The dream lingers, grows and has the possibility of manifesting in the physical realm. Dreams can be expressions of love and divine inspiration. The idea of Paradise is such an inspirational manifestation, which people have imagined and painted for thousands of years. Dreaming is our birthright.

Today, many people dream of community, beautiful surroundings, and meaningful jobs. These people have an inner craving for a more balanced and spiritual life, a loving place for their children to grow up, and a lifestyle which does not force them to leave their children all day as a price for being full members of society. A place full of life, joy and sharing, of living close to nature with plants and animals around them, where love is more possible. All the necessary wisdom, knowledge and technology are available to help this dream come true for everybody on this planet. Ecovillages are emerging attempts at realizing it, or at the very least parts of it. They are paintings in progress, of an envisioned Paradise on Earth.

If we build this "Paradise" to live in, it will not be problem-free. That would be too boring. But it will be a place reflecting the best of our knowledge and insight, and a place where we feel happy to raise our children. And there is not just one, but a host of different possible versions of it: it can be a place where one learns how the physical realm works (i.e. the laws of nature); how to connect with the spiritual realms; how to become love and experience the unity of all living beings; to be co-creative in preserving and developing three million years of "bio-logical" evolution; and how to create an integral society, making the local a holographic reflection of the whole. An American group formulated the vision as follows: we want to make a place where we would like to incarnate as children in our next life.

This book looks at the building of the ecovillage dream, which can be realized in many ways through intentional sustainable communities (family-scale or village-scale), earth or people restoration projects, sustainable neighborhoods, localization efforts or integral transformative practices.

We do not know of any ecovillage which claims to have reached perfection. All of these settlements are works in progress, exhibiting constant improvements and renewal in their physical, social and spiritual/cultural setup. Enjoy your journey in their midst.

What is an Ecovillage?

by Karen Svensson

Ecovillages embody a way of living. They are grounded in the deep understanding that all things and all creatures are interconnected, and that our thoughts and actions have an impact on our environment.

Ecovillages are communities of people who strive to lead a sustainable lifestyle in harmony with each other, other living beings and the Earth. Their purpose is to combine a supportive social-cultural environment with a low-impact lifestyle. As a new societal structure, the ecovillage goes beyond today's dichotomy of urban versus rural settlements: it represents a widely applicable model for the planning and reorganization of human settlements in the 21st Century.

The deep motivation for ecovillages or intentional communities is the need to reverse the gradual disintegration of supportive social-cultural structures and the upsurge of destructive environmental practices on our planet. Underlying the concept of the ecovillage is the desire to take responsibility for one's own life; to create a future which, contrary to the depleting energies of the "mechanical" world dominated by organizational giants, is regenerative for the individual and for nature, and thereby sustainable into the indefinite future. A future which we would like to bequeath our children, so they, and in turn their children, may grow up as balanced and healthy human beings.

Ecovillages embody a way of living. They are grounded in the deep understanding that all things and all creatures are interconnected, and that our thoughts and actions have an impact on our environment. Based on this philosophy, ecovillages build on varying combinations of three dimensions:

> ### Ecology
> ### Community (the social dimension)
> ### Culture-spirituality

Today there are as many different versions of the ecovillage as there are ecovillages. Each has reached its individual level of development, and reflects the particular creativity and inspiration of its builders. Although some ecovillages have been in existence for over 20 years, and are starting to present the picture of quite complete experiments in sustainable living, others are just starting to emerge. Though in the past ecovillages may sometimes have been seen as rather marginal and idealistic settlements, we are gradually witnessing the advent of the "mainstream ecovillage", which integrates ecovillage principles while also fitting in with mainstream lifestyles and expectations (e.g. streamlined architecture; a mix of rental and privately owned housing; both shared and private facilities, including common and private gardens; mixed backgrounds, occupations and ages). These ecovillages allow for a diversity, both in societal composition and in people's individual focus and degree of participation in the community, which reflects mainstream circumstances.

The following section presents an overview of the three main dimensions of ecovillages, which are integrated with varying emphasis in different settlements. These dimensions also represent the three areas we can choose to focus on when establishing more sustainable lifestyles for ourselves in other settings (e.g. our family, neighborhood or organization).

The Ecological Dimension of an Ecovillage

The ecological dimension of ecovillages denotes people's connection to the living Earth: the soil, water, wind, plants and animals. It ranges from an expressed intention to save energy and recycle waste to a more all-round commitment to low-impact living, integrating village-based energy systems, water treatment plants, Earth restoration, permaculture (e.g. for food production) and ecological building.

Ecology means, among other things*:
Growing organic food as much as possible within the community bioregion
Creating "living" homes out of natural, locally available materials, and using local (architectural) traditions
Using village-based integrated renewable energy systems
Ecological business principles (local green business)
Assessing the life cycle of products used in the ecovillage from a social/spiritual and ecological point of view
Preserving clean soil, water and air through proper energy and waste management
Protecting and encouraging biodiversity and safeguarding wilderness areas

* Partly from What is an Ecovillage? *by Hildur Jackson, Marti Mueller and Helena Norberg-Hodge*

The Social Dimension of an Ecovillage

The social dimension of ecovillages refers to people's desire to spend more time together, and to create a supportive environment where one can thrive both as a free individual and as part of a group. Ecovillages are small enough that everyone feels empowered. In the Western world, among the deafening noise of industrial concerns, over-communication and political megastructures, the voice of the individual person is often not heard. In an ecovillage, this voice is loud and clear. People are able to participate in making decisions that affect their own lives and that of the community on a transparent basis (i.e. with total openness). For children, ecovillages provide a loving environment where they are involved in daily tasks such as gardening and building. This enables them to learn a variety of skills through practical experience. Learning to function as responsible members of a community also helps them think for themselves while at the same time remembering their place in the whole. Generally, ecovillages are able to foster a balance between personal freedom and one's responsibility to others, creating free and purposeful human beings who learn to identify and meet their own needs as well as those of the society they live in.

Community means*:
Recognizing and relating to others
Sharing common resources and providing mutual aid
Learning to make good decisions and solve conflicts
Emphasizing holistic and preventive health practices
Providing meaningful work and sustenance to all members
Allowing for a whole life for children, the elderly, and marginal groups
Promoting unending education
Encouraging unity through respect for differences
Fostering cultural expression
Green Economics

Economic Ramifications

The economic setup of ecovillages is often designed to fit a supportive social and family life by reducing financial requirements to allow a shift in lifestyle. One can cut down on commuting time by seeking work closer to home, even if it means a lower income, and reducing external work hours altogether. This in turn allows more social and family time, and can leave room for building up a local business. In practice, this setup often means adopting principles of voluntary simplicity, increasingly integrating work- and private lives, and creating income-earning occupations within the community. Partial self-sufficiency in the form of local food and energy production – combined with a strong communal network – provides an added sense of security for individuals or groups to dare tackle a change in economic setup. Sometimes a community will help launch new ventures by supporting its initiators during rocky beginnings. In many cases the creation of an alternative economic system can add to an ecovillage's independence from the global systems, and strengthen the community. Alternative economics are

At the ecovillage of Torri Superiore, Italy, community members and volunteers help restore the roof of a house on top of the hillside, passing each other building materials from terrace to terrace: the principles of community at work. Photo: Torri Superiore.

often based on the principle of gift giving and exchange, and therefore also directly related to social parameters and values.

Economic principles to support ecovillages encompass:
Complementary currencies (LETS systems, Friendly Favors, ecovillage currency)
Alternative banks
Voluntary simplicity
Local income-generating activities (green businesses, consulting)
Expanded informal economy (communal meals, services)

The Cultural/Spiritual Dimension of an Ecovillage

Through the integration of Cultural and Spiritual principles into their fabric, many intentional ecovillages echo the re-birth of cultural traditions throughout the world, and return to a way of living where harmony with all living beings, including our Earth, is the backbone of daily life. Ecovillages embody a sense of unity with the natural world. They foster recognition of human life and the Earth itself as part of the larger cosmos. Though some ecovillages choose a well-defined spiritual path, many do not place the emphasis on spiritual practices as such. However, observing natural cycles, and respecting the Earth and all living beings on it, they tend to maintain, re-create or find new cultural expressions of humans' connectedness with nature and the universe.

Culture and Spirituality are expressed through*:
Fostering a sense of joy and belonging through rituals and celebrations following natural cycles (e.g. maypole, harvesting feast, Midsummer)

Emphasizing creativity and the arts as an expression of unity and interrelationship to our universe
Expressing a spiritual world view of global interconnectedness
Respecting that spirituality manifests in many ways
Respecting the expression of different cultures
Facilitating personal growth and integral spiritual practices

Traditional Villages

In the northern hemisphere, ecovillages are mostly of an intentional nature, as they try to re-build communities from scratch based on their chosen focus (ecological, social and/or cultural-spiritual). In the global South, 50-75% of the population is still living in villages whose social, cultural and spiritual fabric remains intact, and whose inhabitants largely survive on subsistence economies (supported by self-sufficient agricultural production). Farmers are increasingly forced to shift from polycultures to mono cultures on the land.

The ecovillage concept provides viable alternatives to popular exodus and growing monocultures in the southern hemisphere: networks of villages (e.g. Sri Lanka, Senegal, Burkina Faso, India) and progressive governments are today seeking to integrate ecovillage principles into the traditional village structures, to achieve a form of village-based sustainable development which meets people's basic needs with local resources, while also adapting to more modern requirements and market demands.

Because of their particular configuration, we have reserved a separate section to ecovillages in the southern hemisphere (see page 134).

Picture below: painting by Hildur Jackson of Fjordvang in Denmark, where the Global Ecovillage Network originated. © Hildur Jackson

Ecovillage Design Patterns

by Hildur Jackson

Varying the focus on one or more of the three dimensions of ecovillages results in different patterns of village design.

In other words, people's motivation for building the village will to a large extent determine the design pattern which they opt for:

Ecologically oriented ecovillages start from the perspective of developing a low-impact lifestyle, often alongside Earth restoration. The use of permaculture analyses for studying the land scape and designing the future ecovillage is becoming more and more widespread. Permaculture designs include placement according to the four directions, exposure to sun and wind, observation and use of rainfall, capacity to retain water, etc. The placement and architecture of houses are decided based on these observations and other ecological principles. The same is true for the placement and methods of food production activities, energy production, water treatment facilities, the recycling of waste, green business and the building process itself. Crystal Waters Permaculture Village in Australia is an example of an ecologically inspired ecovillage, based on permaculture. It is largely designed to preserve and restore the environment. A number of North American projects have used permaculture as their organizing principle (see resources, page189). Other ecovillages have combined permaculture design with social or spiritual elements (Hertha, Munksøgaard). The most important thing to remember is that each projects needs to define their priorities clearly.

The socially motivated cohousings have the community house as their center and focus. The residential houses are built closely together along a street/path or around common areas (playgrounds, terraces). Often the houses are subdivided into clusters to create more interaction and community within each cluster. Cars are kept outside at the entrance of the cohousing/ecovillage.

Picture above: the plan of Crystal Waters Permaculture Village in Australia is based primarily on ecological considerations (see article page 21). Map: courtesy Max Lindegger.

Houses are typically not higher than 1½ - 2 floors. Socially inspired ecovillages are built largely around the same principles, including other considerations. In Hertha in Denmark (inspired by Steiner philosophy) the whole village is based on reversed social integration, where "normal" people are integrated in the lives of mentally handicapped youth. The houses are built around the youth homes, and the communal facilities (theater/meeting room, kitchen, dining room). Hertha runs a biodynamic farm, a bakery, a silversmith and a Steiner research laboratory manned by the "young people" and their teachers. It also houses the office of LØS, the Danish Association of Ecovillages. In this, it is a good example of how a social structure impacts on, and actually generates, an economic setup which works well for residents. Also Zegg in Germany is famous for its social experimentation. Zegg women have researched the spirit of womanhood in community. The ecovillage also focuses on raising children in community. Their "sister" ecovillage, Tamera (Portugal), focuses on the creation of healing biotopes and Peace processes (see Tamera and biotopes page 16).

Ecovillages, which focus on a cultural dimension, may choose to have a theater in the middle of the village (Huehuecoyotl, Mexico, built by artists) or another type of cultural/celebration hall (for dancing, music, arts and seasonal celebrations). In traditional villages in the Southern Hemisphere, there is often a central meeting place (a tree, a well, a celebration hall) where villagers seek advice from elders, tell stories which are remembered from generation to generation, and celebrate (e.g. seasonal festivals). In traditional Scandinavian villages the church (spiritual), the inn (social), and the assembly hall (cultural) were placed next to the village pond/well.

Spiritually oriented ecovillages can be built around a meditation hall, so it is easy for everybody to access. This is true for Auroville, with the Matrimandir as its center, including a meditation hall and meeting rooms.

Peter Dawkins in England proposes energy line analyses (landscape temples like a chakra structure) as a pattern for placing the different functions of a community and as a way of building according to spiritual and natural laws. The underground temple of Damanhur is situated where three energy lines cross each other in a special mountain, so they can communicate better with the whole world. Some spiritual groups (Maharishi) want to build the village in the shape of a mandala. For many cultural and spiritual villages, Vastu Sastra principles (Indian architecture), Feng Shui or other similar design systems are important to incorporate.

No matter what the focus is when starting an ecovillage, nothing is right or wrong. This introduction is just to help you clarify what you think is important, and to bear in mind that careful design is a necessity for sound organic growth in the long term. Many ecovillages start with existing structures (buildings, proximity of a village, city neighborhood) and planning stipulations, or other factors, which partly determine their pattern of development. In many cases, discrepancies between ideas and reality also place certain restrictions on the realization of original design plans. However the important thing is to achieve a process which is as fluid as possible, and in this respect we can learn from others' experiences. Assimilating the experiences and the advice of veterans is what can help us accelerate the process of establishing sustainable settlements. Today, there is fertile ground for the expansion of sustainable lifestyles. Where the ecovillage concept previously may have seemed like the rather marginal venture of a happy few, it is now gaining momentum and being embraced by increasing numbers of people the world over. We are gradually approaching the advent of the mainstream ecovillage, a form of sustainable community, which harmonizes with modern requirements and lifestyles, while at the same reflecting our interconnectedness with all of life. This is an expression of the age-old holographic worldview, where each part is a reflection of the whole (microcosm/macrocosm): likewise, the ecovillage microcosm is starting to reflect an urge emerging in the macrocosmic world to re-shape our reality according to basic human needs and laws of existence.

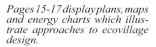

Pages 15-17 display plans, maps and energy charts which illustrate approaches to ecovillage design.

Left: *plan of Hertha ecovillage in Denmark, based on the social principles of Rudolf Steiner (Anthroposophy). The project features main living quarters in the center, surrounded by rental apartments and privately owned houses. The rest of the land is reserved for biodynamic farming.*
Illustration: courtesy LØS

Right page, top: *map of Auroville.*
Bottom left: *map of Europe, showing two of its greatest energy systems, the Grail Temple (left) and the Heartline of the Bull (right). There is also an energy stream crossing Europe from Santiago de Compostella to the Black Sea.*
Bottom right: *the principles of Zoence developed by Peter Dawkins, at Findhorn in Scotland – showing a double Chakra system at play.*

Page 16: the Tamera biotope in Portugal.

Page 17: permaculture plan for Tlholego ecovillage in South Africa

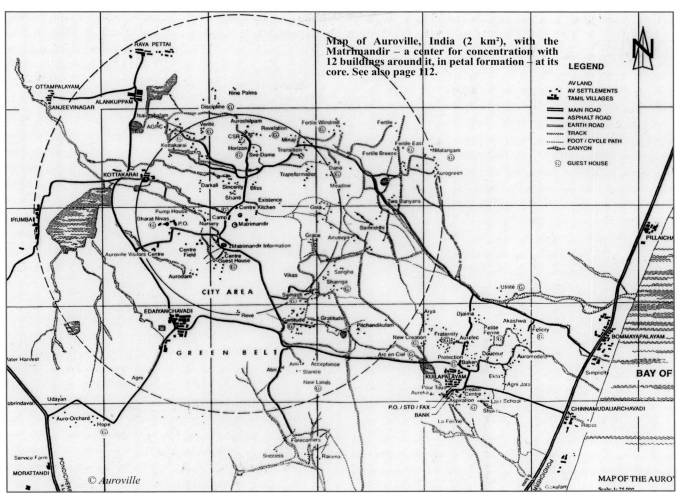

Map of Auroville, India (2 km²), with the Matrimandir – a center for concentration with 12 buildings around it, in petal formation – at its core. See also page 112.

© Auroville

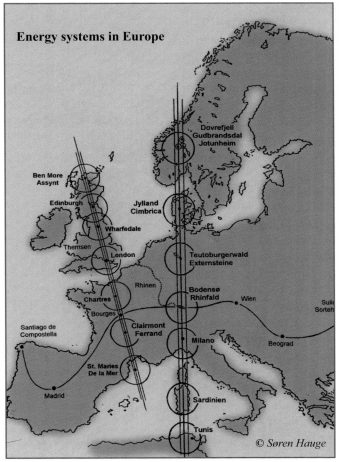

Energy systems in Europe

© Søren Hauge

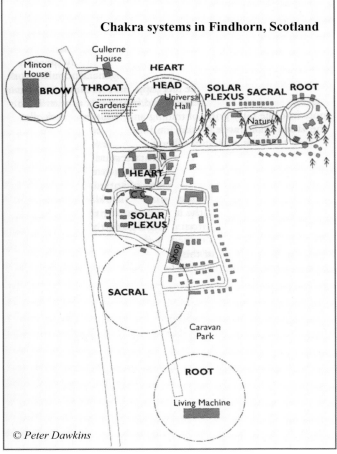

Chakra systems in Findhorn, Scotland

© Peter Dawkins

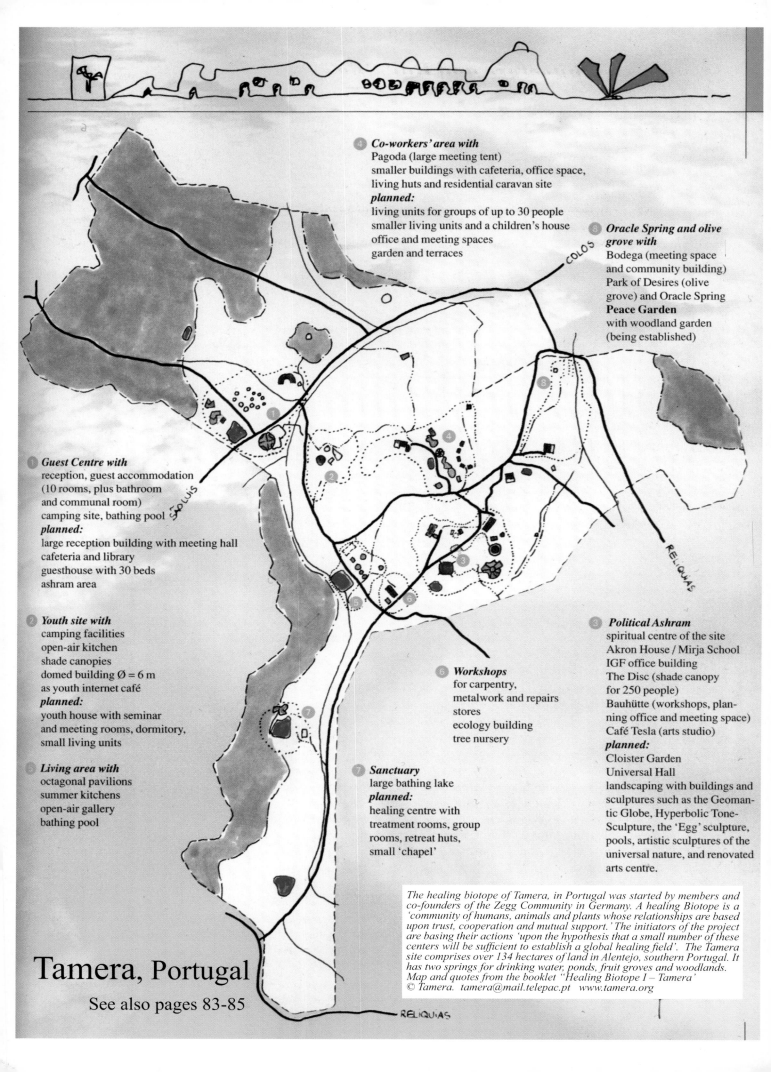

④ Co-workers' area with
Pagoda (large meeting tent)
smaller buildings with cafeteria, office space,
living huts and residential caravan site
planned:
living units for groups of up to 30 people
smaller living units and a children's house
office and meeting spaces
garden and terraces

**⑧ Oracle Spring and olive
grove with**
Bodega (meeting space
and community building)
Park of Desires (olive
grove) and Oracle Spring
Peace Garden
with woodland garden
(being established)

① Guest Centre with
reception, guest accommodation
(10 rooms, plus bathroom
and communal room)
camping site, bathing pool
planned:
large reception building with meeting hall
cafeteria and library
guesthouse with 30 beds
ashram area

② Youth site with
camping facilities
open-air kitchen
shade canopies
domed building Ø = 6 m
as youth internet café
planned:
youth house with seminar
and meeting rooms, dormitory,
small living units

⑤ Living area with
octagonal pavilions
summer kitchens
open-air gallery
bathing pool

⑥ Workshops
for carpentry,
metalwork and repairs
stores
ecology building
tree nursery

⑦ Sanctuary
large bathing lake
planned:
healing centre with
treatment rooms, group
rooms, retreat huts,
small 'chapel'

③ Political Ashram
spiritual centre of the site
Akron House / Mirja School
IGF office building
The Disc (shade canopy
for 250 people)
Bauhütte (workshops, planning office and meeting space)
Café Tesla (arts studio)
planned:
Cloister Garden
Universal Hall
landscaping with buildings and
sculptures such as the Geoman-
tic Globe, Hyperbolic Tone-
Sculpture, the 'Egg' sculpture,
pools, artistic sculptures of the
universal nature, and renovated
arts centre.

Tamera, Portugal

See also pages 83-85

*The healing biotope of Tamera, in Portugal was started by members and
co-founders of the Zegg Community in Germany. A healing Biotope is a
'community of humans, animals and plants whose relationships are based
upon trust, cooperation and mutual support.' The initiators of the project
are basing their actions 'upon the hypothesis that a small number of these
centers will be sufficient to establish a global healing field'. The Tamera
site comprises over 134 hectares of land in Alentejo, southern Portugal. It
has two springs for drinking water, ponds, fruit groves and woodlands.
Map and quotes from the booklet "Healing Biotope I – Tamera'
© Tamera. tamera@mail.telepac.pt www.tamera.org*

INSTITUTE AND VILLAGE DETAIL

TLHOLEGO DEVELOPMENT PROJECT
RURAL AND REGIONAL SELF RELIANCE

0   20   50   100 M

terraced orchard

scholar housing

residential village

staff housing

agro forestry

food processing

botanical grain samples here

research garden

Tree nursery

seed bank

apothecary

daycare

admin

Studio Library

classrooms

marketing

market

path to Molokwane

conference parking

conference center

public entrance

Tlholego center parking

markilot

off season regeneration

apprentice housing

market small industry

Tlholego Village

agro forestry

path to school

road to agricultural fields and small farm

The Ecological Dimension of Ecovillages

Permaculture

Permaculture is increasingly being used as a basis for the design of ecovillages, cohousings, neighborhoods and other communities. Bill Mollison, the father of permaculture, defines the concept as follows: "Perma(nent Agri)culture is the conscious design and maintenance of agriculturally productive ecosystems, which have the diversity, stability and resilience of natural ecosystems. It is the harmonious integration of landscape and people providing their food, energy, shelter, and other material and non-material needs in a sustainable way. Without permanent agriculture, there is no possibility of a stable social order." (From "Permaculture: A Designer's Manual"). Permaculture is as much about beneficial design as it is about values and ethics, and making "the decision to take responsibility for our own existence and that of our children" - Bill Mollison.

Permaculture Design: Philosophy and Practice

by Jan Martin Bang

Photo: Hildur Jackson

Wheat and clover at Svanholm, Denmark

Jan Martin Bang developed the concept of the Green Kibbutzim in Israel. He is currently living at the Solborg Camphill Community in Norway. He co-founded the Bridge Building School (for ecological building and design) with architect and builder Rolf Jacobsen (see page 52).

Introduced in Tasmania by Bill Mollison during the seventies, permaculture soon caught on as a way of helping to plan smallholdings in Australia, and has since developed into a worldwide design system, used also by planners in some well-publicized instances like Village Homes in Davis, California and Crystal Waters in Australia. The emergence of the ecovillage concept in the early 1990s came at a time when permaculture had been developed sufficiently to make a significant contribution to the planning of ecovillages.

Permaculture is about designing sustainable human settlements. It is a philosophical and practical approach to land use integrating micro climate, functional plants, animals, soil, water management and human needs into intricately connected, highly productive systems. Permaculture means thinking carefully about our environment, our use of resources and how we supply our needs. It aims to create systems that will endure not only in the present, but also in the future. The idea is one of cooperation with nature and each other, of caring for the earth and people and presenting an approach to designing environments that have the diversity, stability and resilience of natural ecosystems, to regenerate damaged land and preserve environments which are still intact. Permaculture is right design based on right ethics. It is being used throughout the world to plan buildings, farms, gardens and villages, and has been used for business, industrial, organizational, social and educational design.

When it comes to planning on the ground, permaculture uses the idea of Zoning, further modified by Sectors, and then Vectors. Zoning is based on the need to locate activities in sensible concentric circles, the most intensively used being the ones nearest to the home, and the least used or visited being the furthest away. To quote Rosemary Morrow:

Zone 1 – Homes and food (security) gardens
Zone 2 – Close Public Spaces and Orchards
Zone 3 – Larger open spaces and community gardens
Zone 4 – Reserves, fuel forests, windbreaks etc.
Zone 5 – Wildlife corridors, native plant sanctuaries

Sectors are parts of these circles having specific attributes, such as the sunshine generally coming from a southern direction in the northern hemisphere, the prevailing wind direction, and fire risk areas adjacent to the site. Vectors are dynamic flows cutting through the previous two, such as watercourses, existing or planned roads and tracks, wildlife corridors and the hills and slopes of the site.

The collective ideology of the community in question must first determine the physical layout. I would like to briefly illustrate this by comparing the planning of the ecovillage at Clil in the Galilee in Israel with that of a Green Kibbutz.

Clil is a small village of 170 people settled originally about 25 years ago. It was inspired by ideals such as Gandhian pacifism, organic food production, independence, spirituality and self-sufficiency. Clil's members did not want to use the existing rural community models then available in Israel, and they were extremely successful in developing their own style. Today, each family is responsible for building and maintaining their own smallholding, and the community focus has been reduced to common roads, a kindergarten, and overall decision-making on topics such as the size of the village and the admission of new residents. In this case, the permaculture zoning concept only has relevance at the household level, while the location of each household is largely dependent upon the availability of land. Clil may be thought of as a cluster of zones with a deliberate refusal on the part of its inhabitants to apply any overall planning concept to the village as whole.

In the Kibbutz system, the planning of the community as a whole has always been paramount. The individual family has historically been of lesser importance here. Indeed in much of the Kibbutz' history, children were housed and educated separately from their parents, and even today most meals are eaten in the communal dining hall. Apart from a few square meters of personal garden by the front door of each house, it would be inappropriate to apply the Zoning concept to the family home of the individual Kibbutz member. The Zoning concept has to be applied to the community as a whole. Given the extremely radical starting point of Kibbutz society, and even with the changes going on today – toward greater autonomy for the family – we must regard the Kibbutz as one large household, with the concomitant Zoning implications that this has.

So before we can begin with such physical planning as is implied in the Zoning concept, we must first define our ideals, aims and social parameters as a community and as individuals in the community. These will then be reflected in structures on the ground.

Jan Martin Bang   brobygg@start.no

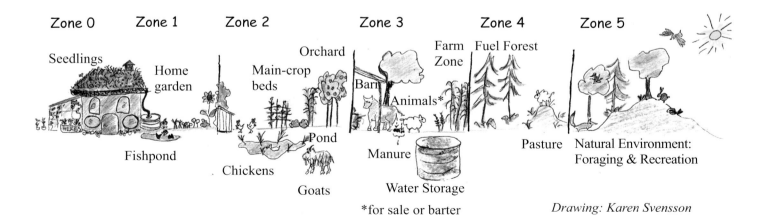

Picture above: an illustration of the zones defined in permaculture, according to the principles of Bill Mollison (as found in 'Permaculture: A Designer's Manual'). **Zone 0** is the house area (with components such as glasshouse, sod roof, roof gardens etc.). **Zone 1** components are what one needs and tends to on a daily basis. They are placed within 6 meters of the home: chicken laying boxes, fully-mulched and pruned gardens (where one can produce most of the foods necessary to existence), rainwater catchment tanks. **Zone 2** is the place for less intensively managed spot-mulched gardens and main-crop beds, chicken and other poultry, small ponds, forage ranges for domestic stock, a home orchard. **Zone 3** is the farm zone for commercial crops and animals for sale or barter; green manuring, large water storages, barns and little-pruned trees belong here. **Zone 4** borders on unmanaged natural areas (forest, wilderness). There is still some management (fuel forest for household use, pasture or range; unpruned trees). Dams are a possibility here, with piping to other zones. **Zone 5** is unmanaged environment, for foraging and recreation. Bill Mollison says of this area: "This is where we learn the rules that we try to apply elsewhere." – Permaculture: A Designer's Manual.

Permaculture for Ecovillage Design

by Max Lindegger

Max Lindegger is the chairman of GEN and one of the world's leading permaculture teachers and consultants. He lives at the Habitat Award-winning Crystal Waters ecovillage in Australia, which he co-founded. He is the Regional Coordinator of the Global Ecovillage Network (Oceania/Asia) Inc., and teaches courses on ecological sustainability, eco-village design and permaculture. To date he has provided his expertise in over 35 countries around the world. In the following article, he explains the principles of site observation, observation assessment and design associated with permaculture principles for looking at the environment and creating ecovillages.

Our ability to change the face of the earth increases at a faster rate than our ability to foresee the consequences of such changes."
– From Bill Mollison's Permaculture, *1990*

"Work with nature, rather than against it"
– Bill Mollison

I believe that the above principles are a good start for ecovillage design. They remind us that ecovillages and 'green' development have an impact on the environment, and that this impact may turn out to be negative if not carefully planned to work with nature; that development as such need not be bad, as long as the positives outweigh the negatives. If we want to make sure that any changes we effectuate do indeed affect the environment positively, it is important to have a good understanding of ecological design principles, to recognize the laws of nature, to realize what we don't know, and to ask others; so is learning from others' mistakes and not repeating them if at all possible. A good knowledge of engineering principles is useful, as is the understanding of natural processes. However, designing ecovillages does not necessarily come easier to an "expert" than to a novice. The most beneficial pre-requisites are a reasonable understanding of most of the disciplines involved in design and the realization that the different aspects of design have to connect. Possibly the most beneficial attributes of all are good observation abilities and a willingness to work with others as a team. Individuals may occasionally be the inspiration for an ecovillage, but they rarely design and implement it (they often provide the inspiration but rarely the perspiration!). The implementation part is more of a group process. In the case of Crystal Waters, the core team consisted of Robert Tap, Geoff Young, Barry Goodman and myself (Max Lindegger). Many others helped with advice and suggestions or simply offered themselves as "sounding boards".

Observation:

I found observation the most important element in creating a sound, ecological design. This takes time. Sadly, in this profit-driven world we live in, time is money and extra time potentially means less profit. But is it not feasible to insist that more observation time will result in a better outcome, and potentially more profit? Observation is the skill to note a number of outcomes and work out the process. It is also a matter of putting two and two together and seeing a solution. Under the heading of "observation", I would also include the task of researching a piece of land, its history, talking to neighbors and people skilled in various aspects. Many observations can be measured easily, such as temperature fluctuations between seasons, the flow rate of a river, and the pH of the soil, wind speed and rainfall. But we cannot stop at the basic measurements. By measuring, we are collecting our paints, but we are not yet composing our picture. We are "observing", but we are not yet "designing". If we jump into action too quickly, abbreviating the observation stage, and skipping a true design stage, we will have regrets later. For instance, it will be too late when the first building goes up and it is found that the soil cannot absorb the inhabitants' waste, or when re-using the old buildings turns out to be a bad idea because they are found to be contaminated with asbestos. It is also possible that we create disasters, which we may never learn about. If we never observed an eastern gray grass owl, I guess we will never know if we destroyed its habitat. If we never test the health of our rivers and creeks, we won't necessarily know if we pollute them. I could go on. The observation stage for Crystal Waters took approximately nine months of part-time work. Don't expect Brownfield sites to take less time or be cheaper – as an example, testing the site for the Olympics 2000 in Sydney cost a fortune.

Observation Assessment:
"In chaos lies unparalleled opportunity for improving creative order." – Bill Mollison

The collection of data which results from concentrated observation can be quite confusing. We may find apparently contradictory information in nature (e.g. lots of predators and an abundance of potential victims). For some observations, we may never find an explanation, while for others a pattern emerges.

It would be foolish to discard information simply because it makes "no sense" at the time. This may be an

Crystal Waters   Permaculture Village Australia

Crystal Waters Permaculture Village is a multiple award-winning ecovillage located in Queensland, Australia. It was established in 1987 by a team of initiators, including permaculture expert Max Lindegger. Crystal Waters spreads out over 83 lots, which take up 20% of the 259-hectare property. It houses many different types of businesses ranging from a cheese production facility to ecovillage design consultancy. Students from all over the world enroll for ecovillage design courses at Crystal Waters College, which has recently expanded its venue with an ecological education facility comprising demonstration solar panels and waste treatment systems. Web: **www.ecovillages.org/australia/crystalwaters** *Photos: courtesy Max and Trudi Lindegger, Val Oliver.*

Top, from left: *Houses in the early days.* **Right:** *recent picture of the house to the top left, showing how rather barren land turned luscious.*

Left: *Rammed earth dome house with pond (see early picture above left).* **Right:** *Volunteers at work in the field.*

Below: *Crystal Waters' café.* **Bottom:** *Celebrating the birthday of Crystal Waters' oldest resident, Dave.* **Bottom right:** *Students enjoying sunflowers.*

Photo: Hildur Jackson

A permaculture garden combines plants in a way that achieves the highest possible balance. Here a vegetable and herb garden at Fjordvang (DK).

indication that we need to gather more observations.
At this point it is important to sort the collection of information in a manner, which can be easily used. Our preferred method is the 'value overlays', an approach that is explained in detail by McHarg (see Ian McHarg's *Design with Nature*). The process may be quite simple or as detailed and complex as one chooses. In the case of the Crystal Waters assessment, we used relatively few overlays but they felt sufficient for the design. We mapped the following data:

Slope – this map differentiates areas steeper than 30% as suitable for forestry and restricted grazing only. Slopes with a 20 to 30 percent inclination are seen as having considerable limitations for buildings and roads, and creating rapid run-off, but suitable for forestry purposes and tree crops with care. Areas sloping between three and 20 percent are deemed suitable for road construction and generally also building. Agricultural activities need to take erosion potential into consideration. Slopes with a zero to three percent inclination could possibly cause poor surface drainage, but are generally considered suitable for roads, buildings and agriculture.

Hydrology – on this overlay, areas which flood are excluded from development. The creeks and river are clearly shown and buffer zones strictly established. (In this case 20-25 meters from either the high water level of dams and lakes and 25 meters from the center of seasonal creeks). The hydrology overlay also establishes a social and spiritual pattern. Access to all water is public (never private), a fact which has a major effect today on the way residents care for the water.

Vegetation – A vegetation map will always be fairly general but should establish the location of specific plant communities. In the case of Crystal Waters we differentiate between riverine plant communities, open grassland with scattered trees, forested ridges and moist gullies

(small valleys). The vegetation map also should establish the existence of any rare or endangered species.

Wildlife – This is an excellent opportunity not only to establish the diversity and health of the wildlife but also the existence of adequate water, habitats, and species nesting places. While it is not an easy task, existing wildlife corridors and flight paths should be noted, if at all possible.

Agriculture – It is essential that quality food production sites are mapped and preserved not only on Greenfield sites, but – maybe even more importantly – also on Brownfield sites. We generally like to differentiate between different classes (quality) of soils.

The above is by no means a complete list of the important or critical data, which should be mapped, but I think it makes the point here. McHarg suggests many more values, which may be considered for mapping, like geology, drainage, existing land-use, historical landmarks, ecological associations, water table – to mention just a few.

By marking the areas not suitable for development in a dark color, an assembly of the various overlays will show an accumulation of all the dark areas, and, if held over a light box, the areas suitable for development are left clear. I call this the "window". It shows the area which is by all of our criteria is suitable for development.

The Design Stage
At this point we should have an excellent understanding of the land, its strengths and its challenges. The task of understanding the needs and wishes of the people who will live in the ecovillage is equally important, and this process is not an easy one, as the faces of the future residents are not yet known. At Crystal Waters we used market research, surveys and our own brainstorming sessions with a group of people to get a good idea about how we, as designers, could have a positive effect on the social aspects of the Vil-

lage and assist its evolution from a development to a community.

I like to split the process into at least two stages – a draft stage and a detailed process leading to the final design. It is important that the draft stage avoids detail but is clear regarding the rough layout of land and placement of infrastructures. Here, too, many criteria need to be considered, such as:

Land layout: is the land facing north, what is the slope, size etc. As an illustration, for Crystal Waters we had 16 criteria for lot layout.

Roads: how wide should they be, what materials should be used, what speed limit needs to be established etc. In the case of Crystal Waters our roads are a maximum width of 3.6m, and we used a lot of local material as a road base.

Water: what is the volume required (fire hydrants, potable water supply, etc.) Crystal Waters has water pumped from the creeks and piped throughout the village. We have one fire hydrant placed between every two houses. Each home is required to provide its own potable water (usually rainwater collected from the roof).

Other elements include energy (electricity/gas/solar), wastewater, walking paths, dams and lakes, telecommunications and other aspects, which make up the "infrastructure."

At the time of the design and implementation, we produced a presentation folder, The Conceptual Report for Crystal Waters (which outlines many of the principles and philosophy of the design) and the Owner's Manual for Crystal Waters (which was a short description regarding how to be a steward of the land and how to make best use of the environment and the climatic situation).

Final Design

This process should be more than drawing "pretty pictures". It should be well presented and contain a design which brings the various concepts and ideas together as a whole. One may call it Holistic design. Each element should have a reason for being included and be well and thoroughly considered. Ultimately, the connections between the elements are what will make or break the design – the connection of a wildlife corridor from habitat areas to the water's edge, the avoidance of unnecessary crossings of natural patterns (rivers, ridges, valleys) with unnatural flows (roads, drains), and the accommodation of humans into the landscape without destroying a place for wildlife.

Getting a feeling for nature by being in it.

A collection of aerial photos taken at intervals of say 5 or so years should show how the design developed. A project like an ecovillage is never "finished" – people come and go, technology advances, and needs change.

A well-planned design is fairly certain to avoid bad mistakes but it will be no guarantee for instant happiness, spiritual enlightenment or ongoing wealth. However having taken the first step safely, the next one may be a little bit easier … for wealth, health and happiness.

lindegger@gen-oceania.org

Students from Kyushu Lutheran College in Japan learn about permaculture and ecovillage design at Crystal Waters. Photos: Max Lindegger.

Wilderness, Biodiversity, Earth Restoration

We are increasingly aware that Earth Restoration is urgently needed everywhere to preserve and rebuild our natural resources after centuries of neglect. It is an activity which people all over the world can integrate in their daily lives to varying degrees, and is one of the essential motivations for creating ecovillages. In the ecovillage of Auroville, more than 2 million trees have been planted over the past 20 years. The Findhorn Foundation, with Alan Featherstone at the helm, has received numerous awards for their Earth Restoration work. Featherstone's "Trees for Life" charity has proposed that the United Nations declare the 21st Century the Century of Earth Restoration. Hanne Marstrand-Strong from the Manitou Foundation in Colorado has founded the Earth Restoration Corps for sustainability training. She says that ecovillages, through their successful combination of Earth Restoration and sustainable social systems, show the next generation how to live if humanity is going to survive.

Earth Restoration is Living for the Whole

Interview with Hanne Marstrand-Strong

Above: Hanne Marstrand-Strong (center) surrounded by a crew of young Earth Restoration Corps students in Colorado. Photo: courtesy Hanne Marstrand-Strong for ERC.

by Hildur Jackson and Karen Svensson

Hanne Marstrand-Strong affirms that practicing Earth Restoration is not only necessary to heal the damage we've done to the Earth, but is also a part of finding our own identity. It is the first step toward learning where one's place is in the Universe. Hanne advocates Earth Restoration education everywhere on the planet, and sees ecovillages as perfect training grounds for it. Access to wilderness and natural healing biotopes are a necessary part of Earth Restoration training, so that people can get in contact with Mother Earth. This is something, which many ecovillages provide. The "Earth Restoration Corps" is an education initiative started 10 years ago by Hanne as a proposed alternative to military service everywhere and as a way of creating jobs for young men and women, especially in the Southern hemisphere.

Earth Restoration Corps & Manitou, USA

Crestone in Colorado, USA is the home of The Manitou Foundation and the Earth Restoration Corps. The Manitou Foundation supports a multi-religious settlement built on ecological principles and initiated by Hanne Marstrand-Strong, who also started the Earth Restoration Corps (ERC). ERC is an education initiative established ten years ago as a proposed alternative to military service everywhere, and as a way of creating jobs for the young – especially in the southern hemisphere. It offers Earth Restoration training to students who want to learn how to establish a more sustainable way of life on this Earth.

*Photos: **Top:** A group of ERC students on a nature quest in the wilderness in Colorado. For many, this is going to be the first time they are alone in nature. Photo: © Peter Engberg. **Left:** A group of ERC students from Japan and their trainers posing with their backpacks. Photo: © Peter Engberg. **Below left:** Hanne Marstrand-Strong (center) with some of the residents of the Manitou settlement. Photo: Courtesy Hanne Marstrand-Strong. **Below:** Zen Dome at the Manitou Foundation. Photo: Courtesy Hanne Marstrand-Strong/The Manitou Foundation. **Bottom:** The Zen house at The Manitou Foundation. Photo: © Peter Engberg.*

Hanne Marstrand Strong:
The Earth gives us everything, everything comes from her. If you live in a way through which you're destroying the very being that gives you everything, that's not very smart. Basically humanity is committing suicide: we're killing the air, we're killing the water, everything that gives life, we're killing it with our behavior … In the last 60 years, which is my lifetime so far, we have killed much of what it took Mother Earth 100 million years to bring forth. We need, on a massive scale, to start restoring the planet.

Let's face it, we're all caught in the system: you have to pay your taxes, you have to pay insurance … but there has to be an alternative to this system that is destroying the planet. That is what I have seen in Auroville, and in ecovillages around the world: people willing to scale down their lifestyle, to live just by their basic needs, to heighten their level of consciousness. Ecovillages are perfect training grounds for Earth Restoration. Everything we want to teach is already there, including a new social structure where everybody feels part of the whole.

This new social system where everyone lives for the whole is key. Right now, everybody lives for themselves. Selfishness and ignorance are the problem, ignorance of the great loss of the universe, of the great loss of nature. This greed that selfishness brings: greed for all those things we don't need, greed for power, greed for money … We have to embrace the entire family, universe, Earth. Living in the new social systems (in ecovillages) promotes that.

Q: How do we go about Earth restoration?
Hanne Marstrand Strong:
My hope is in the young people. They have to make the change, but for this they have to get to the information. This is why we started the Earth Restoration Corps. The educational program of the Earth Restoration Corps consists of three parts:

1. You learn to restore yourself: your consciousness, morals, ethics – and learn your place in the universe. We hold retreats, to bring out what is in the person instead of putting in. That is what education means. We use the age-old Native American way: vision questing, to establish the connection to mother Earth and the whole universe. You go out in nature without food and water. You pray, you cry, you become more humble. The arrogance goes away. All the stiff structures break down. Sometimes it takes up to four days until you get a vision.

2. You learn how to restore destroyed ecosystems – forests, soils, waters, and the air. That needs to be done everywhere on the planet. Permaculture is a good philosophical and practical basis for this.

3. You find out what livelihoods for the next generation do not destroy ecosystems. We need to teach organic farming, natural building, and renewable energy. In the next 15-20 years there will be 1.7 million new jobs created within alternative energy by windmills. Solar energy will produce ten times that! For 30 years I have traveled all over the Planet. I saw hordes of kids come out of university with only 10,000 available jobs. In the Philippines 65% of the young have no jobs. Kids are being trained everywhere for jobs they'll never get, and the ones who do, get jobs which destroy everything that gives life. So the young end up with drugs, crime, (terrorism), and as squatters. The only thing I can come up with is: we just need to train people totally differently. My advice to young people is: we are in a race that is out of control. If we do not change now, we have no future. You young have a lot to offer. Earth restoration would change your consciousness about these things. After an Earth Restoration program in Colorado, all these students from Japan, every one of them, committed to working either in a field which restored Nature, or in one which at least did not destroy it.

Q: How does the ecovillage curriculum fit with your ideas?
Hanne: It is brilliant. We need a super fund to help communities set up the education program and adapt the curriculum. The first thing we have to do is to train the trainers. We need trainers on a big scale and have to concentrate on that.

Q: How do we fund all this?
Hanne: In the short term, the foundation days are almost over. We can receive funds from major ecologically sound corporations. We've got to get more and more original with how we raise money. Countries will have to give up their armies and set up alternatives. Money will have to be re-directed from arms, and other destructive areas to Earth Restoration.

Look at the healthcare system, for example. Sickness is economic right now. We have to make it economic to be healthy. We need to teach preventive healthcare. People have to learn to take care of their own health. Then the money which goes to healthcare can be re-allocated as well.

The future lies in transforming money from one thing that isn't working but destroying our world, and redirecting it to Earth Restoration. For this, pressure from the people is what's needed. People have to change first. Governments and Corporations will change only once people have changed.

erc@manitou.org

Field in Portugal. Photo: © Peter Engberg

Ten Principles of Earth Restoration

by Alan Watson Featherstone

Alan Watson Featherstone, from the Findhorn Community in Scotland, sees Earth Restoration on a large scale as major necessity worldwide. He proposes that The United Nations declare the 21st Century as the Century of Restoring the Earth, to catalyze the process. "Given the scale of the world's environmental problems today, restoration of degraded ecosystems will take at least a hundred years ... so it is entirely appropriate that a century-long perspective be taken for this," he says. The following article introduces the principles of ecological restoration as he sees them. Alan Featherstone is the founder of the "Trees for Life" project, a Scottish conservation charity dedicated to the regeneration and restoration of the Caledonian Forest in the Highlands of Scotland. "Trees for Life" has received a number of awards, including the Millennium Marque Award in 2000. It was declared the UK Conservation Project of the Year in 1991. Alan received the Schumacher Award in 2001 for his work in helping to restore degraded ecosystems.

1. Mimic nature wherever possible

A simple example of this principle involves our program of planting trees in Glen Affric, Scotland. Under natural circumstances, the trees in the forest would regenerate by themselves, but the artificially high grazing levels maintained by human interests prevent this. So when we plant trees, we do so in patterns which copy the distribution of naturally regenerating tree seedlings in the glen, and in the same soil types and topography as the trees grow in by themselves.

2. Work outwards from areas of strength, where the ecosystem is closest to its natural condition.

This facilitates the dispersal of insects, animals and plant seeds etc. into the adjacent areas being restored, and minimizes the amount of human intervention, which is neces-

sary. In Glen Affric, the fence at Coille Ruigh na Cuileige is an enclosure which protects an area of 50 hectares on the periphery of a remnant of the Caledonian Forest, where mature trees have provided a seed source for an estimated 100,000 naturally-regenerating pine seedlings inside the fence, eliminating the need to plant any trees there.

3. Pay particular attention to 'keystone' species

In conservation biology, keystone species are ones which play a central, critical role in ecosystems, and upon which many other species depend. If an ecosystem can be returned to a state in which the keystone species flourish, then all the other species, which depend on it, will benefit as well. In the boreal component of the Caledonian Forest, such as the pinewoods in Glen Affric, we concentrate Scots pines as a keystone species, and find that the whole forest community begins to recover. Another example of a keystone species for riparian (or riverside) ecosystems is the European beaver, which through its dam building creates microhabitats of still water. These benefit certain fish species and promote the growth of aquatic vegetation, which in turn provides food for mammals such as the moose.

4. Utilize pioneer species and natural succession to facilitate the restoration process

When a forest community colonizes an area of open ground, a process of succession takes place, beginning with the pioneer species. These typically are fast growing short-lived species whose seeds are widely dispersed, and they eventually make way for slower growing, longer-lived species of tree. In the pinewoods, the main pioneer trees are birch, rowan and aspen, all of which grow quickly but only live for 100 years or so, in contrast to the slower growing Scots pines, which reach a much larger size and can live for 350 years. The pioneer trees draw up nutrients from the earth, which are returned to the forest floor when their leaves fall each autumn, thereby enriching the soil for the more nutrient-demanding successional species.

5. Re-create ecological niches where they've been lost

For example, with the conversion of natural forests into managed plantations of tree crops in many parts of the world there has been an almost total loss of standing dead trees (snags) or fallen logs, as they are seen as 'waste', and are removed or burned to make way for 'productive' growing trees. However, dead wood in the form of logs provides the habitat for many invertebrate species which are essential components of the forest ecosystem, while snags provide nesting sites for various types of birds.

Girl in the forest on the island of Kauai. Photo: © Peter Engberg

6. Re-establish ecological linkages – reconnect the threads in the web of life

An ecosystem is a community of interdependent species, all of which are necessary for the health and proper functioning of the whole. When ecosystems become degraded and disjointed, many of the ecological linkages or connections between populations or species are broken. A simple example of this is that the remnants of the Caledonian Forest are very fragmented and isolated, and in some cases where only a handful of trees survive, the gene pool, on which the long term health of the species depends, is now very small indeed.

7. Control and/or remove introduced species

Islands are particularly vulnerable to disruption from introduced species: in the Galapagos Islands, for example, the endemic giant tortoises are seriously endangered by introduced goats, which eat their eggs. The control, or where possible the removal, of such introduced species is an important and essential element of any restoration program for ecosystems affected by them.

8. Remove or mitigate the limiting factors which prevent restoration from taking place naturally

In the Highlands of Scotland, the main limiting factor preventing the Caledonian Forest from regenerating itself is the excessive number of grazing herbivores, mainly red deer and sheep, which eat any young seedling trees that grow above the heather. A reduction in the number of grazing animals is a better approach to forest regeneration than erecting extensive, unsightly and expensive deer fences.

9. Let nature do most of the work

We are implementing this principle in our work through the establishment of small pockets or islands of new forest at strategic locations in the denuded landscapes of West Affric and other areas. When the trees in them reach seed-bearing age, we will rely on natural regeneration to restore the forest outside the exclosures, assuming that deer and sheep numbers have been brought down in the interim. Thus, we are in effect 'kick starting' the restoration process and then letting it develop by itself.

10. Love has a beneficial effect on all life

This is perhaps the one unique principle, which we work with at Trees for Life, and it stems from the early experiences of the original Findhorn Community garden in the 1960s. Working with love and respect, in cooperation with nature, the gardeners were able to grow remarkably large vegetables and flowers. Anyone who has a 'green thumb' and grows especially beautiful houseplants or vegetables is also experiencing this. This principle underlies all our work, as we know that love nurtures the life force and spirit of all beings, and is a significant factor in helping to heal the Earth. In some areas of Glen Affric we've found pine seedlings growing in the most unlikely locations, and we know that in some way that's connected with the quality of love which we, and others, bring to the ecological restoration work there.

trees@findhorn.org
www.treesforlife.org.uk & www.restore-earth.org

Earth Restoration in Colombia

by Claudio Madaune

Claudio Madaune is a founder member of the Sasardí Natural Reserve and Ecovillage in the Darien Region in Colombia, South America. He has practiced and taught Earth Restoration with great success in this remote region, managing to give local people and visitors a sense of the rich natural heritage of this area, and showing them how to preserve and regenerate it.

The Darién Foundation was created in 1993 in Colombia, based on the efforts of the Sasardí integrated reserve and ecovillage. The members of the ecovillage group settled in the region in 1985, having chosen to live a sustainable life in the middle of the tropical rainforest, preserving natural resources and building up their level of self-sufficiency based on conservation principles. Here they have been working with children and adults from local communities in education programs on an informal basis; promoting the exchange of knowledge, experiences, and dreams; stimulating people to internalize human values such as unity, solidarity, respect for all living beings, sensitivity, self-esteem and organizational processes; and helping them recognize their natural surroundings as a very important and special region with unique wildlife and cultural diversity.

The Chocó biogeographic region is one of the areas with greatest biodiversity worldwide, and its ecosystems are threatened with serious degradation.

Above: Claudio Madaune's home in Colombia. Photo: Kailash.

The production systems imposed by the dominant extractive culture originate from the interior of the country. Macro development projects such as the Pan-American route, the interoceanic canal and the construction of international ports planned for this region will contribute to the destructive environmental influences and to the critical social situation in the area (even more critical due to the presence of the illegal armed groups fighting for control of the territory).

Facing these circumstances, the Sasardí group founded the Darién Foundation to build up participatory processes with local inhabitants in order not only to preserve and restore the environment, but also to promote sustainable ways of development which will enhance the living conditions of the local people, and which will provide better conditions for Earth Restoration. The holistic and integrated approach used in the various interrelated projects and programs has enabled us to reach significant goals.

We accomplished the following goals:

Environmental education involving local schools, inhabitants and visitors, which builds up a higher sense of personal involvement to help people value and respect nature around them. Some examples are: workshops led by local medicine men, passing on the traditional knowledge about and value of the various flora species, recognizing medicinal plants and how to care for and use them; design of didactic games with local information in order to learn about the environment, culture, and general situation of the region while the children entertain themselves and have fun; publication of a newsletter with practical information and activities related to environmental and social issues, open to articles from the local people – the newsletter is called "Seeds to the Wind", referring to the planting of many seeds full of life and peace all over, with the wish for them to grow everywhere in the region. Recycling trips with children, to teach them about the problems caused by bad environmental management.

Manufacture of handicrafts with local materials as a form of alternative production, which takes advantage of natural resources from the forest in a sustainable way. We use fine hard tropical wood leftovers from clear-cutting and various seeds from the rainforest, and make earrings, bracelets, necklaces, carved animal figures and wooden kitchen accessories. We also produce bags and baskets out of natural palm fibers.

Establishment of pilot projects for fish breeding, domesticated and wild animal breeding; research in the use of local "promissory" species from the rainforest (i.e. wild species which can be used for commercial purposes as they have good possibilities for generating income: wild flowers, wild fruits, oil essences from trees and plants), as alternative production models.

Promotion of a private natural reserve initiative, the "reservas naturales de la sociedad civil". A regional NGO network called "Red Regional de Reservas Naturales UNGANDI en el Darién Chocoano" has been established. It gathers almost 40 natural reserves, which together cover around 2.000 hectares within the Darién region, for the preservation of local ecosystems, sustainable management of natural resources, observation of biological corridor configurations, and facilitation of joint actions at a bioregional level to protect the environment around the Urabá Gulf area. The Sasardí Integrated Reserve is one of the founder members of the "Red Nacional de Reservas Naturales de la Sociedad Civil" (Colombian National Network of Natural Reserves of the Civil Society).

Ethno-botany research with local midwives and medicine men, identifying plant species used for medicinal purposes, and reproducing the traditional knowledge about the use of plants to cure and prevent illness, as well as saving human lives (for example after snake bites).

Protection program for the Leatherback Sea Turtle (*Dermochelys Coriacea*): activities promoting environmental education and respect of all life forms. The appropriation of the process by the local community through cultural and recreational activities has had valuable results: songs with different rhythms have been written about the sea turtle by locals, graffiti, drawings and even a monument of the turtle are

Photos this page: courtesy Claudio Madaune. Clockwise from above left: Young Turtle Queens; teaching in nature; permaculture training; handcrafts; local flora; climbing the cascade.

some concrete examples of this cultural and environmental process in the main town of Acandí; streets and various stores have been named after the sea turtle, and every year the town chooses its sea turtle queen among local girls between the ages of six and ten, during an amazing ecological and cultural festival. In addition to these, new sustainable production alternatives to decrease the consumption of turtle eggs have been promoted. Further research on the lifecycle of the sea turtle is also being encouraged. Interaction with local and national authorities (the Ministry of the Environment) has been focused on declaring nesting sites protected areas and special management areas, giving these places a legal status with the participation of the people.

International voluntary work camp, carrying out various activities such as: native tree planting, waste management, implementation of appropriate technologies (together with the local people), sharing and cultural exchange. These camps have been coordinated with the International Civil Service (SCI) and other related organizations, bringing young people from Europe to live and work together with us. People come to work on their thesis and research, and to share our way of life (as internships for example).

Ecotourism programs with local communities, as an alternative educational and cultural exchange activity between locals and visitors, help people move toward a more natural way of life.

The facilitation of community processes with an integrated vision – through education, alternative and sustainable production, proper natural resource management, and grass-roots organization efforts – helps people appreciate the biodiversity of their region and realize the importance of changing the attitude of each individual to all life forms, of strengthening the relation between human beings and Nature, and of taking concrete measures to restore Mother Earth.

fundarien@edatel.net.co ecoaldeasnsa@hotmail.com
ena.ecovillage.org/Region/SudamericaNorte/
Ecovillage/Lareserva
Private Natural Reserves : www.resnatur.org.co

Local Organic Food Production, Consumption and Recirculation

Food Production: Locally and in Ecovillage Design

Introduction

by Hildur Jackson

People's wish to produce their own food springs from a basic human need to connect with nature, to provide for oneself, and to play an active, responsible role in one's natural environment. This need can be met in various ways, by cultivating one's own gardens (including rooftops), sharing a plot of land with others, or also growing vegetables and fruit in an ecovillage/community setting.

Also, considering the state of agribusiness today, there are many more reasons for localizing the production of fresh foods and increasing our level of self-sufficiency. The deterioration of industrial food, diseases among cattle and the genetic modification of plants have accelerated the need for alternatives to current forms of industrialized agriculture.

In the Northern hemisphere, farms have become extremely large, producing massive quantities of one kind of crop in controversial ways (e.g. using genetically manipulated seeds and pesticides). Reverting to a more ecologically sound production pattern would involve either coming up with new systems, or splitting farms up into smaller holdings again.

In the Southern Hemisphere, land is divided up into plots for subsistence farming and areas for export crops. Export crops (monocultures such as peanuts) are taking up an increasing percentage of the land, even though research has shown that private lots often are very productive, supplying farmers with all basic necessities.

Globally, fear of terrorism may influence politicians to start thinking in terms of food security once again.

Based on these factors, it would be beneficial for every bioregion to strive for self-sufficiency in its production of fresh local foods, and to start thinking of exporting crops and fibers to other regions or countries only once an adequate level of local self-sufficiency has been achieved. This is especially true for countries threatened by droughts, and food and water shortages, where official policies regarding export are called for if local resources are to be maintained or re-established.

Relatively little experimentation and research have been done in the field of local integrated food production systems, and there is room for exciting experiments in order to find alternatives to current models. Ecovillages provide good frameworks for this type of research. As a submission for a Danish competition to identify the best Sustainable Community for the 2100 Century, one ecovillage group in Denmark proposed combining an organic farm with a village, in order to produce food for self-sufficiency and niche products for the external market. This is one possible alternative model. If an ecovillage owns land enough for two farmers to live from its yields, it may become attractive as a working alternative to today's agribusiness practices.

Interesting examples of alternatives to current agricultural practices are offered by: Community Supported Agriculture (CSA), which has gained momentum in many countries as a way of getting a more local fresh food supply (see page 39) and the Integrated Renewable Energy Farm (IREF), a new concept designed by El Bassam in Dedelsdorf, Germany, which integrates renewable energy with organic farming at the village level. The organization is working to integrate an fuel forest, perennial energy crops, oil crops (fuel for cars), animal food crops, cereals, sugar crops, apiculture, fruits, vegetables, spices and medicinal herbs, poultry farming, sheep, grazing, fodder areas, flower growing and a fish lake. Windmills, photo-voltaics, solar and biogas are to supply energy. The project is uniquely multi-faceted (see page 32).

Also, some ecovillage projects have a lot to show in terms of food production. Damanhur produces wonderful wine from its own vineyard, as well as cheese, fruit, olive oil, and vegetables. At Crystal Waters, tropical fruits can be picked off the trees, there are herbs for cooking and drying (teas), and a cheese production facility is in place.

Many projects, however, have experienced disappointments with food production systems and have not been able to perform as expected.

Peter Harper (Center for Alternative Technology, Wales, UK) and Bo Læssøe (Svanholm, Denmark) tell us about their experiences in the articles which follow.

The Importance of Permaculture

A permaculture course will answer many questions about designing food systems for new ecovillage projects, and is strongly recommended. It will help you decide on what crops to grow or animals to keep out of the following list of essentials, and where to place the different areas in your design:

1. Herbs and flowers for cooking, infusions and other medicinal purposes: these date back to the monastic tradition. An ecovillage without herbs is difficult to imagine. The same is true for flowers.
2. Berry bushes: black and red currant; blueberries; raspberries; and gooseberries are natural in temperate climates, where they are easy to grow, freeze and preserve. Rosehips can be included in this category
3. Fruit trees are also a must in most ecovillages and are often the first to be planted.
4. Shelterbelts with a wide variety of tree species.
5. Different types of willow are easy to grow (often up to 10-15 species with differently colored stems). They are often placed with water treatment systems, where the recycled water provides nourishment for these fast-growing trees. Making baskets has become increasingly popular, and is a meaningful and useful hobby. It is a frequent course topic.
6. Nut trees are good for hedges and much appreciated by children.
7. Bamboo is useful for building and furniture, among other uses.
8. Fodder trees and olive trees are part of the natural vegetation in subtropical climates.
9. Vegetables are grown in most ecovillages, either as a common project or individually.
10. Chickens are often placed beside vegetable gardens, as some synergy exists: they are fed food remains and produce manure. They need feeding twice a day, and should be placed close to the house.
11. Bees will be placed close to herbs, the shelterbelt (blossoms) or in wilderness areas.
12. Looking at existing projects, you can see that you often have to choose whether to have animals or not; and which animals to keep, for which purposes. Cows for milk and cheese and sheep for wool are accepted by most; so are chickens for eggs; horses for riding are common; dogs and cats may be unwelcome because they frighten the wildlife away; but animals for meat consumption are not always accepted and may cause big problems.
13. Wilderness, Earth Restoration areas, and meditation areas may be defined.

The above-mentioned crops and animal husbandry activities are most often placed outside the formal economy of an ecovillage, and therefore seen as "leisure" occupations. If one opts for more intensive farming, the ecovillage will need quite a lot more land and resources (both time and finances), and will need to consider farming as labor, which is to be granted corresponding wages (see the following articles). It is possible that more projects will want to take food production out of economic calculations in the future.

Future Farming: Production without Waste

Our fields generously supply a host of products. The concept of waste does not exist. Every link in the chain forms the basis for new production that covers fundamental needs for food, clothing, energy, light and machines, etc. In the long run, any cultivation system must establish a balance between what is retrieved and what is put back into the cycle. Clean groundwater and a living humus layer are both goals in themselves and the means to recreate the necessary sustainability. The new system below was designed by the Danish Folkecenter for Alternative Energy. It includes a number of components which are already well-developed, for example biogas techniques, and self-sufficiency methods using proteins and oil. Such systems need further developing, so that they may provide an alternative to the monocultures which are dominant today, and which have a negative energy balance. Graphic: © *Folkecenter for Vedvarende Energi, Thy, Denmark.*

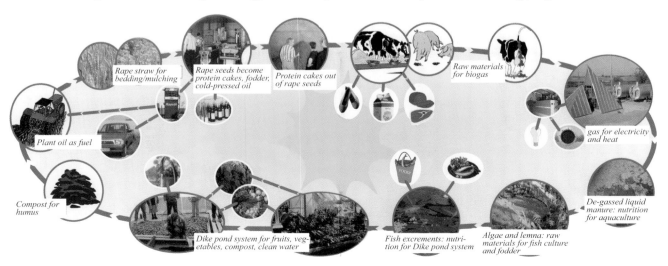

Rape straw for bedding/mulching

Rape seeds become protein cakes, fodder, cold-pressed oil

Protein cakes out of rape seeds

Raw materials for biogas

Plant oil as fuel

gas for electricity and heat

Compost for humus

De-gassed liquid manure: nutrition for aquaculture

Dike pond system for fruits, vegetables, compost, clean water

Fish excrements: nutrition for Dike pond system

Algae and lemna: raw materials for fish culture and fodder

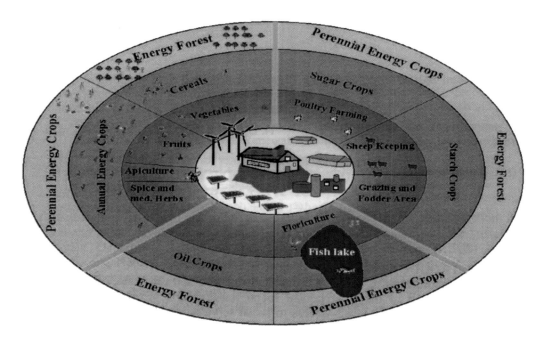

Above: the concept of an Integrated Renewable Energy Farm (IREF) was planned by El Bassam in Dedelsdorf, Germany, in cooperation with the Danish Folkecenter for Alternative Energy. IREF is a farming system model with an optimal energetic autonomy level, including food production and, if possible, energy exports. Energy production and consumption at the IREF has to be environment-friendly, sustainable and eventually based mainly on renewable energy sources. The IREF concept includes a combination of different possibilities for non-polluting energy production, such as modern wind and solar electricity production, as well as the production of energy from biomass. It also provides a decentralized living area from which the daily necessities (food and energy) can be produced directly on site, with minimal external energy inputs. The land of an IREF may be divided up into compartments for growing food crops, fruit trees, annual and perennial energy crops and short rotation forests, along with wind and solar energy units within the farm. *Graphic: © IREF by El Bassam*

Left: a stable designed by architect Anne Ørum for cattle at her farm in Erø, Denmark. The light, compartmentalized house is a functional stable (for 40 cows and their offspring, in the present case). The building profile makes support rooms possible on either side. In this picture, one can see the gable with the grain storage and rolling room below. If one's needs change, the smaller wing can easily be adapted for other purposes, for example accommodation.

Photo and drawing: Anne Ørum

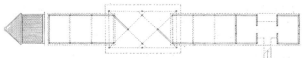

Right: hen coop at Fjordvang, Denmark. It was built on an old wagon and can be moved where it is needed. Eggs can be fetched from the outside by opening the black lid. The house is cleaned via a lid which can be opened on the other side. Manure is scraped off the plates under the pegs directly into the wheelbarrow for use in one's vegetable garden or greenhouse. Several pegs are placed at small intervals on the outside, and the chicken use them to get into the coop at night (height: 180 cm).

Design: Hildur Jackson and Peter Schmidt-Jensen.
Photo: Hildur Jackson

Self-sufficient Food Production: A Veteran's Advice

Interview with Peter Harper

by Hildur Jackson

Peter Harper is the Director of CAT (the Center for Alternative Technology in Wales), one of the oldest demonstration Centers of its kind in the world, situated on top of an abandoned slate quarry. As a professional gardener and a pioneer in growing fresh local foods, he is well positioned to advise us on food systems in ecovillages. We interviewed Peter in the underground dome of the Folkecenter in Thy (Denmark), during the Summer 2001 meeting on Renewable Energy Centers in Europe attended by 60 international leaders in the field.

Peter Harper. Photo: Hildur Jackson

Q: If an ecovillage startup group came to you for advice on how to create local fresh food systems, what would you answer?

Peter Harper: I would begin by asking: what are your reasons for doing it? I have been looking at self-sufficiency from many angles for 30 years. It sounds very nice, and it can be lots of fun if you don't take it too seriously. But when you want to produce food in large quantities, you realize it takes a lot of skill and time to build up your resources, and it involves a lot of hard work. People all over the world are leaving farming because they are not making much money on it relative to other sources of income. That says something about the modern world. In money terms, food takes up a relatively small part of our economies: just a few percent of GDP, and between 10% and 15% of household expenditure. Even if a household or community could produce 100% of its food, economi-

cally it would only cover a small part of their total expenditure. So we can ask again, why do it, or at least, why do it to such an extent?

> *"In money terms, food takes up ... between ten and 15 percent of household expenditure. For me it is not about economics ... The most important thing is recreation"*

I did a two-year study growing vegetables in my own garden, and measuring everything. It happens that I am a professional gardener, so I know what I am doing. I used a 70 m² plot, which is quite common for urban gardens. The soil was good, and there was plenty of compost. My yields were in the region of 20 tons per hectare, worth about £15,000 per hectare, and most farmers would be very pleased with this kind of yield. But on my plot its value (after deducting costs) was only about 6% of my expenditure on food, and less than 1% of my total household expenditure. The return on my time investment was about £1.50 hour, which at least is positive, but very low compared with other things I could be doing. It's using up a lot of my time. It is fair to ask why am I doing this at all, when the local organic grower can do it more efficiently ...

For me it is not about economics. It is about culture, and environment. I am trying to design a multipurpose garden that will combine all the ecological functions and maximize the garden's value as a contributor to environmental quality. The most important thing is recreation. That might sound surprising, but gardening is a tremendous source of spiritual strength. There is no better hobby. It is cheap. It keeps you fit, physically and mentally. It spreads out to the rest of the family. I always insist on making my garden child-friendly. And other people come to enjoy it. All this is an alternative to recreational shopping and traveling about in cars, so is having a positive environmental impact. The diverse activities in an ordinary garden lead to biodiversity, especially if you follow organic practice and include a pond. Oddly, if you abandon the garden and leave it to 'revert to nature', biodiversity will usually go down.

Waste treatment is probably more useful in environmental terms than growing small quantities of food. Fifty to 60% of all household waste is biological, more than you normally think. This should be processed at home, as far as possible. It is important that your biological waste does not end up in a landfill. It makes a big difference. Gardens are good at treating this kind of waste, and it all adds to the biodiversity.

Waste processing generates lots of compost and you might as well use that for appropriate food crops. As

> **"Ask yourself: what can you produce that the (local) suppliers cannot? … They are not so good at producing vitamins, minerals and flavors. You can do that."**

I've already argued, simply maximizing the tonnage of food production is not rational, so what kind of food is best grown? Ask yourself: what can you produce that the suppliers cannot? They are very good at producing cheap calories and proteins. They are not so good at producing vitamins, minerals and flavors. You can do that. Only a small fraction of your diet needs to be of that quality, but most gardens can meet the need. Play to your strengths: herbs, salads, and fresh stuff.

I am especially thinking of micronutrients. Scarce elements we need like selenium and cobalt. If we are composting, putting it back in the soil, we are eating from it and getting the correct vitality. We might need to supplement with occasional dressings of rock-dust for scarce minerals, but generally speaking adding organic matter from compost derived from food waste will build up a complete range of essential minerals, and then we will get these rare elements through our food – much better than pills! The important point here is that you don't need a lot, just regular small amounts, including edible wild plants and "weeds".

Q: So you can save money by not buying vitamins and other pills, and probably not having to see the doctor quite as much. Should that not be part of the economic calculation?

Peter: You are absolutely right. I lived in Iran for some years. They started a meal by eating lots of greens out of the garden, just raw on the table (well, on the floor actually!). They told me with a smile, 'These are our vitamin pills'.

But if you want to have the greatest possible impact on sustainable food, looking at your diet is likely to have far more impact than growing your own. Low meat, (or no meat), locally grown, organic food, which has undergone minimal processing: that is the eco-diet. Good for the planet, good for your health. Look at the whole food

The vegetable garden at The Farm, Tennessee, USA. Photo: GEN.

system in your area and then see how growing your own might fit in. You should know the local growers and not compete unnecessarily with them.

Q: So what do you advise us to do in terms of local food production?

Peter:

1. Research. Think of something we do not know. If you want to grow a certain crop, divide it into several plots with different treatments, record the results, and report them. You still get the stuff to eat, but you move our knowledge forward. Otherwise we are stuck repeating gardeners' fairy-tales from the 1950s.

2. Conservation of scarce varieties and special strains is important, because we are losing them. That is valuable for everybody. You can adopt a variety and look after it, be a resource bank.

3. Generating your own varieties, adapted to local conditions, by saving seeds from selected plants and gradually evolving new strains.

4. Storing and preservation. Look to things that are easy and fun and have cultural significance. Like jam, elderflower drinks, pesto, lavender bags. You can work it into a ritual that is especially nice, like pumpkins made into lanterns at Halloween.

> *Low meat, (or no meat), locally grown, organic food, which has undergone minimal processing: that is the eco-diet.*

Q: What is your advice for people in the Southern Hemisphere: what about self-sufficiency versus joining the global market?

Peter: My answer may not be what you would expect to hear. I do not think producing food should figure as large in our imagination as we are used to thinking. Traditionally in self-sufficiency thinking that is what obsesses everybody, but there are lots of other things we need to do. In modern societies only a small proportion of the people are engaged in serious, proper food production. And they do it properly, professionally, organically, sustainably and everything else. I disagree with those who think that the global South should continue as basically a subsistence economy. I do not think this is sustainable. There is going to be progress towards a kind of modern society, which is much more specialized, in which fewer produce food and people all have diverse, modern lives. There has to be a certain movement of food over long distances. I think "fair trade" is important, working out fair relationships between producer and consumer. That could help bring about development quickly. I know I am at odds here with lots of other thinkers in the green movement, but I do think 'modernity' in a broad sense is the only future. We cannot have a world divided into two parts, one affluent, dynamic and modern, and the other poor, static and traditional.

True, we do not want to transport huge quantities of bulky stuff from one end of the world to the other. We should localize as far as possible. Trade in light, high value things is good and the value should be added where it is produced. Now the way chocolate is produced in Europe, we have to alter that. But on the other hand a Danish study shows that less energy is used transporting winter salads from Italy to Denmark than producing in Danish greenhouses. This is odd, but we have to look at the hard numbers. Just 'food miles' is not an accurate reflection of the energy or environmental costs. Shipping potatoes from Cyprus for example, takes little energy per ton.

Q: But they are flown in!! And what about all the fresh winter vegetables that are being produced on the Canary Islands? The water is desalinated by huge wind turbines, and the produce grows in artificial soil with the use of many pesticides.

Peter: All this is complicated, and there is no single easy solution. I think we have to develop high social and environmental, fair trade and organic standards etc., and help developing countries meet these standards. I don't think we should pull up the drawbridge and refuse any trade links.

On Sustainable Modernization:

Peter: The big problem is sustainably modernizing the whole world. Traditional societies are sustainable, and post-modern societies can in principle be sustainable. It's the ones in-between (now a majority), which – temporarily we hope – are not. Leaving any societies behind is not sustainable. This is the transition century, and it is not optional! It is in this century that we will have the largest environmental impacts before things calm down. Some impacts are irreversible and we should pay most attention to these. They are: climate change; habitat and species loss (biodiversity); tropical soil loss; and ground water (pollution and scarcity) in some areas.

These matters are urgent, but other environmental problems might be less so, or are ones that can be remedied in the future. There might be a case for substituting irreversible problems for non-urgent and reversible ones as a kind of temporary 'overdraft' to get everybody through. We can mend these reversible problems later; the future, after all, has lots of time, as long as it is basically in a sustainable, non-deteriorating, condition. We may have to make some difficult choices in order to reach that stable, sustainable state from which we can clean up the messes of the past.

Center for Alternative Technology, Wales, UK
www.cat.org.uk
info@cat.org.uk

Svanholm Ecovillage, Denmark

In 1978 Svanholm Manor, with its 400 hectares of land, was turned into a farming community with ecology, self-sufficiency and shared economy as its main goals. Today, the 70 grown-ups and 40 children living at Svanholm have gone a long way toward realizing their dream. Svanholm supplies the Copenhagen area with ecological potatoes, carrots, onions and frozen peas. The project has a packaging plant for fruits and vegetables. Other businesses at Svanholm are: catering, dairy production (milk), a packaging production plant supplying wooden crates and pallets made from Svanholm's own trees. Other activity centers are: a windmill, biological waste water treatment, a joint car park with a repair workshop, a kindergarten, a community kitchen where the permanent cooking staff make delicious meals and add to the high standard of living (despite a community economy dating back to the early years, which only allows members a fixed amount of pocket money every month). Svanholm receives visitors, trainees and volunteers from all over the world. **www.svanholm.dk**

Right: Bo Læssøe takes Gaia Trust members and professor Niels Meyer on a tour of Svanholm during an international seminar.
Far right: *Children and parents playing in the courtyard, in front of the community dining hall.*

Right: Svanholm's free range cows. ***Far right:*** *Picking ecological carrots in the fields.*

Bottom from left: *Milking cows. Eating the ecological produce together (left, Christian Coff, a young farmer). Meeting in the celebration hall.*

Photos: Svanholm, Hildur Jackson

Self-Sufficiency and Production at Svanholm, DK

by Bo Læssøe

Svanholm Ecovillage in Horns Herred, Denmark, was founded in 1978, and is located 55 km from Copenhagen. Some of the estate's buildings date back to the middle ages. Svanholm owns 230 hectares of farmland, 130 hectares of woodlands, and 50 hectares of fields, parks, lakes and buildings. Farming, including cattle and forestry, provides jobs for approximately 15 people. Vegetable and fruit packing activities, including the packaging production plant (wooden crates and pallets), also employ 15 people. Of the available land, professional vegetable production takes up 20 hectares, grain takes up 5 hectares, potatoes 15 hectares, seed production 5 hectares, oil production (rapeseed) 8 hectares, and peas for deep freezing 10 hectares. Timber from the woodlands is sold outside Svanholm, while branches are used as wood chips in the central heating system. 167 hectares are reserved for free-range milking cows and their young (110 cows). Svanholm currently houses 65 adults and 35 children, plus varying numbers of guests. The estate is run on ecological principles.

"Self-sufficiency" has always had a positive connotation at Svanholm. By "always", I mean since 1978. In the beginning, we had great ambitions of becoming 100% self-sufficient, although our experience with food production was almost non-existent. We started a herbal garden and a fruit-tree plantation of one hectare each. We bought ten cows for milk and meat production, and rented an old mill to grind our own grain. The amount of spare time that had to be used on these activities, and the number of things we had to learn to ensure safe and sufficient food production, came as a shock to many. Squash prepared in 100 different ways is fortunately a thing of the past. The fact is that after the pioneer phase and the excitement of digging with our hands in our own soil, we realized that there was little time left over for producing our own food if we also had to take care of our income-generating activities, be they professional farming or industrial work at Svanholm, or jobs outside the ecovillage. We ended up delivering basic food items from our professional production activities to our community kitchen (milk, carrots, potatoes, meat, onions and flour), and combining these with various vegetables and fruits from our "self-sufficiency" cultures. To ensure the proper use of our food products, we introduced a permanent kitchen staff on all weekdays, and had them bake bread and churn butter as well. Everyone at Svanholm is very satisfied with the quality of our food (served in the communal dining room), and it is a good feeling to know that the basic provisions are produced in our own backyard.

However I would like to use some examples to illustrate how we have had to compromise on some of our high ideals in favor of more pragmatic approaches. At Svanholm, our ideal is that all crops which can't be sold as Grade A food products should be consumed at Svanholm, as a way of showing that vegetables are good enough even when their appearance does not top the charts. Also, we support the idea of manually gathering the good vegetables spilled in the field by the industrial harvester, thereby demonstrating frugality and respect for the fruit of the Earth. Reality is different. The cost/benefit relationship does not only come into account in our pro-

duction activities. The time and energy spent on putting a good meal on the table is not negligible. Do you peel four small onions or two large ones? Do you have to cut away blemishes on every potato, or only on one out of ten? We have come to the realization that when raw materials are cheap, we eat the Grade A products and lower quality vegetables are used as compost or fodder. When raw materials are more expensive, we sort them and use the lower quality vegetables, which can be eaten, even though this requires a bit more work.

The need to focus on the costs of market-driven food production influences the way we look at self-sufficiency within our community. The food items which we don't produce professionally, and which we as a community have not agreed upon producing to complement our self-sufficiency cultures, are much more time-consuming to cultivate, and would therefore be much more expensive to produce if paid labor were to be used. So we have chosen to organize the growing of herbs and special vegetables; fruit and berry pricking; cheese production; and the keeping of chickens as voluntary work, to be carried out in our spare time. I use the word "organize" on purpose, as most people have long working days and different daily rhythms, and nature doesn't let itself be ruled by our timetables: we have to take into account when the spinach is ready to be picked, so that a team of volunteers can be ready for harvesting, washing and freezing the vegetables. Coordination is key for good voluntary work.

The task of making Svanholm sustainable is a never-ending process, and it doesn't happen by itself. We routinely review our ecological goals (once a year), holding them up against our lifestyle and our production activities. Each year, we have to agree upon changes, which improve our practices in the light of our ideals. This may sound a little fundamentalist, but it would be unlike Svanholm to fall into such an extreme behavioral pattern. We see delight and joy as the best guarantee of a sustainable future.

bo@svanholm.dk

Food Consumption:
Fresh Local Foods
Community Supported Agriculture

Market in Rajastan, India. Photo: © Peter Engberg

by Helena Norberg-Hodge

Helena Norberg-Hodge is known for her ardent activism in support of the global environment and her 20 years' work in Ladakh (see p. 175) to save an extraordinary culture. She is President of ISEC (UK), the International Society for Ecology and Culture.

Society today is faced with a choice between two diverging paths. The path endorsed by government and industry leads towards an ever more globalized economy, one in which the distance between producers and consumers will continue to grow. Trillions of dollars are being spent creating superhighways and communications infrastructures that facilitate long-distance transport at the expense of local trade. In the last decade, vast sums of taxpayers' money have also been spent on research for biotechnology – with the aim of allowing food to be transported even greater distances, survive even greater doses of pesticides, and ultimately to be produced without the troublesome need for farmers. Large corporate producers are given further advantages by policies that promote 'free trade', such as Maastricht, GATT and NAFTA. The result has been the further centralization of political and economic power in huge transnational corporations, global joblessness, the erosion of community, and the rapid depletion of natural resources and further breakdown of the environment.

However, there is an alternative path, a significant counter trend that, despite a lack of support from government or industry, continues to flourish. Throughout the world, particularly in the industrialized countries, increasing numbers of people are recognizing the importance of supporting the local economy. Within this countercurrent, attempts to link farmers and consumers are of the greatest significance. A local food movement is sweeping across the world.

The benefits of local food systems are enormous; they help to rebuild community, strengthen local economies, foster diversity and protect natural resources. Local food systems take many forms: from farmer's markets to cooperatives, from box schemes to local shops. One local food initiative gaining popularity around the world is Community Supported Agriculture (CSA). The basic principle of CSAs is simple: consumers pay the farmer in advance and receive a certain share of the produce in return. Farmers benefit by getting a better price for their produce, while consumers are able to buy fresh and nutritious food at an affordable cost. Because farmers are growing for people's needs, rather than for an abstract market that demands larger and larger quantities of a single product, they tend to grow a greater variety of produce. The absence of packaging means a significant reduction in the huge amount of non-reusable, non-biodegradable waste that is daily thrown into waste dumps all over the world. Meanwhile, the shorter transport distance means a reduction in the use of fossil fuels, less pollution, and lowered amounts of greenhouse gases released to the atmosphere.

The local food movement has already provided real benefits. But lasting progress will require changes at the policy level as well. For national economies and local communities to flourish we must rethink 'free trade' policies that favor transnational corporate producers, and question the direct and indirect subsidies that are used to continually expand the transport infrastructures and corporate agribusinesses. We need to oppose government support of biotechnology and other environmentally risky, job-destroying technologies. Finally, we have to actively promote shorter links between producers and consumers – a process we can start today by publicizing the incredible social and environmental benefits of local food. We can honestly tell people that eating fresh, delicious food may be one of the most effective ways of saving the planet!

Building

See p. 180, natural building resource centers

Introduction

by Lynne Elizabeth

Lynne Elizabeth is Editor of New Village, the national journal of Architects, Designers, Planners for Social Responsibility (based in the USA), and co-editor of the book "Alternative Construction: Contemporary Natural Building Methods," John Wiley and Sons, 2000. **lynne@newvillage.net**

Ecological architecture and construction, and in particular non-industrialized building, is often viewed skeptically by those trained in mainstream industrial systems. The language alone can evoke prejudicial resistance, as I experienced while working on a book about alternative construction methods, when I was warned not to use the term "natural."

Concerns about ecological architecture include its applicability, durability, availability, and cost. Although appropriate natural building systems, just like any other systems, should be selected with consideration of site, climate, culture, and availability of materials (all building systems are not ubiquitously applicable), earth and straw-based systems have been built quite successfully in modern urban settings. While the demand for trained architects, contractors, and craftspeople trained in alternative building still outstrips availability, there are significantly more now than ten years ago.

Documentation of standardized testing on alternative natural and green materials within various construction assemblies is growing, despite the continuing challenge of funding such research. And, regarding the economy of ecological building, hard evidence of the benefits is spreading, including respected institutional reports about the broader effects of various construction practices on the quality of air, water, and forests.

Making a Compelling Case for Ecological Building

by Lynne Elizabeth

As vanguards of an ecological ethic and lifestyle that is fringe to the dominant culture, we are vulnerable to occasional discouragement, if not despair. The gap between ideal and reality may seem unbridgeable, or the movement toward change may feel fragmented and too feeble to maintain itself. Often we are wanting too much too fast. Or we have focused on obstacles rather than developing the vision of what we want to achieve.

People can be suspicious of change, so the best revolutions are made gently, step by small step. We must, of course, make a compelling case for needed change, yet conduct ourselves with all the skills of good communitarians in the process. Showing our impatience, disrespect, or extreme frustration, gets us nowhere. We need to strengthen our own faith in positive alternatives, and one of the best ways to accomplish that is to educate ourselves thoroughly. Through the learning process, we can naturally assemble a support system of experienced people, as well as a library of valuable references.

Sometimes we underestimate the enormity of our ambitions. The difference between appreciating a beautiful violin and being able to play that instrument is vast.

Imagine now training a few dozen friends to perform as an orchestra when you yourself are still learning to read music. Introducing an entirely new building genre to your community and then completing a structure is no less of a feat. Architectural systems that have taken centuries to perfect, and construction skills passed down through generations, can hardly be transferred in a single weekend workshop. Yet, that is often the expectation.

Obtaining plan approvals from building departments unfamiliar with wall systems such as strawbale, rammed earth, light-clay, or cob can also be pushing for the impossible, unless diplomatic efforts are made to bring building officials through an educational process. Building officials, too, may be constrained by codes requiring mechanical systems for heating, cooling, and ventilation, when you want to specify only natural systems. Presenting professional documentation of the efficient performance of such solutions in a similar context may save you the expense of being required to install dual systems.

Fortunately the resources to help architects, contractors, craftspeople, and owner/builders are abundant and improving every year. Educational centers offering technical assistance in natural, ecological, sustainable, environmental, healthy, and green building can be found throughout the world. Training programs, conferences, and wall-raisings are popular, as well. Four new books have been published in the past 18 months alone that give an overview of the many promising ecological building methods. Manuals on individual alternative construction systems are still proliferating and being regularly updated. Handsome picture books that show off the beauty of natural building are also enriching the field, and the Internet helps many find technical assistance every day. Popular media, too, have moved beyond depicting ecological building as sensational, and are more mature and practical in their coverage. Reportage within the mainstream building profession is increasingly in-depth, as, for example, the International Congress of Building Officials (ICBO), which has devoted three issues of its magazine "Building Standards" to ecological and natural building methods.

Above: House of Culture (Kulturhus) at Järna, Sweden, built according to Steiner principles. Architects: Asmussens Arkitektkontor. The house is part of the Järna village, which comprises residences, a clinic for complementary medicine, shops, a university, and much more. Photo: Martin Voss-J.

Some of the best guidance to shepherding non-standard architectural plans through a building department for permits has been written by David Eisenberg of the Development Center for Appropriate Technology (DCAT) in Tucson, Arizona. In summary, David recommends appreciating the plan checker's responsibilities, mustering infinite patience, and starting as early as possible to provide your local building official with the most authoritative information on the particular building method you will be using. He points out, too, that the first people to present an ecological alternative for permits should be mindful that they are not only working to get their own structure approved, but laying the groundwork for all who follow.

Because non-industrialized building systems do not have the advantage of underwritten research, development, testing, and advocacy afforded to industrial materials, it is easy for them to be ignored in the written codes. DCAT has been working with the primary organizations of building code officials in the United States, not only as an advocate of ecological construction, but initiating a re-examination of the underlying principles of building health and safety so that they now encompass global sustainability.

After all, what good is a weatherproof house if the air in it is unbreathable?

Below: left, light shaft at the ING bank in Amsterdam showing the integration of more natural, human building principles in mainstream construction. Architects: Alberts & Van Huut. Photo: Martin Voss-J. Right: natural housing with a mainstream look in Germany. Photo: GEN

Natural Building:
An Alchemical Approach

by Rolf Jacobsen
Translation Karen Svensson

Rolf Jacobsen is a member of the Gaia architect group and one of the initiators of the Bridge-building school in Norway (see page 52). In his essay, The Alchemy of Building, *he connects natural building to the human spirit. He establishes that today, alongside rampant materialism, we also find that people are on an inner search for inner truth. He says that these apparently contradictory drives can connect in the alchemy of building: "Alchemy sees physical reality and the metaphysical world as related, and we can transfer this to ... natural building". The search for inner truth can happen by shaping our own environment through the homes we build, and the materials we use. Rolf Jacobsen talks about the alchemy of building because, like the alchemist, the natural builder uses original raw materials (prima materia), which can be found in nature around him, to build a bridge between our physical reality and metaphysical existence. The process of transformation goes through experimentation, knowledge of chemistry and physics, trial and error. At the end of it, we find "gold" in the form of natural buildings, which are healing, provide space for human growth, and are the "human-made picture of the universe", or also the picture of who we are. A living, ecological architecture can represent what we know, believe and dream of. The process of building (our own home), participating in it body and soul, overcoming the many practical difficulties that arise, exercising our will to realize our dream, can be a most effective teacher in life. The following are passages from Rolf Jacobsen's essay.*

The alchemy of building: the "prima materia"

Natural building starts with the use of original raw materials, which can be found locally. This is our "prima materia": it can be stone, wood, clay, earth or straw. Natural building is also about getting to know these materials through experimenting, again and again, and researching. The alchemy of building will turn the practical exercises into inner exercises. We build a house with a soul, and we build a soul with strawbales, a hammer and a trowel and by stamping the earth.

"Genius loci"

The alchemy of building originates in the observation of where we are, in ourselves and in physical reality. We must under-

Roof of the Eurythmeum at the Gotheanum Institute (Switzerland), founded by Rudolf Steiner. Photo: Martin Voss-J.

stand "Genius Loci", the soul of a place. This includes physical, concrete parameters such as resources, soil, climate, vegetation, topography etc., as well as less definable qualities: light, atmosphere, smells, air etc. We must try to understand, observe, listen, sense, we must analyze and be quiet. What is this place - in the world? When we have interpreted and used that which we have in us to understand the soul of a place, we have the necessary foundation to create an architecture, which fits in naturally; a house, which belongs. We must also get to know our inner landscape, and seek to find out where we situate ourselves in it. Where is our "place of the soul?" Here again we have to search, feel, observe and be quiet to understand. Alchemically, we are talking about "prima materia" in both the inner and outer form. We start from the bottom with our raw material and begin building it up in the outer world. A little bit of humility helps. We are all novices in the world of alchemical building.

Reconquering Our Immediate Environment

Without a basic knowledge of natural laws, chemical reaction patterns, physical properties, and symbolic characters, the alchemist would never be able to reach his noble goal. In alchemical building, one of the crucial things is insight and participation in one's close surroundings: where one lives, natural circumstances, the social space etc. We must reconquer our immediate environment. If something new and sustainable is to emerge, it must find its source in the living local community. The alchemy of building aims higher than just the individual natural house. It is about developing community, healthy social forms, a vibrant relationship between house and people, and closely-knit neighborhoods.

The Dynamics of Transformation

The alchemist's project was a slow process of transformation on several levels which required patience, perseverance, comprehensive studies and countless experiments. The alchemist found that creating gold, be it physical or spiritual, was difficult. Within the alchemy of building, it is the vision that represents the alchemist's gold: beautiful, natural buildings, fruitful permaculture gardens,

A different way of forming models is to create them in clay and subsequently cast them in plaster. This gives a good feel for the three-dimensional reality of the design. Many Steiner-inspired architects use this technique. Here, casts of the Goetheanum buildings in Switzerland. Photo: Martin Voss-J.

living ecovillages, and a sustainable and just society. That is the vision that will inspire us, and lead us further ahead. We build, learn new methods, new angles, experience and create reality. Step by step we bring about change. The alchemy of building is about gradual change, about ennobling the outer and inner, the hand and the heart. The vision of the gold leads us forward.

Clay is a traditional building material much used by ecological builders. It offers a host of beneficial properties, such as a high absorbence factor, malleability, temperature regulation, humidity regulation, and much more. Here, a mosque in Djenné, Mali, built in clay and straw. Photo: © Peter Engberg.

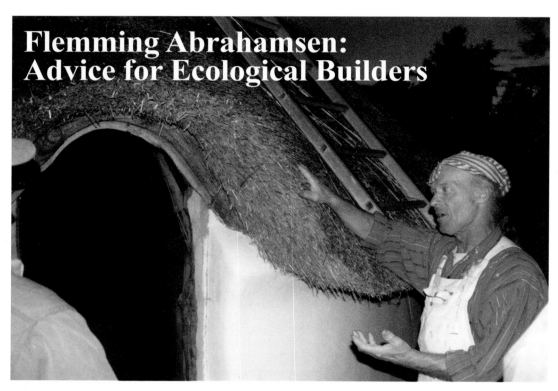

Flemming Abrahamsen: Advice for Ecological Builders

Flemming Abrahamsen explaining a cob building to course participants. This circular cob building is one which Flemming and his crew built at his home in Stenlille, Denmark. Flemming's home and the surrounding buildings are demonstrations of ecological building practices.
Photo: Hildur Jackson.

Interview with Flemming Abrahamsen
by Hildur Jackson, translation Karen Svensson

Flemming is one of the pioneers of ecological building in the North. He introduced modern composting toilets in Denmark, as well as the Finnish 'mass stove' (a type of storage heater where a convection stove is encased in a brick 'mass' – up to three tons in weight – which stores heat for up to 24 hours). He has been instrumental in training the next generation of ecological builders (see Kolja Hejgaard page 46). Flemming founded Denmark's first ecological building and renewable energy company, 'Renewed Energy' which has a policy of equal salaries and responsibilities.

Q: What's your advice for people who want to build their own house?

Flemming Abrahamsen: In ecological building, there is a tendency for people to build their own houses. I believe it's a good thing, but would advise them to work together with professionals. A lot of people, when they're already far into the building process, find themselves saying: "I wish I'd known ... We could have done this and that, and then we could have avoided catastrophes." Professional ecological builders should not be afraid to talk with self-builders, and self-builders should not be afraid to contact professionals. The two should mix.

Q: What types of houses would you advise self-builders to construct in our climate (Denmark)?

Flemming: To understand what to build in Denmark, you have to look at history over the past hundreds of years. Weather conditions here include a strong west wind, heavy rain, ice on the walls. Walls have to be strong enough to withstand such influences. In Denmark, houses have to be windproof, not humidity proof. For my part I support natural building, which to me means experimenting with natural and local materials.

Here I'm thinking for example of minimizing the use of concrete. (This is one of the areas in which one has to start breaking building regulations, and to influence the Ministry of Housing toward adopting new natural solutions – which actually are the traditional ones.) Typically, people start the building process with the house's foundation, which is concrete, dug down to a depth of 90 cm. Here you have to think about what the concrete has to be able to do for you: it has to be able to bear the house. For the family homes we need to build, the foundation could actually just as well be a stone fascine. There is no reason for it to be made of concrete. We have to break with our habitual thinking. We should just go back to the principles of the old country church: it rests on a stone fascine, not a concrete foundation. It hasn't been dug 90 cm down into the ground. But it's been standing there for 800 to 900 years! So it's worth looking up the local registers to identify buildings which have existed for 900 years. This applies all over the world. The worst that can happen (to building) is that academics forget to be humble in front of local people's traditional creations, achieved through trial and error and much hardship. Generation after generation have found out how things have to be built to last. It's wrong to bypass this knowledge.

Q: So what we need is for people to make it "modern" to build ecologically, using old traditions?

Flemming: Yes. Compost toilets are the best example of this: there is so much trouble with authorities for the introduction of compost toilets in Denmark, yet we know that this is the only right way to go. However these same authorities don't have a problem with us exporting the solution. I say that we will never get compost toilets exported to China to save the world situation if we don't use them locally. We have to show that it's modern here first. Only then can it be seen as modern in China. We can't skip that link in the chain, and say: "Others have to do it, but not us".

Q: What materials would you use for building in Denmark? Straw, cob, stone, clay?

Flemming: I would use the four materials you mentioned together. I wouldn't want to leave any of them out. The same applies to energy systems: I would never rely on just one energy system. It's important to interweave systems, so you use them in the best possible way. You can never solve it all with one thing.

As for building options in Denmark, I'd build the side of the house which faces North in timber. This side is where most heat is lost, so straw would be a good insulator there. Where the West wind comes in, I'd give the wall clay plaster. In some places you will only need plaster and in others you can have a cob wall. I really like mixing these in a house. There are all sorts of hybrids, and many different ways of combining them. You can make the prettiest things with firewood, like low walls built with clay mortar. It becomes so beautiful ... Natural stone walls are also beautiful. And clay floors, there's real substance in those.

Q: What type of heating system would you recommend for an ecovillage?

Flemming: A communal heating system is most likely the most ecological and least polluting in the long run. However in the case of Torup (northern Zealand, Denmark), engineers intended to "do magic" with a central heating system, but it went to pot because it became too expensive. If a communal heating system can't be set up, then we work with mass stoves, which we are very happy with. There is an added bonus to mass stoves, which is that you have your fire inside the house. Most people start off thinking in terms of energy systems, and find out that actually the emotional appeal of a living fire in the house, which one tends, and which is so close to one, is of the greatest value and wins all arguments. Also, a bread oven incorporated in the mass stove is a lovely thing to have, it's all ready for baking when one comes back from school or work.

Q: Would you use the mass stove to heat water?

Flemming: I have nothing against putting in a heat alternator – we do this in many cases, heating the water in the upper section of the oven. But it should be relatively easy to get to for repairs.

Q: How many square meters can a mass stove heat up?

Flemming: If we're talking about a house, which is well insulated, it's no problem heating up 125 m², but no more than that. It also depends on people themselves. Some feel they can just put on a sweater when they walk around the house. Others want the ambient temperature to be 21°C at all times. The latter is not very ecological, though. It's a modern comfort, which we've adopted over the past 40 years. All during history the rich people's castles had heating in three rooms, the rest was 0°C.

Q: You talked earlier about a three-ton mass stove?

Flemming: We build three-to-five ton mass stoves with smoke shafts, which are built on the spot with stone materials. Only the door and the ash drawer are cast iron.

Q: After the mass stove, what's the next best solution?

Flemming: If we're thinking of complementing our heat supply in December-February with alternative energy, and we live in Denmark, we could have a windmill for heating: There's almost always wind in this country, so a mill can heat the house. It's a windmill with a whisk, which heats the water for the heating system. Small windmills, which can do this for individual households, can be found. But I find it difficult to imagine a Danish landscape with such a windmill beside each house.

Otherwise, firewood is also a possibility here in Denmark. Here (as opposed to most of the Southern Hemisphere), it is a form of renewable energy. It grows over and over, and it's CO_2 neutral, and we love surrounding ourselves with bushes and trees, so why not use wood?

Q: What is your opinion on wastewater and toilet systems?

Flemming: That's the issue on which I'm really tough. According to me the only right thing to do is to compost wastes and to retain and separate urine and feces. The biggest problem is that we try to lead urine and feces out through pipes and into the waterways, and to me this is a catastrophe. In the meantime we've been brought up to think that the water closet is the most modern and hygienic solution: correct, until the waste comes out of the house, after which we consider that the rest of it is not our problem. Only it *is* our problem.

We think we are so smart, but I'd say the level of intelligence has gone down a lot since the time when people knew about nutritional balances in nature; the times when people knew about the use of feces and urine in nature. The waste from water toilets represents 90% of the individual household's environmental pollution.

What's left is 10%, and here washing products are naughtiest of all, so one should use those that are as neutral and harmless as possible.

The Elements of Ecological Building

Interview with Kolja Hejgaard
by Karen Svensson

Kolja Hejgaard is a Danish eco-builder who studied and worked with Flemming Abrahamsen, among others, and traveled around the world to learn about natural building techniques. Today, he designs and builds with natural materials, using alternative energy techniques and holistic architecture.

Q: What are the elements one should consider before starting to build an ecological house?

Kolja: Look at what your needs are, now and in the future. Draw a clock dial (see drawing p. 49). Pencil in when you get up in the morning (up until that moment you've used the bedroom in the house), and when you have breakfast (kitchen). If you don't work at home, mark when you come back and eat in the evening (kitchen/dining space). If you work at home, write down the hours spent in your office or workshop. Mark all the needs you have during a fortnight (on weekdays and weekends) on the dial, including extra needs when you have guests over. Looking at the dial drawing, you can infer your personal requirements:

Respect for nature and its beings is one of the basic principles of ecological building. Here, Kolja with a curious duck.

for example when to have daylight in which rooms, what rooms require most heating, how large the rooms need to be, and how the rooms need to be positioned in relation to each other (which of them need to be interconnected).

To determine your building style and use of materials, look at local building traditions in your area, because these are adapted to your region and its climate. From traditional buildings in your area, you can derive information on what roof, foundation and materials to opt for. A good rule of thumb is: Keep It Simple (KIS), especially if you are building a house yourself, and have limited experience. Every time you have an angle/corner, all your materials have to meet at the junction. The more angles/corners you have, the more complicated your building process will be. Also, follow the nature of your chosen materials: if you build with timber, don't try for rounded shapes, while clay is ideal for round shapes.

You also need to look at your climatic position in the human comfort zone. The further away you are from the human comfort zone in terms of heat, cold, dryness, and humidity, the more demands will be placed on your house (see page 49) to make up for imbalances.

Last but not least: don't be afraid to question locals and other ecological builders. The rule of thumb here is: "There are no stupid questions, only silly answers."

Q: Can you give us some more tips for roofs and foundations?

Kolja: I like the saying: "A good house needs a broad hat and a strong shoe." It sums up some basic construction truths.

A good foundation is dug down in the ground (except in humid tropical climates). You dig until you have removed the top soil, and have reached subsoil, a layer which by its composition is able to support the building. In Denmark, you reach subsoil at a depth of between 10 cm and 2 meters (swamp areas). You have to reach frost-free depth, so you don't get ice under the foundation (which causes cracking). Alternatively, you can make sure that you build your foundation so as to drain water away (another way of avoiding ice formation under the foundation). Insulate the foundation with as much care as you would the walls (heat frame).

Above: strawbale house at Torup, Denmark, by Kolja Hejgaard. The house is octagonal, and its outer walls are protected with a layer of plaster made of Perlite (vulcanic expanded clay) and lime. The grass roof has an octagonal light shaft in its center, wich casts light inside the house over two floors. To the right, there is a cooling room for food storage. Photos: left: Kolja Hejgaard. Right: Hildur Jackson.

When mapping out your foundation, you also need to think of heat storage. If you want to have insulated heat storage in your foundation, you need to build it in from the start. You typically place the water pipes in a sand layer, ready to be connected with solar panels and possibly a mass stove.

When choosing a roof, you need to consider whether you will use the space under it for living. If yes, it needs insulation against heat and cold, wind and damp. Your roof construction needs to be ten times as dense on the outside as on the inside. This rule is also applicable for walls, to avoid condensation and humidity inside the construction.

On the inside of your house, as under your roof (if it is used as living space) there needs to be a vapor barrier. Use a material which slows down the transference of vapor through the wall/roof (the material used will depend on what you choose as external covering). One possibility is a special type of paint (for example a mix of whitewash with a bit of latex). Insulation materials need to be hygroscopic (absorbing humidity). If you use wood in your construction, hygroscopic insulation materials will prevent the wood from absorbing all the humidity.

On the outside of your insulation layer, you need a layer that can break the wind. If wind penetrates your insulation, the insulation won't have any effect.

Then you need an open layer for ventilation. And on top of that, your roof covering (tiles, sheets, wood shingles). If you want a thatched roof, the inner construction is the same, except for the ventilation layer: the straw needs to lie right on top of your insulation, with no air in between (in the eventuality of a fire, this prevents spreading).

If you want a sod (grass) roof, you need a very sturdy construction to support it. Grass/sod roofs can serve to cool a house down in summer and prevent heat loss in winter. The construction of the roof is the same as the one described above, plus a damp shield over the ventilation layer. The damp shield is typically polyethylene, upon which you spread soil for grass to grow on. Traditionally, people used birch bark as a damp shield.

Q: What are the easiest materials to use ?

Kolja: This depends on the climate you live in, and on the materials that are readily available. Generally, there is a good reason why 60% of the Earth's people still live in clay constructions: it's cheap, strong, healthy, and easy to use. If you don't build in the humid tropics (where your house is elevated on pillars), your foundation should be made of mineral materials: stone, concrete, or bricks. You can avoid using concrete by opting for bricks and stone, however bricks require cement mortar and plaster (on the outside) anyway. Using stone requires very good skills, as you have to get the building's pressure to spread evenly over the foundation (especially in the case of a heavy construction such as a house in stone and clay). Realistically, it's difficult to avoid concrete altogether in the Western world, but that doesn't mean you have to use concrete slabs. Use a frame or a point foundation instead. This minimizes the use of concrete. It's difficult to sum up materials just like that. I'd rather make a table to include different variables that are to be taken into account (see p. 48).

Q: Are there particular things to remember for the Southern Hemisphere?

Kolja: In the global South, it's good to spread the message that one of the fanciest building materials to use in the West at the moment is clay. It's what Hollywood movie stars want to live in, because it gives the best indoor climate, it's beautiful, and it's a luxury: around here, it is often expensive to buy a house built in clay, because it requires craftsmanship and time. We're not only reverting to building with clay and other natural materials because it's fashionable, but also because many so-called modern construction materials and coatings have given us allergies and other diseases. There is nothing fancy about concrete. The only thing to be said about it is, that concrete and cement production account for 10% of the world's CO_2 emissions, and that it is neither healthy nor a good insulating material. Another point to remember for the Southern Hemisphere (as everywhere else in the world) is, that it's important to advocate the use of compost toilets for hygiene and for reducing the use of water.

Material		Composition/Properties	Used for	Climatic conditions where used
Clay		Indefinitely recyclable; breathes (air throughflow); accumulates/regulates heat and humidity; permeable; high absorbence	floors; walls; roofs; dome construction	all
	Pisé	Rammed clay + gravel	floors; walls	all; found everywhere but in Greenland
	Adobe	clay + straw + fine gravel for blocks, brick-laying	walls; vaulted constructions (parabolic); floor separation	all
	Cob	clay + straw + fine gravel	floors, walls, internal fire protection for thatched roofs	all
	Bricks	clay, burnt; absorb less humidity than dried/compressed; more impermeable; higher tensile strength; lighter than unburnt clay as crystalline water components are evaporated; irreversible process (lower recyclability).	floors; walls; roads; terraces; ceilings; roofs	all
	Compressed Earth	clay + gravel, compressed; high compression/low tensile strength; easy to handle and produce	walls; vaulted constructions	all
Wood		Cellulose; easy to work with (soft); relatively light; high tensile strength; flammable; renewable (to which degree depends on local conditions and abundance)	load-bearing construction; floors; walls; roofs; foundations; stairs; windows; doors; inventory	places with no deforestation, below the timber line. *Note* in humid tropical climates, use wood only in elevated constructions. Rot and vermine pose problems. In arid regions, use wood ony for roof construction, windows, doors (dryness). Wood provides no temperature regulation.
Straw		Cellulose; easy to work with; good insulator; lightweight, though flammable in itself, more fire resistant than concrete when properly baled and plastered; high earthquake and wind resistance; high strength in relation to weight	walls; composite for floors; walls	everywhere where straw is naturally available; low suitability in humid tropical climates (problems with rot).
Stone		Mineral composition	foundation; walls; roofs	all
	Pumice Stone	lightweight; easy to work with (soft); relatively insulating; porous (high air throughflow, breathes)	insulation (also in pulverized form in insulation)	can be used everywhere, but is not found in many places
	Sandstone	lightweight; easy to work with (soft); porous	walls; foundation; inventory	vulnerable to cold and humidity, not in humid/cold climates
	Granite	frost-proof (zero humidity penetration); hard; heavy	walls; foundation; tiles (floors and walls); inventory (sink, table top)	all places where found
	Slate	layered stone	roofs; outer wall coverings	all places where found

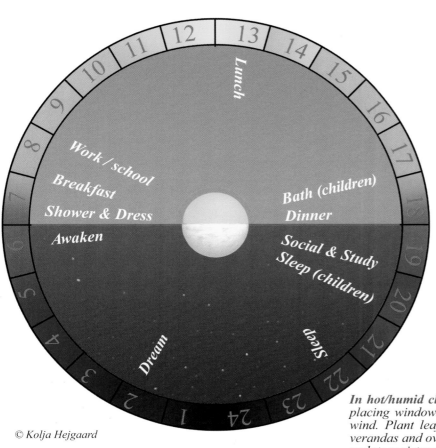

© Kolja Hejgaard

Need Evaluation
for Building Design

The dial shows how one can mark the times when particular rooms are in use. This helps determine the orientation and interconnection of rooms according to the need for high/low temperatures, daylight and access. Use separate dials for weekdays and for weekends.

Bioclimatic Index

In cold climates, build compact constructions turned towards the sun. Use heavy, dark materials for passive heat accumulation, as a humidity buffer and against overheating. Protect the house against cold winds by erecting a shelterbelt. Place rooms with lowest heating requirements on the shadow side (north side) and avoid building in cold pockets. If snowfall is frequent and abundant, use it constructively as insulation, since it has the same qualities as good insulation materials.

In hot/dry climates, you need to catch cool winds and reflect sun and light with white. Plant on the sun side to create shadow for walls and roof. Use heavy materials to level out daily temperature fluctuations. Use natural cooling techniques such as double roofing, reflective roof covering, cooling of incoming air (e.g. filter through a drain below ground level), cooling shafts/chimneys, wind catchers, overhanging roofs and dams to humidify the air.

In hot/humid climates, ensure air movement (cross-ventilation, e.g. by placing windows on two opposite sides of the building) and catch the wind. Plant leafy trees on the sun side, create shadow with trellised verandas and overhanging roofs. Use light materials which do not accumulate moisture. In an extremely warm/humid climate, it is best to build houses on stilts. Wood is not recommended.

Drawings: Kolja Hejgaard, Alexander Svensson

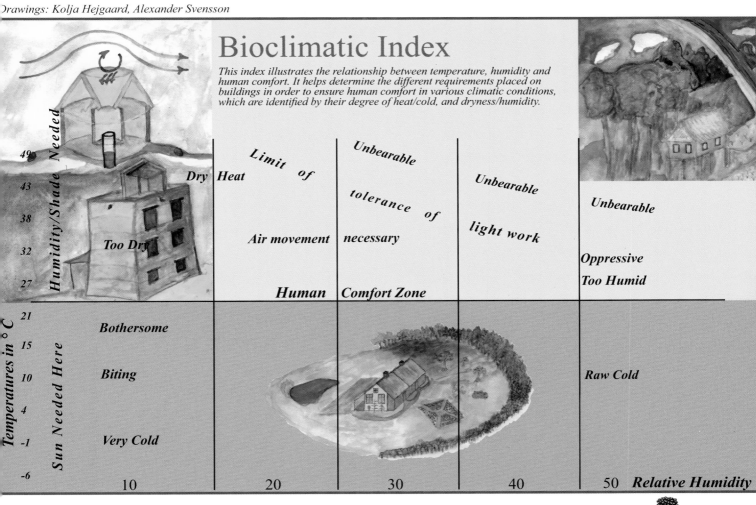

Bioclimatic Index — This index illustrates the relationship between temperature, humidity and human comfort. It helps determine the different requirements placed on buildings in order to ensure human comfort in various climatic conditions, which are identified by their degree of heat/cold, and dryness/humidity.

Ecological Buildings

Above: Houses at Dyssekilde Ecovillage in Denmark. Here, architects and builders experiment with different styles and materials, creating a composite picture of ecological constructions. To the front, left: Brick houses with greenhouses and solar panels. Front right: Flemming Abrahamsen's "Folkesolhus", with its low overhanging roof. In the middle, background, the group of dome houses which can be seen from the road several kilometers away as Torup's own landmark. Photo: courtesy Allan Elm and Troels Dilling, LØS. Below: Flemming Abrahamsen's cob house at Dyssekilde-Torup (Summer 2002). Photo: Hildur Jackson. Below right: House in straw and clay at Gyurufu, Hungary. Photo: Philip Snyder.

Left: Wooden house at Sieben Linden ecovillage, Germany. In the foreground: Silke Hagmayer, one of the founders of Sieben Linden, with Ross Jackson, co-founder of Gaia Trust and GEN. Photo: Hildur Jackson

Below: New building finished in 2001 in Lebensgarten, Germany. The house provides great exposure to sunlight, and is built out of wood. Photo: Karen Svensson

Above: This street at Findhorn, Scotland, shows how mainstream ecological design can look while providing the advantages of natural building. Materials used are wood and clay tiles, roofs are equipped with solar panels. Photo: © Findhorn Visuals. Above right: Schoolhouse in Järna, Sweden, built by Prisma architects, out of loam loafs (clay rolls) with a shingle roof. The lively, playful colors and the organic design which fits the materials all play together to create a unified whole. Photo: Martin Voss J.

Above: Workshop at Goetheanum (anthroposophical university founded by Rudolf Steiner in Switzerland). Though this building was not made out of natural materials, its design is an early attempt at building expressive forms which work with the environment: Here, form and colors blend into the blue sky as if reaching out to it. Above right: Christopher Day's Christian Retreat Center, "Ffad-y-Brenin", Pembrokeshire, Wales. Stone building designed to fit snugly into the surrounding nature. In the foreground, a chapel built around a rock (see page 108). Below left: Kindergarten with sod roof, "Nant-y-Cwn", Wales, by Christopher Day. Right: Home in Järna, Sweden, Prisma Architects. Fairytale design and shingle roof. Photos: Martin Voss J.

The Bridge-Building School, Norway

by Jan Martin Bang

The Bridge Building School is located at Solborg Camphill Village in southern Norway, an hour from Oslo. The School's goal is to build a bridge between the heart and the hand, between the world of spirit, where ideas arise and creativity is stimulated, and the world of materials, where our hands fashion our surroundings with a variety of tools and materials. We also strive to create a bridge between East and West, between Western Europe, Latvia and Russia.

Recognizing that Camphill Villages are ecovillages, we want to create a link between people's rising ecological consciousness and life as lived in Camphill, by teaching permaculture and creating strong links with the Norwegian Ecovillage Association, "Kilden", and with the Norwegian Strawbale Building Association.

Our main educational program is a five-month course in ecological building. This program was first offered in the year 2000, with twelve students spending two months in Rozkalni Village in Latvia, building a strawbale house, and incorporating many other ecological features such as a "kakel" heat-retaining wood stove, passive solar heating, mud and log walls and earthen floors. The program was offered again in 2001, with a focus on a small strawbale family house needed at the Waldorf School connected to Svetlana Village in Russia. The course is projected to expand to a full ten months.

In addition to this, short courses are offered for Camphill Villages. So far we have held introductory courses, a story telling festival, permaculture courses and professional seminars in curative education and social therapy. This part of the School will be developed and expanded in the future, to include biodynamic farming, nutrition and other subjects. Teaching is in Norwegian and English.

brobygg@start.no

Natural Cooling Cabinet and Ventilation

by Jørgen Løgstrup   www.rootzone.dk

Natural cooling is as big a problem in many places as heating is in others. Jørgen Løgstrup is the founder of "Rootzone" and "Transform", two Danish companies which design and implement root zone systems. He has developed a system to cool down the indoor climate for general housing, and provide cool air for food and beverage storage at a low energy cost. We thank him for the use of his material.

The natural cooling cabinet and ventilation system is based on utilizing the cool air found below the ground surface. The cooling effect of humidifying air over a water surface is combined with the energy potential available in warm air, all integrated into a non-energy consuming air-conditioner. In Australia, this method has allowed a low 14°C indoor temperature to be maintained with an outside atmospheric temperature of 55°C (see diagram on opposite page).

Foods and beverages are generally kept at temperatures below what is optimal for products such as wines, cheese, fruits and vegetables, which keep their flavor and quality better at 8 to 10°C than at the 2 to 4°C we maintain in our refrigerators (in order to keep the meat, fish and various dairy products). "Transform" developed the Natural Cooling Cabinet which, at a negligible energy consumption (only occasionally to be powered by a small solar panel), can keep a temperature of 8 to 10°C at all times of the year.

The cooling effect is obtained by filtering the air first through a humid plant wall, and then through a drain placed just below ground level. At a depth of only one meter below ground level, the temperature is a cool 6 to 10°C (or less) throughout the year.

The force pulling the cooled air up into the cabinets is a combination of thermodynamics and aerodynamics, utilizing the sun chimney effect, where the sun heats the exhaust shaft from the cabinets. The exhaust is shaped 'aerophonically': exposure to wind causes a vacuum to build up in the exhaust, thus creating pulling power to withdraw warm air from the system.

As a curiosity, "Transform" has built in a fresh drinking water supply cooler in the cabinet, to ensure that water from this tap will be cool from the very moment the tap is opened. In conventional tap systems one may have to let the water run for some time before it is cool enough to refresh, causing considerable water waste.

Compost Toilet

A generalized, continous-process toilet. The baffle prevents fresh material arriving prematurely at the retrieval point.

Graphic from "Lifting the Lid", by Peter Harper and Louise Halestrap. Publisher: the Center for Alternative Technology Publications. ISBN: 1 898049 79 3 © CAT, Peter Harper.

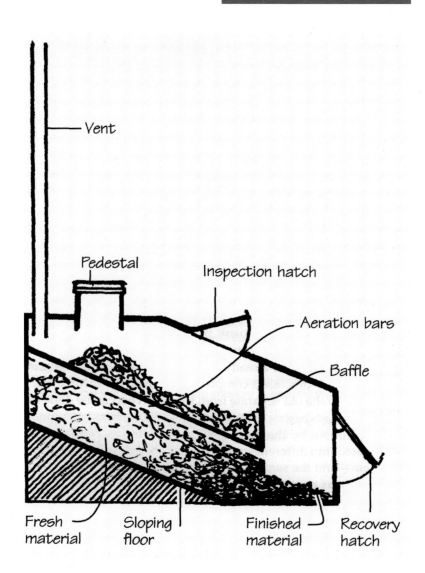

Natural Cooling Cabinet

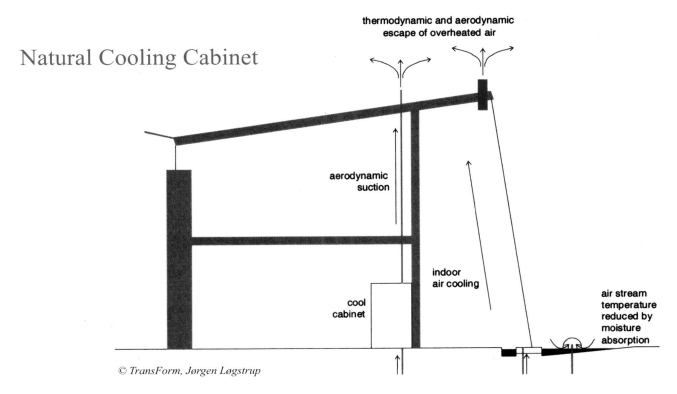

© TransForm, Jørgen Løgstrup

Energy

Integrated Renewable Energy Systems for Villages
Interview with Preben Mægaard

by Hildur Jackson

Preben Maegaard has fought for over 25 years for the introduction of renewable energy worldwide. He has founded the Folkecenter for Renewable Energy in Thy (Denmark), a research, demonstration, and education center for windmills, biogas, solar thermal, and photovoltaic systems, and most recently wave energy systems. The Folke-center's field of competence also includes integrated farming. Preben Maegaard's lobbying is proving successful: in Thy, on a windy day, windmills cover 150% of the consumption of electricity. Wind energy is the region's big-gest export item. Sixteen thousand new jobs have been created within the future-oriented industry of wind energy. Thirteen years ago, Preben hosted the first global conference on renewable energy with participants from 28 coun-tries. He is now one of the central figures of a global network of renewable energy organizations, offices and centers. Today, the Center's survival is threatened by the retroactive withdrawal of all funding by a recently elected conservative government. It is our hope that the Folkecenter will be able to continue their admirable work.

Q: What is the future of energy production?

Preben Maegaard: "One real challenge for the future is the transition from fossil fuel to renewable energy. It is unavoidable, because within a few decades the remaining oil, gas, and uranium resources will be close to depletion. We have very little time to make the transition. Twenty years back there were no options to choose from. The development within renewable energy over the last few years has given us many more possibilities and new opportunities, which we now can combine in interesting models. No single model is the right one.

Q: How do you determine what model to opt for?

Preben: Around the world the available natural resources vary. Some areas have plenty of wind, others have sun or biogas. In this region (Thy) there is no doubt that wind energy is the most suitable. A development plan for eco-logical settlements here in Thy would use wind as its main energy component, but not exclusively: biogas can be stored well. Wind energy is more difficult to store, but we do have to store it and may use hydrogen as the medium.

You store wind energy under pressure in a tank as hydro-gen. It is a completely clean gas. The only residue when you burn the gas is clean water. Then we can run our vehicles on hydrogen, use it in our home for our stove (gas burner) and for combined heat and power produc-tion. It is such mixed systems we are dealing with.

Not so long ago, I was in Northern Siberia, north of the Arctic Circle. There was too little sun to base solar sys-tems on, and no possibility for biogas. But wind energy was abundant. The only alternative to wind energy was to fly mineral oil in, which would make it cost 3 times the normal price. So wind energy is the obvious choice there: ten percent of it can be used for electricity and

90% for heating. In tropical areas, sunshine is abundant. Solar cells can provide for all electricity needs there.

Q: What can an integrated renewable energy system look like for an ecovillage of about 100 families?

Preben: To some extent that depends on what you want energy for. You have to adapt your systems to the needs of individual settlements. First, analyze the demands, and then design the supply systems. You have to analyze the individual energy elements of the system thoroughly, both the potential resources and the technologies (i.e. straw and wood; wind, solar, photovoltaic, biogas systems); then you have to combine the elements you opt for in a suitable way. You have to base the system on the energy sources that are predominant in your specific location. Your solutions will differ a lot according to climatic zones. You should note that solar and wind energy are unpredictable to some extent, and should be combined with other supply systems which can be stored, such as wood, plant oil, and various gases under pressure (hydrogen, biogas).

Co-generation (combined heat and power production) is the first level of integration. Here are some basics: in all combustion systems, whether you burn oil, wood or gas, you produce both electricity and heat. You typically get a maximum of 40% electricity out of the combustion process, the rest will be heat. Use the cooling water, and not electricity, for heating (except as I just said near the Arctic Circle, where you would have to fly oil in if you didn't use 90% of the produced energy for heating).

Excess wind can be converted into hydrogen, which you can compress and store. The problem is still to get the power conversion units for the use of hydrogen for small-scale application – but they will be available for households within a few years. Hydrogen has been used

The Folkecenter for Renewable Energy, DK

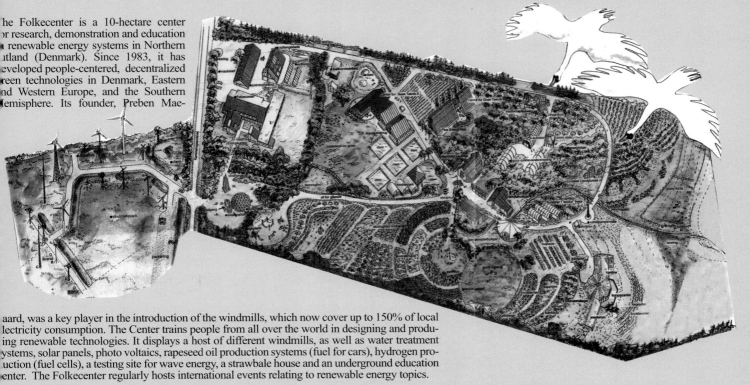

The Folkecenter is a 10-hectare center for research, demonstration and education in renewable energy systems in Northern Jutland (Denmark). Since 1983, it has developed people-centered, decentralized green technologies in Denmark, Eastern and Western Europe, and the Southern Hemisphere. Its founder, Preben Mae-

gaard, was a key player in the introduction of the windmills, which now cover up to 150% of local electricity consumption. The Center trains people from all over the world in designing and producing renewable technologies. It displays a host of different windmills, as well as water treatment systems, solar panels, photo voltaics, rapeseed oil production systems (fuel for cars), hydrogen production (fuel cells), a testing site for wave energy, a strawbale house and an underground education center. The Folkecenter regularly hosts international events relating to renewable energy topics.

Top: Map of the Center. Below, 1st row from left: Preben Maegaard talking in front of the entrance to the underground education center (center picture). Right: The dome-shaped meeting room inside the education center can accommodate several hundred people. 2nd row: Rootzones (left and middle). Right: Meeting participants at the Summer 2001 conference for International Energy Centers: Jane (Preben's partner and co-director), Galal Osman, Egypt (African Wind Energy Association), Preben, Wu Libin, Chengdu, China and Ulla Vandbæk, EU Parliament Member. Bottom row, left: Partial view of the Folkecenter's grounds in the early '90s (overlooking the Limfjord). Right: Testing facility for wave energy in the Limfjord. Bottom: Several dozen people demonstrate the span of the wing of a windmill. Photos: Folkecenter for Renewable Energy, DK; Hildur Jackson; Lucilla Borio.

for industrial applications for many decades in the chemical industry. It is a well-known technology.

Q: Who can design these systems, and how do they work?

Preben: A systems engineer can design them. Here at the Folkecenter we combine wind, solar, and hydrogen energy systems, plant oil, and wood pellets, giving us a 100% level of self-supply. Hydrogen production only kicks in when there is a surplus of electricity, and we avoid selling electricity as long as we have some storage capacity available for hydrogen. By the way, hydrogen can also be used for cooking.

We also have another type of integrated system. We have a facility for the production of plant oil. We use rapeseed oil for transportation by car, or for co-generation (combined heat and power production). This combined production leaves a protein cake as a residue, which is given as a concentrate to animals: chickens, cows or pigs. (Most countries import their proteins from developing countries, which is not appropriate. Developing countries need the proteins themselves.) The next step in this combined process is biogas derived from the excrement of the animals.

Three-step management systems for energy consumption

We have to implement management systems for energy consumption, by which we adapt our energy consumption depending on how much and what types of energy are actually available. This way we live according to seasonal and day-to-day fluctuations in the availability of natural resources.

1. As an example, if you produce electricity with windmills, you only start the washing machine when the wind is blowing. You develop people's sensitivity so that they only use energy when the renewable energy source is available.

2. In addition, you implement a system of differentiated prices, by which prices are lowest when the natural resource supply is abundant (wind or solar), and highest when there is no wind or sun, and you have to tap into your hydrogen storage. The difference in price range could be a factor of ten, meaning that electricity would cost 10 times less on a windy day than on a day with no wind.

3. Finally, in order to prevent overload, this integrated supply management system must have a built-in possibility of switching off some resistance heating appliances, which consume a lot of energy--like a sauna, toaster, electric stove, or iron--when the renewable energy source is not available. A well-designed freezer can also be switched off for several days without a critical temperature increase. A minimum level of energy supply will cover lighting with low-energy bulbs and communication (these are minimum necessities). In all cases, integrated supply and consumption management systems should be well-balanced, and users need a high level of awareness of their principles in order for basic energy needs to be

covered optimally at all times.

Q: Who is working to make these systems a reality in the future?

Preben: the University of Aalborg has been a leader in renewable energy system design for many years, but legislation and tariffs are not in favor of advanced systems integration. There is also the "Integrated Renewable Energy Farm" project (see page 33), which is being developed by four partners in Europe. At the Folkecenter, we are approaching promising, new integrated systems for food, fiber and fuel. Have you seen our brochure on "The Future of Agriculture" (see page 32)? It shows what the energy cycle can look like. The fodder cake goes to animals, to manure, to biogas, which becomes heat, and electricity. The fermented slurry (digested) from the biogas is going into ponds and here you can grow azolla, lemna and other water cultures of high productivity. With this you feed the fish. Fish excrements are nourishment for the dike-pond system, which produces fruits, vegetable, compost and clean water. The compost ensures productive soils.

I believe this is the future: an entirely new systems approach, a new way of living following the rhythms of nature.

www.folkecenter.dk
energy@folkecenter.dk

The EU still grants nuclear power R&D seven times as much funding as it does renewable energy, in spite of a political climate favorable to renewable energy. To promote renewable energy, several new global non-governmental organizations have been created:

INforSE is the oldest. It is an NGO giving out a global newsletter: *Sustainable Energy News* from Denmark. inforse@inforse.org www.inforse.org

WCRE. World Council of Renewable Energy. It has a chairman in all continents with Dr. Hermann Scheer as general chairman. They are in constant contact via telephone conferences. Main office is in Bonn, Germany. See under : www.eurosolar.org

WWEA. World Wind Energy Association. Preben Maegaard is the president. www.wwindea.org

EUROSOLAR. Dr. Hermann Scheer is the president. www.eurosolar.org

The WCRE's primary mission is to start up IRENA, the International Renewable Energy Association, a future UN organization in support of renewable energy. It is hoped that governments will use IRENA as a tool for the promotion of renewable energy and transfer of technology. For further information about IRENA: www.irena.dk

Local Water Supply and Watercare

Introduction

by Hildur Jackson

Local water supply and watercare is an increasingly pressing issue, as the groundwater table is diminishing – or even disappearing – in some places in India and Africa. Even though water is a scarce resource in many parts of the world, fresh water consumption in the industrial countries has risen because it is used as a cleaning and waste transportation system. Human consumption only accounts for a minor part of our total water usage. No matter where one lives, it is a precious resource, which needs much more respect and protection than it is currently being given.

One way to honor the water cycle is to learn how to retain rain on its way to rivers, lakes or oceans. Permaculture solves this by building ponds, lakes and swales. Another possibility is to use water-catchment from roofs.

We also need to find ways of minimizing our water usage. When we look at this issue, we have to distinguish between high quality water, rainwater and recirculated water. Wastewater can be recirculated, and used for purposes such as washing. Rainwater can be used for crops. To obtain high quality water out of wastewater, sophisticated wastewater treatment solutions have been designed, such as the Living Machines in Findhorn (Scotland) and Jørgen Løgstrup's energy-saving water cleansing systems (see page 58). High quality water is used for drinking, cooking and bathing.

The questions to be asked for the future are, among others, how to spread the use of local, no energy/chemicals water treatment systems and composting toilets (no water is used), what to do about water usage in big cities, and how to increase our willingness to reshape our lifestyles and follow a more natural cycle that respects one of our most precious resources: fresh and sweet water. What can be done in big cities needs new systemic thinking, and is beyond what we can discuss in this context.

The river at Torri Superiore, Italy, is ideal for swimming. It is fresh and clean, and alive with energy. Photos: Kolja Hejgaard.

Local Water Treatment:
Turning an Environmental Problem into a Production Tool
Interview with Jørgen Løgstrup

by Hildur Jackson

Jørgen Løgstrup started setting up, and experimenting with, local wastewater treatment plants 30 years ago. His companies, 'Danish Rootzones' (reedbeds) and 'Transform', are now creating energy-efficient local water treatment systems all over the world, and employ a total of 80 people. They have built 700 facilities in Europe, Africa, Asia, Australia and America, which treat water without chemicals, save water, create local jobs, and are local resources in many respects. Jørgen starts the interview with the comment that regenerating the water supply is as important as treating water.

Q: How do you calculate the optimal size of a waste water system for an ecovillage?

Jørgen: We normally calculate 3 to 5 m² of rootzone per person in Denmark, based on the low temperature during the winter season, for treating about 200 liters of mixed sewage per day or about 1000 m² for 100 families. In tropic and subtropical regions you only need half the area. For an indoor system you can come down to about 1 m²/person.

Below: root zone at the Center for Alternative Technology in Wales, UK. Schoolchildren are shown around the demonstration center. In the background, rental cabins for short stays, where groups can measure their energy use. Photo: CAT.

Q: What is the optimal system for an ecovillage?

Jørgen: There are various options for designs:

Rootzones, subsurface wetlands and sand filters are a simple and compact design with very low operational costs.

Folkecenter and Living Machines (by John Todd, USA) are intensive and more productive systems, which need active care and interest in the production process.

Camphill and Rensekilden (Torup, Denmark) offer a more creative process from a design perspective and have an attractive form from a landscaping perspective.

It has been demonstrated that a soil-based treatment is a very stable method for processing. Nature can be activated or manipulated to take care of most of our environmental problems in water contamination. At the same time it demonstrates that human and animal pathogens, germs etc. are destroyed in a subsurface treatment system.

Q: Should the system separate feces and urine?

Jørgen: You should always use separation systems. The sanitary risk of reusing urine is less than of reusing feces. Nearly all risk of infection is connected to feces and very little to urine. To use urine as fertilizer you have to dilute it 10 to 20 times: normally this is done with greywater (water from the kitchen and washing/bathing). I would recommend composting toilets, because it is easier to reuse the dry composted material. An alternative is the low flushing in separation toilets (three to four liters per fecal flush).

Q: At the Folkecenter in Denmark you are working on an indoor water cleaning system for a pool. When is such a system appropriate?

Jørgen: The Folkecenter's systems and Living Machines (like the John Todd model at Findhorn) are relevant where you have very little space. It is easy to connect a 5 to10 m² greenhouse to the house to harbor a cleaning system. I see good potential for these indoor systems in the temperate and arctic areas. In addition it is possible to produce some fruit, berries and vegetables indoors, where they grow fast (greenhouse conditions), and pick up rich nutrients. At Camphill and Dyssekilde (Torup), the water treatment systems are based on setting up several treatment steps. You pump the water to the top and let it trickle down through several steps. Results show that it is the first two steps that give 95% of the main treatment results. From a treatment perspective, two or three steps would be enough. The next steps are treatment zones where one can grow flowers, willows or create some nice landscaping. This type of eco-landscaping on rootzones can be like a logo for ecologi-

Swimming lake with a rootzone for water treatment. Photo: Jørgen Løgstrup.

cal living and permaculture (creates a recognizable identity), and it can be inspiring. Note that if you have to pay for labor to keep the flower beds and the landscaping section, it is an expensive solution. If you can do it yourself, the cost is surmountable, and it is a creative outlet.

Q: Is it possible to create an artificial lake and achieve a proper sanitation standard even if many people swim in it?

Jørgen: I have been very reluctant to adopt this approach. In Holland, we built an artificial swimming lake for a national workers' organization's course center. The bottom is all sand. Out in the middle of the lake, we have built a rootzone system for water treatment (see picture this page). It is being controlled, and functions well. The base of the rootzone is bentonite, a natural material that expands by a factor of 10 to 15 when it becomes wet. It closes off the entire pore system and becomes impermeable. The system has been in place for four to five years. I am still treading carefully when talking about this, but our experiences are positive. We've also established the system in Australia. We haven't had the resources to find out why there is no formation of colibacteria.

Q: Do you see recirculating water as an option?

Jørgen: In most parts of the world, mainly in arid and semi arid areas, clean water is scarce. At the same time, water consumption has risen. It doesn't make sense to use your best drinking water to flush toilets. In my opinion we have to reuse part of the water or make double use of the water. In our office we have the sink for hand washing placed on top of the toilet cistern for flushing. That is a direct double use in the Japanese tradition. Every visitor in our office who uses this toilet comes out smiling. This tells us that, even in our consumer world, it makes us happy to take care of natural resources. So the answer is yes. Definitely.

Q. Are there scientific studies available that may persuade local authorities?

Jørgen: Authorities increasingly approve low-technology solutions or decentralized sanitation and reuse. The Danish Environmental Protection Agency has developed guidelines for rootzone, sand filter and filtration systems. With this document it is possible to persuade local authorities. In India, the government promotes soil-based rootzone systems for sewage as well as for industrial wastewater. Local authorities increasingly accept well-documented and -designed projects.
Rootzone and sand filter treatment systems are well-proven technologies and it is possible to get projects guaranteed and insured.

Q: In which way can local water care contribute to production and local jobs?

Jørgen: Wastewater treatment can create a production area of 200 to 500 m² per person, based on our water use and outlet of what is called wastewater (which actually is fertilizer!). This is enough to produce your own vegetables and have some small animals. Based on wastewater, a village with 100 families could have approximately 10 hectares of green production (vegetables etc.) and this could create more than ten jobs. Taking care of our own contamination has to be seen as a big potential for production instead of an environmental problem.

www.rootzone.dk   transform@rootzone.dk

Rootzones: How Do They Work?

From *Transform's* Documentation Files

The rootzone bed (reedbed) is a biological filter, through which water is treated in a volume of soil, which is penetrated by the roots of plants. The principle of the rootzone method is to activate the microbial processes that actively stimulate the breakdown of the toxic compounds in a specific wastewater situation. When organic matter is transformed, it produces metabolites such as organic acids and lactates. These compounds assist in mobilizing iron and aluminum, which bind phosphate. The breakdown of slowly transforming carbon compounds is likewise stimulated.

The rootzone method was developed during the 1950s and thereafter. The basic idea was that by binding phosphorus from wastewater in the soil, it could be used as a fertilizer for agricultural vegetation. It should be noted here that certain soil types have a high absorption and capacity to bind to phosphorus. For example, the higher the content of Calcium and Magnesium in the soil, the greater the phosphorus precipitation. Also, the larger the admissive soil surface, the greater its binding capacity.

The rootzone's root network must be composed of suitable plant species, and it is beneficial if the optimum varieties of these species are selected. Most often varieties of Reeds – Phragmites Communis/Australis – that have horizontal clusters of roots in their root mass, are used.

Jørgen Løgstrup with Bent Petersen from the Danish Ministry of the Environment. Photo: Hildur Jackson.

This structure ensures that there is a wastewater flow horizontally through the soil mass. In addition to this, vertical flows are also part of the process. In this wastewater flow, the nutrient elements – carbons, phosphorus, nitrogen and heavy metal compounds – are bound to the soil colloids.

The decomposition and breakdown of organic compounds occurs with assistance from a wide range of microbe activity in the soil – both aerobic and anaerobic. (Note: Anaerobic decomposition processes normally cause development of odorous gases. These gases, however, are bound to soil clay particles by the aforementioned colloids, which have high absorption characteristics and thus prevent bad odors from being released to the atmosphere.)

The aerobic micro-organisms are oxygenated by the plant roots and the surface respectively, whereas the soil strata further away and deeper in the ground sustain the more anaerobic processes. This mosaic of oxygen-rich and oxygen-deficient regions sustains bacteria of both varieties in great numbers, and is necessary for the transformation of organic waste substances. The processes are quite similar to the aerobic and anaerobic steps in conventional wastewater treatment facilities. In biological treatment plants, the aerobic and anaerobic processes normally take place in separate steps. In the rootzone/filter system, the above mentioned mosaic structure permits all processes to occur in the same soil mass.

Complete wastewater treatment, with Rootzone, Sandfilter and clarifying pond, and integrated sludge treatment.

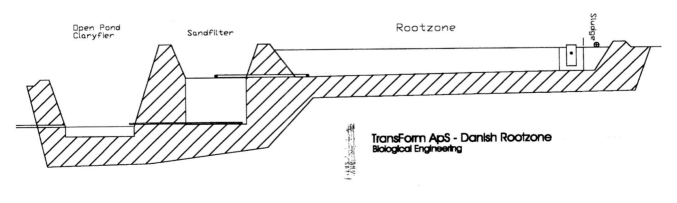

Open Pond Claryfier   Sandfilter   Rootzone   Sludge

TransForm ApS - Danish Rootzone
Biological Engineering

Photos: courtesy Max Lindegger.

The Biolytic Filter System

Excerpts from *Ecocenter at Crystal Waters*

The Ecocenter at Crystal Waters in Australia (see above) uses a biolytic filter system for waste water treatment. The Ecocenter is a newly built education facility, which incorporates examples of environmental technology in building, water, wastewater and energy. It functions as a demonstration building, and is an educational experience in itself.
www.crystalwaterscollege.org.au   lindegger@crystalwaterscollege.org.au

The biolytic filter system is a compact water treatment solution which enhances natural processes of waste treatment. The name "biolysis" combines the component "bio", meaning life, and "lysis", to indicate the chemical decomposition of organic matter. The system demands a pump for water circulation (that may be activated by photovoltaic energy), and uses worms for digestion. A biolytic filter has been installed at Crystal Waters' ecocenter for waste treatment.

Max Lindegger says: "In Crystal Waters we have many generations of the Biolytic Filter System. We have been testing and improving it for years. The latest system is able to treat human waste with near to nil involvement from the user – in other words, with the high quality expected from a modern system (low flush, no smell, near maintenance-free). The system is ideal for ecovillage installation in a subtropical zone. Its suitability in a temperate climate should be checked with the manufacturers: Dean Cameron or Boris Danilchenko."

The system uses organic waste matter, including toilet waste, household food waste, and paper products, as a source of energy to sustain millions of bacteria, a balanced mix of larger decomposer organisms, their predators and prey. The system uses actively decomposing solid organic matter and fully broken down matter to filter wastewater. The solids are constantly digested and redigested by this complex ecosystem, and eroded by the action of flowing

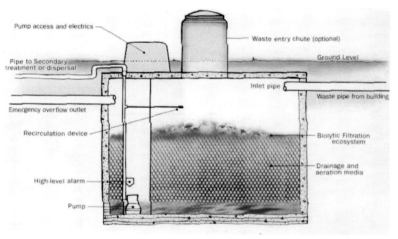

Above: the Biolytix filter manufactured by Biolytix International, as shown in the Ecocenter brochure. Illustration: courtesy Max Lindegger.

wastewater. The outcome is a continuous reduction in particle size until stable humic colloids are formed. Every cubic meter of the filter has an approximate internal surface area of 450 square kilometers to ensure the effective treatment of the waste passing through.

The process involves:
1. Automatic, in-tank separation of solid and liquid waste flowing directly from the house.
2. The addition of putrescible kitchen waste to the separated solids and treatment for the combined solids using a vermiculture process. The addition of kitchen waste is preferable but not mandatory.
3. The aerobic treatment of the separated liquid by slow controlled passage through a porous vermiculture matrix comprising a supporting media, with fine product solids passing from the solids treatment stage and a natural and robust ecosystem of bacteria, insects, worms and other invertebrates.
4. The supply of sufficient oxygen by passive ventilation and air in the sewage/flush water influent to maintain aerobic conditions.
5. The provision of power to recycle the separated liquid through the vermiculture matrix and into the reticulation system.

bordan@optusnet.com.au

Infrastructure

Rationalizing and Humanizing Infrastructure Design

by Roger Kelly

Roger Kelly is a UK-registered architect with 25 years' experience in the creation of sustainable rural communities, including 10 years as Director of the Centre for Alternative Technology in Wales. He now acts as a consultant to public and private bodies as well as grass roots organizations in all aspects of the design and development of sustainable settlements, with a specialization in ecological building.

One of the challenges for ecovillage developers is to both rationalize and humanize the process of infrastructure design, finding the most appropriate solutions for the desired end results. There are many ways in which infrastructure can be categorized, but for the purposes of this article we will look at the three sometimes overlapping networks or patterns:

Roads and paths for motorized vehicles, pedestrians, cyclists and animals.
Cables for electricity and telecommunications.
Pipes for water supply (including possibly hot water) and wastewater/sewage.

1. Roads and Paths

The desired end result of this network is the easy movement of people and goods between the village and the outside world and within the village itself. We can start with a fundamental principle that the use of private motor vehicles should be strictly limited, which suggests :

Choosing the location of the village to be close to a public transport network

Having a car-sharing scheme

Limiting roads and parking areas (small, well landscaped) to the perimeter of the village

Having centralized distribution points for incoming goods and

Centralized collection points for outgoing recyclable materials

Within the village there can then be a network of paths designed to connect the different parts by foot, on bicycle or animal, with handcarts, rickshaws or small electric buggies. Besides providing a stable, comfortable and well drained surface, the design of paths needs to consider the use of locally available materials and low maintenance requirements as well as the fact that a good path is not just a means of getting from A to B, but can also provide places to stop, relax and socialize. Remember too that there may be emergencies when an ambulance or fire engine needs to get anywhere in the village and plan accordingly.

2. Cables

Most ecovillages will plan to generate a high proportion, if not all of their electricity, from renewable sources, mainly wind and solar. Given this and the end goal of an efficient, uninterruptible supply of electricity, there are two strategic decisions to be made which will affect the electrical cabling network:

A. Will the system be:

Grid-linked (i.e. importing electricity from and exporting to the local/national network), or
Stand-alone, depending on a storage system (usually batteries) to cope with variations between supply and demand?

A grid-linked system will have to comply with local electricity authority regulations concerning cabling and control equipment; stand-alone systems are free of such regulation but may be more complex because of differing voltage requirements and storage technicalities.

B. Will the generation and distribution systems be:

Centralized for the whole village, as in most conventional development,
Localized, with generation, distribution (and storage) at the housing neighborhood level, or
Autonomous, with each individual house having its own self-contained system?

There can of course be combinations of the above, for instance a centralized group of wind turbines feeding the whole village (and exporting at times) with photovoltaic roofs on individual houses linked together at the neighborhood level.

Finally, telecommunication cabling also has to be planned, bearing in mind the speed at which Information Technology is changing. Many ecovillages will want to be in the vanguard of this technology, which may involve fiber-optic cabling, satellite receivers and other yet to be developed systems.

3. Pipes

The basics of local water care have already been described, the end goal of which is to have as near as possible a closed cycle of water supply and use; this section deals with the physical infrastructure needed to support such systems.

Gravity is the simplest and most energy-efficient way of moving liquids, so an ecovillage which is lucky enough to be located on sloping land where freshwater storage can be created at the top level, wastewater treatment and irrigated land at the lowest level, has a head start. Otherwise pumping (and an energy source to power it) will be needed at some point in the system.

Rainwater collection and storage is likely to become an integral part of most ecovillage development and has to be carefully planned in at an early stage. Again, the degree of centralization or localization has to be considered from a technical and economic point of view, as well as the merits of above or below-ground storage: can earth excavated in the creation of storage tanks be used as building material, for instance?

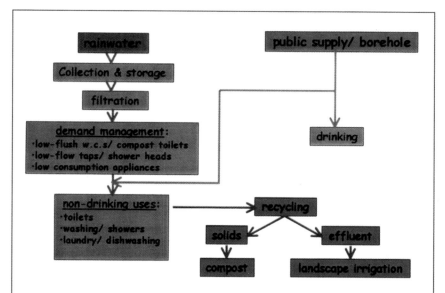

This diagram shows a schematic layout devised for an actual ecovillage development, where rainwater collection is complemented (as it will normally have to be) by water from a public supply or a private well/borehole. In an area of relatively high rainfall where irrigation is not needed, treated effluent could be returned for use in flushing toilets or even laundry.

Integration

Although we have looked at three distinct infrastructure systems, they can be integrated to a large extent in practice. The ideal is probably to have a network of paths into whose construction is designed a duct, which can carry cabling and pipe work of all kinds. The duct should run along one side of the path and have access covers, which will allow simple replacement of pipes or cables with the minimum of disruption and the maximum allowance for system changes. Easier said than done!

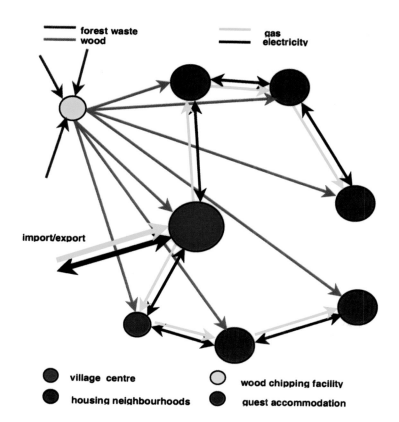

Left: This final diagram shows the distribution network planned for an ecovillage, which was to have a grid-linked electricity system with a single wind turbine close to the village center and photovoltaic roofs on most buildings. Heating was to be provided by localized wood-chip boilers in each housing neighborhood, the fuel for which was to be provided by waste from forestry operations (part of the ecovillage economy) processed centrally. Gas for cooking would be stored in a central tank and distributed to each local area.
Illustrations: © Roger Kelly.

Green Businesses at Ecovillages

Introduction

by Hildur Jackson

Ecovillagers often accept a less material lifestyle as part of the process of community building. Even when their needs are diminished this way, they still have to find ways of keeping themselves afloat financially in the long run. In most of the ecovillages which have survived over the years, people have been successful in planning and creating income-generating activities close to home. In many cases, their willingness to lead a simpler life has allowed them to scale down on their expenses and thereby reduce their income needs, freeing up more time and energy to explore new avenues for sustenance close to their heart and hearth. Partial self-sufficiency in the form of local food and energy production, coupled with a strong communal network, provide a sense of security for individuals or groups to dare tackle a change in their economic setup. Sometimes a community helps launch new ventures by supporting its initiators during rocky beginnings.

From the outset, it is a good idea to plan the development of local businesses when designing an ecovillage; to be realistic as to the ecovillage startup group's experience and ability to create a local income; to allocate a reasonable time frame for the development of income-generating activities; and to set up some guidelines as to how many residents should work outside the ecovillage (one Danish project, co-developed by Steen Møller, has got one person in each family working within the ecovillage on a daily basis, while others work outside, in order to keep the place alive during the day, see p. 159).

Guy Dauncey (see page 79) proposes to start the design of an ecovillage by planning businesses to attract entrepreneurs. New projects might give this some thought, so that the need for attracting businesses is given enough energy from the beginning.

Fully developed ecovillages may eventually mirror the activities and professions one finds in industrial society, but on a local scale, with a different kind of organization (i.e. co-ops), and based on principles of human and environmental ecology. Many of the products and services, which one usually has to outsource and pay for in mainstream society, can be manufactured and carried out within an ecovillage setting.

This reality has further economic implications: instead of having to involve hard currency in the equation, one can keep transactions within the informal economy (gift or love economy), and outside the formal economy (see page 76). The gift economy, which involves exchanging goods and services outside of formal economic registration systems, will be discussed further under the social dimension of ecovillages, since it is based on a community's social network, and is instrumental in strengthening the community by making it less dependent on society at large.

To make this alternative economy visible, a community may want to include community dinners, child- and healthcare and other elements such as entertainment into a kind of "welfare accounting system".

Certification/Lifecycle analysis

Alternative ways of producing goods and providing services are on their way to being certified by national and international authorities. Organic farming spearheaded this development, following consumer and producer demand. The assessment of consumer goods is happening through lifecycle analysis. Alternative healthcare systems are gradually being approved by mainstream institutions: hospitals in Germany provide acupuncture, homeopathy and foot zone therapy alongside Western medicine. Chiropractic treatment is subsidized in many countries. Traditional Chinese and Ayurvedic medicine, and other practices are being integrated with orthodox Western treatment systems, with good results. Ecovillages could play an important role in expanding the official application of ecological assessment and certification to other technologies, such as alternative energy and building, and in having such assessment include social and spiritual parameters. As an example, "ecological eggs" are today being produced in chicken houses of over 5000 chickens! Research shows that the chickens suffer severe diseases and display socially undesirable behavior. Ecovillages could help define and introduce a sustainable way of producing healthy eggs, which allows for a natural life for the animals.

The Farm

USA

When Stephen Gaskin toured the US with public talks in the late sixties, he collected an ever increasing trail of buses filled with people who wanted to learn from him. Eventually, the buses stopped in 1971 in Tennessee, where their occupants founded an ecovillage on three square miles of untouched land, and called it The Farm. The number of residents at The Farm peaked at a high of several thousand, but has now settled at a more conservative count of 200. The Farm has been very inventive in setting up businesses. Among the most famous are the Spiritual Midwifery clinic headed by Ina Gaskin, a Geiger counter production, many different Tofu products, and a wide variety of mushrooms produced by The Mushroom People. Albert Bates has developed the Ecovillage Training Center into a model education facility, providing immersion courses in ecological building and sustainable technology. www.TheFarm.org

Left: artwork done by residents. Middle row, from left: Strawbale building with students in front of greenhouse by the vegetable garden (in the background). The Farm staff explaining the principles of water treatment (standing on the reedbed). Childcare. Strawbale building in community. Bottom: Ecological Building Master Ianto Evans (3rd from left) doing miracles with cob. Photos: The Farm, Albert Bates.

Business Activities in Ecovillages

by Hildur Jackson and Karen Svensson

In order to avoid repetition, we drew up a list of the locations of the main ecovillages and projects mentioned under different headings in this article: Crystal Waters, Australia; CAT (Centre for Alternative technology, Wales, UK); Findhorn, Scotland; Lebensgarten, Germany; Damanhur, Italy; Dyssekilde (Torup), Denmark; Svanholm, Denmark; The Farm, TN, USA; Sarvodaya, Sri Lanka; Auroville, India; Twin Oaks, VA, USA; Ladakh, Kashmir; Tamera, Portugal; Zegg, Germany; The Folkecenter for Renewable Energy in Thy, Denmark; Gaia Argentina, Argentina; Sirius Community, Mass, USA; HueHueCoyotl, Mexico; Ithaca, New York, USA.

The examples mentioned in this section only represent a sample of the total number of ecovillage and community projects with business ventures.

Ecovillage design, ecological building, permaculture consultancy, renewable energy, and water treatment:

These skills are often gathered and/or implemented in the process of building an ecovillage. The years of trial and error, and the knowledge acquired through experience, research and education in these matters provide a basis for starting up local businesses. Establishing local circulatory systems (wind, water, soil) can create workplaces. Local water treatment systems alone can create three jobs per 100 families serviced by the systems.

Crystal Waters, Lebensgarten, Findhorn, Torri Superiore and the Ecovillage Training Center at The Farm teach and consult in Ecovillage Design. Auroville, The Farm, Crystal Waters, Findhorn, Dyssekilde (Torup), Snabegaard, and Hertha specialize in ecological building. Auroville, CAT and the Folkecenter work intensively with renewable energy.

Consultancy in community skills:

Conflict resolution, meeting facilitation and Future Workshops are other possibilities for local income-generating activities. They are taught at Lebensgarten, Christiania, Dyssekilde (Torup) and Huehuecoyotl.

Home-based work:

Internet businesses are independent of location and fit in well in an ecovillage setting. More and more companies accept home-based work. The percentage of home-based workplaces has grown enormously the past few years. If you live in an ecovillage, you are not isolated when you work from home (as in so many other cases). You are able to interact with others during your workday, and can find inspiration for your work in the ecovillage environment. In busy periods, you may be able to employ other residents on an ad hoc basis.

Education:

This is probably the most widespread and fastest growing money-earning activity in ecovillages. Many ecovillages are teaching or have the ability to teach some or all of the 15 modules of the Ecovillage Curriculum (page 4). Coordination between ecovillages in this area is likely to give a boost to these educational efforts. Some of this coordination could happen via the Earth Restoration Corps set up by Hanne Marstrand Strong to educate and create jobs for young people (page 24). Permaculture or ecovillage design courses are excellent introductions to ecovillage living and are found in many ecovillages. They are also design tools, which can be used by landscape artists, city planners, agriculturists or other individuals interested in ecological cultivation methods. The Farm (see previous page) teaches immersion courses in sustainability at their Ecovillage Training Center. The Folkecenter teaches renewable energy to people from all over the world. *Sustainable Futures* at Crystal Waters teaches ecovillage design and permaculture. Other frequently offered topics are health and spirituality (Findhorn). Competition in this field is fierce. However, ecovillages differentiate themselves in that they implement what they teach in their living environment (experiential education).

Living and Learning centers:

The principles of Living and Learning Centers are increasingly being used to form the pedagogy and content of ecovillage education, both in the Northern and Southern Hemispheres. These centers, such as Crystal Waters College, The Ecovillage Training Center at The Farm, Findhorn, Tamera and Zegg, The Folkecenter for Renewable Energy, Sarvodaya, Associacion Gaia, Colufifa and Ecoyoff, provide students with hands-on experiential learning environments, where they apply newly acquired knowledge as they go.

Ecovillage tourism:

This activity is partly related to education, as many ecovillage visitors stay in ecovillages to help build and expand them, or to complete educational modules of the ecovillage curriculum. Even a short stay in an ecovillage is a form of experiential education, immersing the visitor in the world of ecovillage living. The GEN Europe secretariat in Italy started an ecovillage tourism project called *Ecovillage Travels* in 2001. This service can be expanded globally to include all ecovillages which have organized the necessary task force and developed their capacity to receive visitors by building guest houses, sanitary systems and eating facilities. Auroville is a force in the field, with a continuous flow of visitors staying at guest centers, restaurants, shops, and cafés. There is a central booking system and a local bank, where visitors can leave their money and receive special credits to be used for purchases on the grounds. As a note, it must be said that receiving visitors on a regular basis can be a strain on a community, and should be planned and agreed upon by all members. Some communities may initially think it a good idea to build the ecovillage as a living demonstration center open to guests, but experience shows that this can be the downfall of a community's social life, (see page 151).

Above: café at Auroville, where ecovillage tourists from around the world find good and abundant guest facilities all year round. Photo: Philip Snyder/GEN. Below: Marti Mueller from Auroville in Damanhur's wholefoods store. Photo: Hildur Jackson.

Food production:

This is an area in which it is difficult to earn or save money, though some have been successful in striking the right balance between self-sufficiency and commercial production. Svanholm in Denmark generates good revenue for their community by producing fresh foods such as carrots, potatoes and onions for the Copenhagen area. Damanhur in Italy produces wines and cheeses, and Crystal Waters has built a successful cheese production facility. Munach in Denmark has the most wonderful herbal garden and produces herbal teas. At The Farm, the Mushroom People have many different species of delicate mushrooms on offer (see articles on food production pages 31-39).

Healthcare, psychological and physical:

Ecovillages increasingly integrate healthcare services in their activity pool. These activities can provide an income (though in the case of Gesundheit!, founded by Patch Adams in the US, healthcare is planned as a non-profit service), and enhance a village's potential for building up a healthy lifestyle supported by professional practitioners. Some of the ecovillages, which have developed this aspect are the Gesundheit Institute (Western medicine and alternative healthcare); Findhorn, Dyssekilde (Torup, p. 72), Crystal Waters and Damanhur (pages 21 and 107). Integrating handicapped residents or building hospices may attract funding from the state.

Health Products:

Essential oils, herbal medicine and other health items are produced and sold at Findhorn, Associacion Gaia in Argentina, Torup (DK), Lebensgarten, Auroville (IN), Crystal Waters (AUS) and Damanhur (Italy).

Above: hands-on testing of Damanhur's own wine. Photo: HJ.

Photo: Svanholm

Above: farming, Svanholm. Below: weaving, Damanhur.

Photo: Damanhur

Arts and Crafts:

Pottery, painting, theater and other forms of artistic expression are often part of ecovillages' lifestyle and can be offered for sale directly to visitors or through local shops (export is a possibility, as in the case of Sarvodaya). These activities are also part of the educational curriculum offered by ecovillages.

Damanhur produces glass, pottery, jewelry and handwoven shawls. Twin Oaks in Virginia, USA, produces hammocks and casual furniture, which generate most of their income. Auroville is famous for its crafts, which range from silk scarves to paper supplies. The Farm sells Celtic jewelry, hemp bags and crafts from South America.

Media, printing and publishing :

Some ecovillages produce music CDs and tapes, as well as films and photo exhibitions. Findhorn and Damanhur produce music and videos. Auroville has an array of CDs for sale. The Farm, Crystal Waters, the Manitou Foundation and many others have produced videos about their projects. Lebensgarten produced a photo exhibition for Expo 2000.

The Findhorn Foundation has published its own books for many years, as do the Centre for Alternative Technology in Wales and the Folkecenter in Thy. Sarvodaya has its own printing shop, which services both internal and external customers.

Shops:

Many of the products manufactured in ecovillages are sold through ecovillage shops along with other ecovillage-related products. Lebensgarten and Snabegaard have green building stores. The Phoenix store at Findhorn offers books, tapes, health foods, natural medicine and natural foods. Damanhur has shops for organic foods and crafts (most of them, including a café, are gathered in one building, a sort of mini-mall). Torup's Taraxacum (grocery/alternative supplies store) has been a center of attraction for years, and the ecovillage is now getting ready to build a business center including a bakery, alternative therapy clinic, and the new Taraxacum store (see page 72).

Mail Order Businesses:

The Farm (USA) and Auroville have functional mail order catalogues. The CAT mail order catalogue is especially successful, with a yearly turnover of £ 400,000 (page 74). Websites: www.farmcatalog.com and www.cat.org.uk www.damanhur.org

Although many income-generating activities are located within particular ecovillages, ecovillage businesses need not be limited to individual projects. Many of these endeavors would benefit from cooperation and exchange between ecovillages, which would strengthen ecovillage business everywhere. All around the world we can use our communication systems to build on each others' successes, and expand ecovillage trade.

Businesses at Lebensgarten Ecovillage, Germany

by Agnieszka Komoch

Agnieszka has lived at Lebensgarten since 1997, and was President of GEN Europe (2000-2002). She is Polish/Danish and speaks many languages. She has a growing interest in group processes, organizational (and personal) development and the re-building of communities.

When people started to resettle in Lebensgarten 16 years ago, few probably knew how it would affect their lives. During the first years, Lebensgarten residents carried out an thorough renovation of the houses and the community center, and discussed the overall purpose of the ecovillage. The first period was marked by idealism and the attitude that we could change the world, but soon the basic questions of how the community should function and, above all, how its members should make a living, became central issues.

Steyerberg, the closest village, is located 50 km from both Bremen and Hanover. With its traditional focus on agriculture and industry, it didn't offer opportunities interesting enough for people who came here to do something different. A lot of good energy was needed to make things work at Lebensgarten: the settlement had been under military dominance since 1939 and functioned as a labor camp during the war; it was abandoned 10 years before the community moved in.

With this background, it seemed natural that healing and teaching should become two important activities in the community. In 1985, the first seminar took place in Lebensgarten, and soon many members began to give courses on subjects mainly related to self-realization and healing. Members built new seminar rooms, a guest house was opened, and the accommodation office and the kitchen got more professional. Today the association of Lebensgarten Steyerberg holds three-to-ten day courses practically every week. The adult education program is a great source of income. Apart from members who rent rooms to guests (Lebensgarten can comfortably host up to 60 guests), there are about 10 persons permanently employed by the association: kitchen staff, accommodation office, bookkeeping, cleaning staff and housekeeping. All these functions, necessary to run a more or less professional seminar center, are employment opportunities for our members.

Last year's development has shown that fewer members from our community are interested in giving courses themselves. There is nonetheless a steady demand for course venues from teachers from other German-speaking countries. This again presents a challenge, as it requires a stronger professionalization, increased financial investment and further development of our facilities. For this purpose, a team of CEOs was created in 1999, whose job is to make sure that the economic aspect of the seminar program is sustainable. This way, employees have a very active stake in the smooth "running of the company", because as we have noticed, the number of guests is proportional to the service they get. It turned out that we couldn't escape the basic laws of the market.

What about the rest of our community? Not everybody is a part of the seminar center. About a third of our members (the association has 70 active members), work in the nearby towns and villages, mainly in the fields of therapy, teaching and pedagogy, and are happy with it. Others have decided to form their lives according to their own values, quit their formerly mainstream professions and search for what they really wanted to do with their lives. This kind of process does not happen without a certain degree of personal transformation. It so happened that an optician decided to specialize in voice healing, a social worker opened a shop selling ecological building materials, a lawyer and a biotechnician started the first school for conflict resolution in Germany, a TV-technician opened an esoteric book store, and so on. Almost everybody can tell stories about how their life changed.

It would not be an exaggeration to say that living in a community is about discovering our own talents and putting them into practice. It helps us realize our skills, think about our values, and see if those "new values" really hold up in practice.

Today Lebensgarten, apart from the initiatives mentioned above, has a rehabilitation clinic, an architects office, a food cooperative, one psychotherapy and two natural healing clinics, a jewelry store, a souvenir shop, a small bakery and the GEN-Europe consultancy office. Lebensgarten provides workplaces for about 20 persons. In many respects, this wouldn't have happened without the support of the community: many have started by providing services to their neighbors and slowly expanded from there.

This was the case with the green building store, Ökologgia. Joachim Kreutzer, who joined the community in the early days, was asked to take on someone's load of natural paint back in 1989. He started selling it, first in the community, and later to people in the local

Lebensgarten Ecovillage, Germany

The ecovillage of Lebensgarten in Steyerberg, Germany (North of Hannover), was founded in 1986. Lebensgarten's initiators bought the 44 residences that had served as living quarters for workers in a Third Reich arms factory, and turned them into private homes, community facilities and education/business spaces. The big hall was turned into an exhibition and seminar space on the occasion of Expo 2000 in Hannover. All the buildings were refurbished according to building biology, inspired by architects Margrit and Declan Kennedy. Today, there are 70 grown-ups and 40 children living at Lebensgarten. Outdoor circle dancing, singing and meditations are part of daily life. Lebensgarten offers courses in conflict resolution and personal development topics, and houses many consultancy and business ventures. There is a carshare system including a solar car for local transport, and the community kitchen serves lunch as well as dinner. Web: **www.lebensgarten.de** *Top: Houses by the central square, with the entrance to education facilities in the glass house.* **Right:** *Monica's shop (inset and on the walls: one of the angel which she started her shop with).* **Below, from left:** *Declan Kennedy with Lebensgarten's design, and a model of his house. Agnieszka Komoch in the solar car. Ökologgia, a store for ecological building materials. Bottom, from left: Theater on the square. Dancing around the maypole. View from above, with Declan and Margrit Kennedy's house on the foreground.*

area. The demand for his building work was so great (the news that these perceived 'hippies and freaks' could actually do a good job restoring old houses spread) that he quickly started to build up his capacities as consultant and builder and started having customers from outside of the community. Ökologgia, the shop he opened, was the first store of this kind in the region and performed pioneer work in many areas: the first solar panels, solar heating system, co-generator and solar car in the region, were all installed in Lebensgarten and introduced to impressed mainstream companies from the nearby villages. Today these solutions are state of the art. However, some years ago they were unthinkable to many.

Ökologgia is an example of good marketing intuition, future thinking and organic growth. The company started without any financial debt and developed with capital created by the shop. Ökologgia is an example of an expertise that has been created by the condition of the place: ecological building and renovation, converted into liquidity by offering this service to the general public and maintaining the values created by the community: health, stakeholding and future thinking being some of them. Joachim employs three persons from nearby villages, who through their experience of Lebensgarten have the possibility to try and feel the benefits of alternative healing and personal development.

Another good example of products that came out of Lebensgarten is the production of ceramic angels by Monika Hoy. She came to the community in 1994 as a long-time unemployed mother of two girls. She started helping out in a jewelry shop and got the idea of designing and producing angels herself. After some time of trial and error, Monika came up with a design and soon the first 40 angels were ready. A group studying flower remedies in Lebensgarten witnessed the first production process and practically bought it out before the angels even reached the store. In 1996, with some inherited money, Monika was able to start her first shop together with another woman. At the same time she became a circle dance teacher. The angels were sent to many shops in Germany and a couple of years later, when the community center was being restructured, Monika opened her own shop where, apart from the angels, she sells "handicrafts made with love" as she says herself: They are made by friends who are craftsmen and women.

With time the designs got more developed and up to now Monika has created about 32 different angels, all with assigned qualities and colors. New angels "are born" after a time dedicated to inspiration and intuition. Customers are mainly Lebensgarten´s seminar guests, who can also have a chat with Monika about how it is to live in our community, share experiences from a seminar or simply enjoy a cup of coffee from her espresso bar.

There is an interesting dialectic between the small enterprises and the community at Lebensgarten. Lebensgarten interacts with the "outside world" via guests who come here to do courses, and the different services that attract

the local population and contribute to greater tolerance between the community and our neighbors. This way it also helps introduce new ideas and changes into the mainstream. In this process values, growth and money are carefully balanced out, and constantly revised and reinvented. Together they make the GEP: Gross Ecovillage Product, which is closely connected to learning and teaching, or transformation and outreach. In this field of tension created by the two poles, work and money are slowly being redefined and brought back to their original meaning: to fulfill our basic need of happy expression (as work is an expression of our body, mind and spirit) and recognition (= payment), a place within a social structure. This is exactly what the ecovillage vision is about.

Email: agni@gaia.org

Photos page left: *Agnieszka Komoch, GEN, Karen Svensson.* **Below,** *from top: Joachim Kreutzer in his shop, Ökologgia. Photo: Agnieszka Komoch. Terrace and entrance to the community kitchen. Photo: Karen Svensson. Agnieszka Komoch and Karen Svensson in front of Lebensgarten's solar-powered car.*

An Ecological Business Center:
Something New under the Sun

Interview with Leif Hierwagen by Hildur Jackson

My husband Ross drops me off in the late October sunshine at Dyssekilde (Torup) Ecovillage, in northern Zealand (Denmark) to take some photos and interview Leif Hierwagen, who is starting a new business venture there. I have not made an appointment, but he is the first person I see, and he immediately agrees to an interview. He takes me to his house, where he lives with his wife Elizabeth. The house was built by one of the great masters of ecological building, Fleming Abrahamsen (see page 44), and is called the Folkesolhus (people's sun house). Leif's parents live under the same roof, occupying one end of the building. After taking some pictures, we sit down in front of Leif and Elizabeth's store, "Taraxacum", which they started five years ago. They have a huge selection of goods, from woolen attire for babies and grown ups, to books, herbal medicine, soaps, dried foods, vegetables, organic meat and Leif's home-baked bread. I buy a loaf, as they are delicious and difficult to get. In the back of the shop, Elisabeth has her health clinic, where she works with iridology and phytotherapy (herbal medicine). It is evident that the shop is getting too small, and I am here to hear about their new initiative: A social ecological business center, called "Under the Sun".

We have received their brochures with drawings by Flemming Abrahamsen. The idea is to build a 300 m²-center comprising a shop, a health clinic, a coffee shop for the many visitors Torup receives, and a bakery (for Leif, who has baked for 15 years and now wants to operate on a larger scale). At startup there will be four people working at the business center, but this number is expected to go up to eight within a short time.

Q: Do people in the village buy their daily provisions here (at Taraxacum)?

Leif: Some buy everything here, others buy nothing. We have four kinds of customers: locals; summer cottage owners (there is a beach two kilometers from here); tourists; and visitors and friends of the locals. The latter is quite a large group of people who pop by every time they visit their friends in Torup. The business center is designed for all these groups and there may be one more customer group as the bread is going to be distributed all over Northern Zealand. Sales at Taraxacum have tripled since we started. Now Elisabeth can live off the income of the shop.

Above: Drawing on the shares to "Under the Sun", a cooperative business venture initiated by Leif Hierwagen and his wife Elizabeth at Torup (Dyssekilde) in Denmark. Artist: Benn Landrup for Under Solen A/S.

Leif about "Under the Sun"

We have sold 500 shares in the business center by now*, and expect to be sold out in a few months' time, and then we'll begin building. Eighty percent of the shares were bought by locals, 65 people altogether. There are 80 grownups living in Torup ecovillage. "We could not borrow from the credit union," Leif explains. "When we get 1 million Danish Kroner from selling the shares, we can borrow the rest from the alternative bank Mercury or the credit union. This way we combine the best elements of grass roots organization, as many people get actively involved and want the project to become a success. We expect people to get

*Note: What is special about the business center is that they have decided to finance it by issuing shares. One share costs 1000 DKK.

a seven percent interest on their investment, and the value of their shares will increase. Our shareholders are very flexible and we do not carry sole responsibility in this venture. Of course a lot of work was done for free. The plans have been developed by the architect in cooperation with future users, workers and Feng Shui people. It has been a very interesting process. Many potential mistakes have been identified before they were made. The idea of a coffee shop came from the locals: we'd never thought about it.

When I leave to take photos of the cob building that Janto Evans started during a seminar this summer, the West African ecovillage group that I wanted to photograph in front of the building is just approaching. How lucky can one be? I get a warm welcome and some great pictures (see page 139). I manage to get a lift from Leif back to Holte where I live (seems like cosmic planning) and he tells me about his other source of income, meeting facilitation.

Meeting facilitation

"Helping the ecovillage of Torup become a reality taught me a lot about good meetings, as did earlier experiences at the Roskilde University based only on group work and 15 years of communal living. I have just taken on the task of running all the common meetings of our ecovillage. Meeting techniques are different depending on the group of participants, the decision to be taken or other purposes of a meeting. Support systems for deci-

Above: The plans for the new business center, initiated by Leif Hierwagen and his wife Elizabeth, were drawn by ecological building master Flemming Abrahamsen. © Under Solen A/S.

sion-making, involving the evaluation of goals and values of an organization or other group, are central in my work. These systems have been developed for computers and I have translated them into "meeting language". I use many other techniques. I have taken a lot of courses, from NLP (Neuro-Linguistic Programming), to organizational theory and 'suggestopedy'. I have attended university to learn about structural semantics. I think of the meeting as a living being. And people are part of that. They have to adjust to the meeting. This interest of mine has become a business. I give courses to many different groups all over Denmark. My fee varies according to the group. This way I can earn enough with relatively few working days so I can do all the other work I need to do. I am thinking of setting up an educational program teaching people to be group facilitators."

solen@mail.dk

Right: Leif and Elizabeth in Elizabeth's health food store, where she also runs a clinic for irisiology and phytotherapy. The shop is a great success with both local customers and visitors.
Photo: Hildur Jackson.

CAT's Mail Order Business: A Success Story

by Karen Svensson

Sabrina Wise ("as in: very clever," she says, and laughs) took over CAT's mail order business in the early 1990s. At the time, she had just had a baby, and she therefore worked part time for five years, but went on to work full time as the venture grew. The business originally started in the 1980s as a sideline to the CAT (The Centre for Alternative Technology in Wales) shop, when most of the products sold were CAT's own publications. Today the catalogue displays a wide range of products, from candles and soaps to home-composting systems and solar panels.

"At the beginning, we had it all on one sheet of paper, and we used a wax template," Sabrina says. "The business started out behind the counter in our shop. Then we graduated to a small office behind the shop, and now we're located in a separate office the size of the ground floor in a large house." (We can't get to a more precise measurement, and settle for this approximation.)

The one-sheet item list grew into a 30-page black-and-white catalogue, but it wasn't until technology allowed good prices on color printing in the mid-90s that the business made a big jump: "When we were able to scan pictures and send everything to the printer's on a disk, we went full color: Over a few years, we jumped from a yearly turnover of £ 43,000 in 1993 to our current £ 400,000," Sabrina says. Of this amount, ten to 15% is accounted for by e-commerce (sales over the Internet). How do people react to credit card transactions on the web? Sabrina has not noticed any reticence: "People aren't afraid to pay via the Internet, we have a secure site. The possibilities of e-commerce are endless."

CAT's mail order shop maintains a database of 43,000 customers, who receive the catalogue by mail. Some people receive a full color sheet with selected items, others the whole 32-page publication. This year the color sheet was sent to 200,000 people, while the catalogue was mailed to 60,000.

CAT's mail order company employs five people full time, and others on a seasonal basis. Next year, they will add one more person to the full-time staff. Staff members pack and send orders, take orders by phone, and provide customer service, which includes information on products, and on the Centre. Sabrina says she makes sure that her staff is well trained and feels comfortable, so they are relaxed with customers. "It's impossible for us to compete on price, so we compete on prompt, efficient, friendly service. The quality of the phone service is very important. The other day, we had three customers saying

how wonderful we were and how we sorted out Christmas for them," Sabrina says. "People are calling all the time saying nice things, it's very rewarding."

Sabrina's wise tips for setting up a mail order business:

Grow organically: Go carefully. Start the business alongside another source of income. Don't go glossy straight away: it's too expensive. Weigh out the costs of printing (for the catalogue) with your calculated income.

Test out your products if you can. The best is to have a shop, where you can test whether your customers like a product.

Build up a database of customers right from the start. Find new products all the time. When you send out a catalogue every year, you need to have new products to offer.

Go to trade fairs to find products, establish contacts with suppliers, look on the web; consider the possibility of supplying products wholesale.

Keep track of your ideals (CAT's is to be ecologically sound).

Ensure flexibility in terms of: staff (sometimes you suddenly need a few more people to lend a hand); space (stock and packing, office space); inclusion of new items ("sometimes we see something and just decide to include it in the catalogue"); stock ("be prepared for busy times").

Stay abreast of new products (and techniques) Be aware of competition.

Be efficient and friendly: "Treat the customer as you'd like to be treated," says Sabrina. "This is a crucial element for success. Spend time on training your staff, also the temporary employees, giving them knowledge about the products and other things so they can be relaxed and friendly.

Put out a "human", friendly catalogue. "Try to make the texts friendly, to put faces on builders and producers if possible."

www.cat.org.uk and Email: info@cat.org.uk

The Social Dimension of Ecovillages

Introduction

Sustainability is often defined in terms of Earth restoration, natural building and alternative technologies, but it also carries an important human factor. The strength of the ecovillage movement is that social-economic sustainability is just as noticeable and important as the ecological aspect.* Most ecovillages are based on community as a central motivation for their existence. This is one hundred percent so for the cohousings on which many ecovillages build. In ecovillages, people seek a better, more integrated place to raise their children. They want more time for family and friends with common goals and interests, and less time spent on stressful jobs and commuting. For women, ecovillages represent a possibility of integrating professional activities with childcare at home. Ecovillages also provide the possibility for integrating the differently abled, the elderly, other weaker groups, and children in a way that gives them a full life.

The intention to stay present to each other, to stick with it, is the glue of a community. This requires that people concentrate their lives around their living space, re-adjusting their priorities and their lifestyles. Prioritizing the social aspects of one's life in this way has an impact on economic parameters. People tend to gradually build up a local money-earning capacity through local businesses, and to accept some scaling down on income and expenses (as in voluntary simplicity). One way for ecovillages to increase their independence from the global monetary system is to build up alternative currency models, which increase their quality of life without service or product exchange through the regular money system.

An increased sense of community, and of one's human worth in it, also has an impact on how people look at healthcare: while healthcare in mainstream society is turning into a great "machine" which is increasingly top-down and de-humanizing for both patients and healthcare practitioners, people who opt for a more natural life-style tend to lean toward alternative medicine and local, more holistic health practitioners. In most intentional ecovillages, the social aspects of the new lifestyle and its ramifications are some of the most difficult to implement well*. We therefore give much space to the important lessons learned in this field, and to the many attempts to handle the social dimension well, hoping that the following articles will help others.

*Note1: a Danish study by Hamish Stewart and Kai Hansen, "This Is the Way We Want to Live", shows that it is the social dimension which is most important to people.
*Note 2: in the southern hemisphere much of the social fabric is still intact in the existing villages, which comprise about 60% of the inhabitants. Here, the ecovillage as a model for modernizing the existing villages, represents a promising alternative to urbanization and globalization.

Below from left: Dinner at Torri Superiore, Italy, on the terrace which looks out over the valley (photo: Torri Superiore); huddle during a meeting (photo: Hildur Jackson); sharing meals is a beautiful way of communicating (Alcatraz, photo: Lucilla Borio).

Sustainable Abundance, Voluntary Simplicity, Localizing Economics

Introduction

by Hildur Jackson

From left: Ross Jackson; Margrit Kennedy; Declan Kennedy; Bernard Lietaer. Photo: Hildur Jackson.

From the outside, the ecovillage economy may look like yet another version of voluntary simplicity and localization, as energy- and resource consumption decrease following a conscious choice, and resources are created within the community. But in reality it is more appropriate to see it as what Bernard Lietaer calls "sustainable abundance". In his books, The Future of Money *and* The Mystery of Money, *Lietaer describes how Yin money systems (feminine, egalitarian and discouraging accumulation) can balance out the prevailing national and international Yang system (masculine, based on hierarchy, centralization and accumulation) by creating wealth locally (as in ecovillages). He also describes the limitless possibilities of exchanging services, of helping each other. This is the kind of economy which helps sustain successful ecovillages. Through alternative economies, we glimpse the possibility of an evolution which can lead us from the national, centralized, scarce systems, via local economic systems, to a sheer gift economy. In many communities, a gift economy already takes many transactions totally out of the mainstream economic sphere, contributing to the creation of a high quality of life. To make this visible, a new economic accounting system is called for.*

Alternative Economics

Success Is ... A Bulging ThankYou Balance

by Karen Svensson

Sergio Lub, co-creator of the Friendly Favors network, is a citizen of the world, and a quintessential networker. He has traveled to 70 countries, and made friends all over the globe. "My passion is people, making friends," he says. According to Bernard Lietaer (The Future of Money), friends are "those who do favors for each other." This is what Sergio's alternative currency system capitalizes on: it is built on Friendly Favors, and connects generous people to each other.

"Globalization has destroyed the value of favors," says Sergio Lub. The Friendly Favors system measures generosity, not financial wealth. Here, people who take more than they give are the debtors. Even though we are still talking in terms of measurements, we're a long way from traditional bank balances.

The Friendly Favors website, developed by web designer and programmer Victor Grey, introduces the concept as follows: "Friendly Favors is a web-based service to help us stay in touch with the nice people we meet as we live our life. It is also a way to account for the favors that we do for each other. This service

is free and is available by invitation only. Its members behave like an extended family exchanging gifts and favors with each other. Friendly Favors Members offer each other their products or services at a discount rate ranging from 10% to 100% (free). These discounts and gifts are acknowledged with ThankYous. A ThankYou is equal to 1 US dollar saved and is not redeemable. ThankYous are backed up by the goodwill of the person who gives them. When a person writes a ThankYou for savings on services or products received, she/he assumes a moral commitment to return Favors to others in the community." The difference between ThankYous and LETS credits is, that Thankyou are not redeemable, they are just shown on your account to keep track of your activity. Also, you are not obliged to do a favor whenever another member asks for it. Favors are totally voluntary. A lawyer may for instance offer Friendly Favors members a 60% discount on his usual fees. If he grants you four hours at this rate, and his normal fees are $200 per hour, your bill will be $320 instead of $800, which you then

Sergio Lub explaining the principles of Friendly Favors to Karen Svensson.
SLub@sergiolub.com   www.favors.org

in turn will soon do a favor for someone else in the network. "It's too good to be true," one person said at a Friendly Favors presentation in Denmark. "I keep thinking there must be something wrong, but if there is, I can't put my finger on it."

In a world where people increasingly live according to the "me first" principle, where the greedy gathering of money is a rampant disease, and alienation from

acknowledge by sending him 1680 ThankYous for the US dollars you saved. What does your lawyer get out of this? A positive balance in the network (no one will mind doing him a favor, as they can see that he's generous), the pleasure of doing a favor, and the knowledge that you

others is widespread, Friendly Favors provides a first step toward weighing inner values rather than outer signs of wealth, to re-identify the meaning of success, and to maintain a network of Friends all over the world. Are you ready to try?

Microcredits

From Damanhur's documentation

"Microcredit" is a term used to describe programs which extend financial and business services to very poor people – particularly rural women in the Global South. The programs facilitate the creation of income-generating projects and self-employment. The worldwide microcredit revolution started with the Grameen Bank in Bangladesh, which was founded in 1976. Grameen, through the Grameen Foundation, offers training programs and grant money to people and organizations that are serious about starting a microcredit program in their country.

In February 1997, an International Microcredit Summit was held in Washington, D.C. Over 2,900 people, representing 1,500 organizations from 137 countries, attended the Summit. The Summit launched a nine-year campaign to reach 100 million of the world's poorest families with credit for self-employment and other financial services by 2005. To date there are over 225 microcredit lending programs in existence worldwide, reaching approximately 8 million families.

Although the microcredit revolution is designed to reach the poorest of the poor, there are many lessons, which can be used to create innovative financial and entrepreneurial programs, for those wanting a more "human-focused" economic system.

www.microcreditsummit.org or: www.gdrc.org/icm/
www.gdrc.org/icm/grameen-contact.html

MICROENTERPRISE DEVELOPMENT INSTITUTE

Co-sponsored by
CARE, Catholic Relief Services, Christian Children's Fund, Enterprise International, Freedom from Hunger, Katalysis, Opportunity International, Save the Children, SEEP, World Relief and World Vision

JUNE 9 - 28, 2002
School of Community Economic Development
Manchester, New Hampshire

SOUTHERN NEW HAMPSHIRE
UNIVERSITY

The Credito: Damanhur's Own Currency

by Lepre Viola

Lepre Viola lives and works at Damanhur. She is a member of the GEN Europe Board and is instrumental in launching a new ecovillage education initiative. Following Damanhurian tradition, her name is composed of an animal (first name) and a flower (last name). "Lepre" means hare, in Italian, and "Viola" means violet. Lepre takes care of much of the external communication work at Damanhur.

Today, more than 25 years after its foundation, Damanhur feels ready to share its experience with other communities. Damanhur's economic system is fundamentally based on the idea of sharing. It was born and has grown thanks to the consistent application of the principles of common goods and common wealth.

At the beginning, before inaugurating the first community-village, the founders decided to pool their personal savings. In this way it was possible to buy land and build the first houses. The community needed to have immediate liquidity in order to start all the planned internal projects, while at the same time having the money to invest in land and houses. Damanhur's founders decided to use 'vouchers', to substitute for money exchanges inside the community. These "vouchers" – 'Credits' – were to replace money inside the community, and to support its services. As this system worked well, it was decided to issue Credits every time new citizens joined the community. Each Credit ("Credito" in Italian) issued corresponded to the same amount of liras deposited in the bank to be used for other investments.

Thanks to community management of the resources, a central "Treasury" was also instituted for all resident citizens.

Two distinct services were organized:

1. An "issuing authority", which issues new credits with a corresponding value in houses and land. This is guaranteed by a real estate cooperative of which all citizens are members and in which they own shares.
2. A "loans service" to place loans at the disposal of community members in order to support companies in the making. In this case we are talking about activities and services, which have ethical and social goals linked to the ideals of the Federation.

Thanks to this double-service system (issue and loan), all the Credits are backed by real estate, in the event that it would ever be necessary to stop the system.

Community members working outside the community, or with profitable internal activities, were asked to regularly exchange part of their income into Credits. They were then asked to use these Credits in order to increase the value of the exchange system among citizens. Because games and humor are at the basis of Damanhur's culture, it was also decided to produce real coins, to have a system that could be both 'quantifiable' and symbolic. Over the years, Credits have been issued in paper, ceramics, silver, gold and other materials, with a well-defined artistic style linked to Damanhur's tradition. The latest Credits were issued in 1999, the 24th year of Damanhur's existence. The value of the Credit is now linked to the Euro.

lepre@damanhur.org

Left: Damanhur's Credito coins in silver. They are used inside the community, have a corresponding value in real estate and are linked to the Euro. They have become collectors items.
Photo: Damanhur

Localizing Economics

Building an Ecovillage Economy

by Guy Dauncey

Guy Dauncey is the author of Stormy Weather: 101 Solutions to Global Climate Change *and* Talking Cedars. Stormy Weather *received a Nautilus Award at the 2002 New York Book Expo. Guy Dauncey has researched local economics for many years, and summarizes some central points in the article below.*

Can an ecovillage have its own economy, as well as a shared community life? If we think back to villages of the past, there was always a local economy, with the blacksmith, the baker, the farmer and the forester.

Today's world is much more complex, with planning regulations, and centralized cities. Nobody would expect that an ecovillage should provide work for all its members. But if we want to rediscover a more harmonious world, we should at least aim to provide some work locally.

In theory, this is just a matter of people running their own businesses from the ecovillage. In practice, it involves obtaining permission from the planning authorities to conduct commercial or industrial activities, and organizing the layout of the ecovillage so that the noise of working activity does not disturb people.

The simplest way to build a local economy is to plan for home-based businesses, and to make space in the homes for a workshop. Most local governments allow this, but often they will demand that you do not sell anything. An approach which is being explored in the "Talking Cedars" ecovillage on the West Coast of Canada is to build a shared home-based business workshop. The building has been approved in the initial plans, and when there are enough people who want to use it, they will be able to build without complaints from the local government.

Home-based work is only a partial answer. A traditional village has a commercial village center with businesses and shops. In the eco-town of Bamberton, a planned West Coast Canadian project for 12,000 people, which was never completed, we planned to build three village centers as well as a town center, and to have a separate eco-industrial area, where larger businesses could share resources, energy and "wastes". We wrote a 'Bamberton Business Code' as a detailed voluntary agreement by which business owners would agree to act in an environmentally responsible manner. It is our economic activities, not our living and family activities, which cause the greatest destruction to the natural world, and if we want to live responsibly, we must reconfigure our businesses, our manufacturing, our buying and our selling, to make them harmonious with nature.

In the successful "Village Homes" ecovillage in Davis,

California (70 acres, 240 homes), 12 acres were set aside for shared agricultural land, and 372 square meters of space were built for commercial activity. The villagers are the landlords, and the income from the commercial leases goes into a community fund. The village uses edible landscaping (fruit trees and bushes), and the agricultural land enables some families to grow their own food, building a very grassroots economy.

The biggest challenge, which still lies ahead, is to turn the anonymous, boring suburbs, where so many people live, into ecovillages, so that everyone can begin to experience ecovillage life, not just a tiny few. The secret will be the creation of village centers within the suburbs, where there can be a village shop, a bakery, a café and a few offices, creating a focus where people can meet and begin to realize that they are part of a community, not just a suburb. There will be huge opposition at first, as people resist the change, but once the new villages begin to emerge, people will start to love them, just as they did in the past.

www.earthfuture.com/stormyweather
www.earthfuture.com/talkingcedars
www.earthfuture.com/bamberton

Ecological building materials shop at Vrads Sande, Denmark.

Photo: Hildur Jackson

Modernizing Welfare: Integrating All Social Groups

Introduction

by Hildur Jackson

During the past 50 years, the welfare states of Scandinavia and Europe have worked their way toward solutions for social problems: equality for women, childcare, care of the elderly and the handicapped, and support for the unemployed. For my part, I feel happy to live in a country where people generally are able to meet their basic needs for food, shelter and clothing, either through their own income or with state support.

However, for all our organizational advancement, we have learned an important lesson: you cannot buy a sense of community, love or being a part of society. In today's social environment, our children are looked after in childcare institutions, and are losing contact with nature and community; people on welfare are terribly isolated. So are many elderly and differently abled people.

In this respect, cohousings and ecovillages represent to me a necessary modernization of the welfare state. Many cohousings were originally started to create better environments for children. "Children need 100 parents" was the slogan that initiated the whole movement 33 years ago in Denmark. For children, cohousings and ecovillages are wonderful places to grow up in. For women, ecovillages and cohousings are a good solution to the currently existing choice of either having a career (and leaving the children in institutions) or spending their days in isolation at home in the suburbs (becoming financially dependent on their husbands). A new women's movement started by women from the Zegg Community in Germany, advocates the creation of "healing biotopes, peace villages and communities, in cooperation with men". This is an alternative to women's lib – one that many men might welcome. Their goal is to develop a new vision of womanhood in their community, according to the principles they have developed.

Several ecovillages, inspired by the ideas of Rudolf Steiner (in the UK, Iceland, Norway and Sweden), integrate "normal" residents with differently abled youth (and not vice-versa), providing a lifestyle where people live and work alongside each other in a meaningful way, which promotes the development of "whole" persons (see facing page and p. 82).

No one has to live an idle life in an ecovillage; there is always something which needs fixing, a garden which needs weeding, a meal which needs cooking, or other activities which need completing. Everybody who wants to contribute can do so.

In Denmark, cohousings for the elderly are a fast-growing phenomenon. I personally think it is a better idea to integrate older persons in villages, which integrate all ages – but, for the time being, state institutions have caught on to this particular idea, and it is the format which they currently allocate funds for. Speaking for myself, I hope to live the rest of my life growing old in a place where I can contribute, be with my loved ones, close to nature, growing herbs and roses, singing, meditating and having fun.

Reflecting a holographic worldview, ecovillages comprise all the elements of nature and society in their microcosmic rendition of the macrocosm. In this world, which is in the process of being born, children, the elderly, and the differently abled can be full participants in daily life, and can enjoy much that the world has to offer, within close range. Photo: Suste Bonnén.

Hertha, Denmark

Hertha Ecovillage in Herskind, Denmark, is a reversed integration community, where so-called "normal" adults are integrated with a group of differently abled youth called "the young people"). The initiators of the project were parents of some the "young people" who, after 15 years of planning, acquired 20 hectares of land in Jutland, near Århus, in 1996. At Hertha, everyone works according to her/his abilities: at the bakery, the biodynamic farm, the plant nursery or also the weaving workshop. The building style, as well as the prevailing pedagogy behind reversed integration, are based on Rudolf Steiner's principles of Anthroposophy. Hertha researches the advantages of biodynamic produce over chemically treated vegetables and fruit in an on-site laboratory frequently visited by the young people. It also houses LØS, the Danish Association of Ecovillages. **www.galten.dk/hertha** *Top:* view of Hertha from the fields. *1st row down, from left:* new house; the young people and their housemates celebrate the harvest. *2nd row down, from left:* Hertha's resident choir; newly built apartments. *Bottom, from left:* permaculture design of Hertha; at work on the farm (Hertha in the background); stable for free range cattle with a dwelling attached (in the foreground). Photos: LØS, Hildur Jackson.

The Camphill Network

Reversed Integration of the Differently Abled

by Jan Martin Bang

In many cases in mainstream society, mentally handicapped people are peripheralized and "looked after", and so denied an active and useful role. In the world of Camphill, every person has something to contribute, and feels self-worth even when fetching the milk or laying the table. We strive to create fellowship in our economic life, and a flexible equality in our social sphere. In short, we offer an alternative way of life.

The Camphill Network was created in the 1940s by a group of Austrian refugees fleeing from Nazism, who were inspired by the Spiritual Science of Anthroposophy developed by Rudolf Steiner. The Camphill Schools began by working with mentally handicapped children, and subsequently developed to create communities where mentally handicapped adults worked alongside other people to support themselves. Throughout the world today there are about 100 Camphill Communities in over 20 countries.

The farms and gardens in Camphill Villages are always biodynamic, producing food of the highest quality while nurturing both soil and wildlife. Generally the organic waste from the kitchens is composted, usually by a village compost setup. Horse transport is quite common, being very efficient and low-cost at village scale. Villages in England have pioneered wastewater treatment using ponds, reed beds and "Flow Form" water cascades. These are now standard in the Norwegian villages, and throughout Camphill worldwide. Buildings, both communal halls and chapels, and the usually large residential houses, are largely constructed out of natural materials, and avoid the use of poisons and plastics as much as possible.

There is a great deal of self-sufficiency: we eat home-grown, organic food; we recycle, compost and treat our own waste to a great extent; and we attempt to integrate a spiritual worldview into our everyday lives. No money changes hands, and work is seen as something that is freely given within the fellowship, recognizing that some people have higher capabilities than others in certain areas.

brobygg@start.no

Sólheimar, Iceland

From GEN documentation

Sólheimar in Southern Iceland is the first community of its kind in the world, where so-called 'able' and 'differently abled' people live and work together. It was founded in 1930, by Sesselja Sigmundsdóttir, who was inspired by Rudolf Steiner. Sólheimar was also the first community in Scandinavia to practice organic cultivation. Hot springs heat up the soil and allow the growing of plants which would not otherwise be seen in this part of the world. Today, Sólheimar is a village with about 100 inhabitants, 40 of whom are differently abled. The grounds stretch out over 250 hectares, where Sólheimar's residents have recently planted a forest. Sólheimar offers varied cultural, social and sports activities. Sólheimar has a theater group with a choir, a childcare center, a swimming pool with jacuzzi and sauna, a convenience store, gallery and sports hall. There are also workshops, a plant nursery and a greenhouse. Visitors are welcome for stays and for interactive day-tours in the unspoiled nature of the area. The visitors' center, 'Brekkulot', hosts conferences all year round.

Photo: Sólheimar

solheimar@smart.is

Solborg, Norway

by Jan Martin Bang

In my community at Solborg Camphill Village in Norway, we have a biodynamic farm, extensive vegetable gardens, a bakery, a weavery, a large forest for timber and firewood, herb-growing and drying, and have just begun a cheese-making workshop. Most of us live in large extended families: co-workers (both long-term staff with their families, and young temporary volunteers) and villagers (mentally handicapped or otherwise in need of help), sharing our lives, our meals, our living rooms and bathrooms. There may be as many as fifteen people or more gathered around the dining table three times a day. Each house has its own budget, and is run more or less autonomously by a couple of responsible co-workers (the house father and house mother). In the morning and the afternoon everyone goes to work, in a variety of workplaces. Everyone has a workplace, and each person contributes something useful to the running of the village, according to his or her capability.

Solborg is situated in Southern Norway, an hour from Oslo, on the edge of an extensive wilderness area. We are around 40 people, of whom half are people with special needs. Within the village, we have a Steiner school with over 100 pupils, and the Bridge Building School, which offers courses in Camphill theory and practice, and a long course every year in ecological building, specializing in strawbale construction. We are open for volunteers and long-term co-workers interested in sharing their lives with us.

Community and Childhood:
Perception Instead of Child-Rearing

by Leila Dregger

Leila Dregger is a co-founder of the Tamera ecovillage, with stretches over 134 hectares of land in Southern Portugal (see page 16). She is also affiliated with the Zegg community in Germany. Tamera and Zegg have developed their own childcare model, which has resulted in the advent of a "Children's Republic".

"It takes a whole village to bring up one child" – Sobonfu E. Somé of the Dagara people

The Tamera ecovillage in Portugal has issued a Children's Manifesto, 'Shogunga' (Child Peace), which reads:

"Children are cosmic beings. They have an eternal soul and an inner dream and purpose. Even a small child has a large spiritual form. Born free, they should stay free." Based on the understanding that the future of humanity will be decided by its children, Tamera grants an important role to the creation of an environment of trust for children to grow up in. Iris Lindstedt and Ria Zimmerman lead the Children's Project at Tamera. They say: "We need to be observant and listen to the children's souls in order to understand what they need, to preserve their cosmic dimension and greatness, and to reveal their creative treasures. They need as much protection as possible from the adults' meddling and projections. Nonetheless, they need orientation from us, since most children have already lost their innate cosmic sense of direction because of the way they are treated in today's society. Children need adults who establish limits for them, and give them clear directions in order for real contact and real trust to be built up."

At Tamera, as at the Zegg community in Germany, children have their own community as well as their secure nest amongst the adults. They support each other and learn from one another. They have their own area, where adults can only enter when invited. Here, they can try out their own social experiments and remain free from adults' interference. The plan is to establish a Children's Republic. Iris Linstedt comments: "We have said goodbye to the idea that we have to provide separate 'childcare'. (In our community) we set up some of our work areas in such a way that children are welcome there, and can learn from us. They learn from adults how they can cultivate their own creative way of working."

Children also learn by roaming freely in nature, by inter-

acting with plants, animals, light and the elements. In particular, animals are important companions and teachers for them. Looking after pets, watching the animals that are living freely, and making contact with them – these seem to be appropriate for every child, strengthening their souls right from a very early age. The children at Tamera already have their own temporary buildings, and a permanent house for accommodation and teaching will soon be built.

Tamera is presently building its first Healing Biotope. A Healing Biotope is a "Greenhouse of Trust", a community of several hundred people who live in peace among each other and with nature. The political theory of the project of the Healing Biotopes says that a future society of Healing Biotopes will send new, non-violent information into the informational structure of the Earth as an organism.

Some institutions at Tamera are: the Institute for Global Peace Work (IGF), the Political Ashram, the Mirja Peace School, Youth School for Global Learning, Peace Garden, Research for Interspecies Communication, Tamera Arts. Tamera can be visited from April to October (see p. 16).

Tamera@mail.telepac.pt   www.tamera.org

Photo: Tamera

From left: Leila Dregger; Ria Zimmerman (who directs the Children's Republic) and Maria Isabel; Women's conference at Zegg. Photos: Zegg.

Women at Zegg, Germany

by Leila Dregger

The Zegg community in Germany is known for its research in the fields of women and sexuality, and woman-power in community. Their work has resulted in their very own vision of a new woman's movement, which is based on cooperation with men, and solidarity between women. Leila is the editor of a new women's magazine, 'Frauenstimme' (Women's Voice).

Womanpower needs practice. It needs the experience of solidarity among women, and with men, in everyday life. Woman power will arise when we reconnect with our sources of womanhood: intimate relationships to all living beings; a caring and political responsibility for everything which surrounds us; female ways of practicing spirituality; and sexuality as sacred power.

In traditional matriarchies, the prevalent lifestyle was community. A clan felt unity with animals, plants and spirits – all of them being loved and looked after by the Great Mother. Community was a lifestyle where the abilities of women – communication, emotional intelligence, resolving conflicts, integrating differences, sharing, creating a home – determined the fate of a tribe. Power was the power to give and protect life rather than to destroy it.

In today's matriarchal societies, men seem to enjoy their position, too. They don't feel of lesser value, quite the opposite: they feel superior to their male-chauvinistic neighbors, "who have nothing they can really honor". In traditional matriarchal communities, women were linked together by communication about the sacred sources of womanhood: the power of giving birth, the material wealth of the clan, spiritual communication, and sacred sexuality: Sexuality between God and Goddess, represented by men and women.

The patriarchal revolution separated women from each other and from their sources of strength. Suddenly they belonged to one husband, who became their only guarantee for security. Other women became a threat to this security: and so jealousy was born. Today, a communal lifestyle can be revolutionary, when women come

together and create solidarity: not against men, but including their love towards men.

During our research on the topic of woman power in community, we met once a week in a women's circle. We made the room pretty, dressed up nicely, and went to the women's circle as one would to a celebration. We started to do things we enjoyed – massage, music, talking stick circles. We studied women's history, the situation of women in many parts of the world, and tools of womanpower, like intuition and the inner voice. Like the African spiritual teacher Sobonfu Somé says, there is one big difference between men and women: women love to talk. And talk. And talk. We learned to listen to each woman, her needs, her abilities, her very special way of being female. Little by little, we created intimacy among women. Many new activities emerged from the women's circle: rituals, celebrations, and special events for the whole community, like rites of passage.

Some women felt responsible for intimacy, love and sexuality in the community. They tackled questions such as: where do those who don't have a partner find emotional and sexual intimacy, and security? Does a certain couple need help in their communication? Do the young people need more support or protection? Sometimes little wise actions in the area of love – like a true word, a talk, a special event – helped to change the whole atmosphere of the community.

After months of sharing in our women's circle, the dark side of the relationship among women came up: hostility, jealousy, and competition. We have to face it: women were raised with the secret thought that other women have to be fought and damned. The more women start to love men – and love and sexual attraction is something that happens in community – the more difficult solidarity and friendship with other women seem to become. This is not our fault, but a heritage of history. Secretly, we compare ourselves with the beauty, youth or intelligence of other women. This is the hurdle over which so many friendships of women have broken down, so many communities and feminist groups have failed.

We felt that here was the crucial element to overcome for achieving a deeper solidarity. The first thing we needed was humor. And all our communication tools, the understanding of the historical background, love for truth (instead of gentle lies), a vision of friendship, solidarity among women (even if we love the same man), and a vision of a love life where growing and spreading love is not the end of a relationship but the beginning of a deeper level. That was also the time when the solidarity of men was needed more than ever. We had inspired men with our visions about love which is free of jealousy and fear. Now we needed their support to go further.

Telling each other what we like and what we don't like about ourselves was, for a while, more important than any spiritual ritual. But without knowing and feeling that we are supported by our spiritual sources of womanpower we would have been stuck in fights. We found that the more truth can be risked in a community, the bigger its chances of survival are. And truth, spoken with all the humor you can find in yourself, will release everybody.

What we needed in difficult times were common interests and shared responsibilities, which were more important than our small jealousies. These could be caring about the young people in the community; establishing education, job opportunities, and new professions for women; caring for the mental, emotional or sexual benefit of the group; or caring for a special political aim.

I can't say that everything is solved yet. But we have found a solid basis for friendship between us. More and more women at Zegg develop their strength, their beauty and their social or political commitment without depending on the love of one man, while embracing their love. Our finding is that the emotional intelligence of women seems to fit well with the variety of a community and a commitment to life. This is not a law, but our experience. Our aim is not a new matriarchy and a new sexism, but a society of equally strong genders, which complement each other and come together in love and trust.

info@zegg.de   www.zegg.de

In Community, women can integrate all their roles ...

Photos: Max Lindegger, Lucilla Borio, Hildur Jackson, Kolja Hejgaard.

Building Community

Ecovillages are planned and built by their members. They are not developer-led. It is difficult to get a group together and create a rewarding process, but it can be learned. Bonding, mutual respect and harmony do not develop without the sustained involvement and dedication of the people who live in a given community. This section broaches on the subject of building community from the perspective of design and human interaction. (see also pages 143 and 146).

Designing for Community:
The Social Questions

by Jan Martin Bang

Jan Martin Bang lived in a Kibbutz for many years and was instrumental in developing the Green Kibbutzim. He has now settled in Norway, at the Solborg Community (see page 82).

The first and most important principle for community design is that a community must steer the planning process if it is to create a social design. A coherent social policy has to be worked out: a vision statement, a consciousness of what kind of society and community people wish to have. Each group will come up with unique features. A kibbutz-style community will typically have small living units, with large central public buildings like a dining hall and kitchen, a laundry, children's houses, and cultural centers, with workshops, factories and productive farmland on the outside periphery. A loose community of more or less independent smallholders or homesteaders will have large living and working houses, each one set within gardens and orchards with less in the way of communal facilities – perhaps a meeting place or a hall.

The balance between communal and private spaces lies with us, and it will be solved in different ways by various groups. Within the Global Ecovillage Network, we strive for pluralism and diversity, and we would hope that this would be reflected in a wide range of solutions.

So I would suggest that the most important part of the physical design is actually the social development of the community, and design might be seen as a group building process.

This is one reason why a Permaculture design course is such a powerful tool when starting a new ecovillage, whether it be on a Greenfield site or involve the retrofitting of an existing situation. A Permaculture design course will give the group an intense common experience, and appropriate tools to be able to understand enough of the design process to control and direct it as a team.

The second principle for community design is that the more tightly communal a group wants to be, the more emphasis there will be on centralized shared elements, which will in all situations have the effect of encouraging and preserving community. It might be worth considering how a tripartite analysis of society could be reflected in the physical planning. The spiritual, personal sphere, where freedom is essential, could be represented by a non-sectarian place of meditation and contemplation, perhaps slightly set aside from the busy center of

In Volimierz in Poland, the children's playground has been given an important place. Here children stage a play for visitors during an International seminar.

In general, it is a good idea to plan children's places so that they may roam freely and safely within the ecovillage. Photos: Agni Komoch.

Above left: in the case of an artistic community, it is a good idea to prioritize common facilities for creative activities. Damanhur in Italy, a creative/spiritual community, has been building an underground temple for many years (the Tenple of Humankind), which comprises seven main highly decorative halls (see also page 107). This picture shows a concert in the Hall of Mirrors, which is frequently used for musical and dance performances Photo: Damanhur. Above right: how much do you want to share, and in what areas? Many communities and cohousings opt for a communal kitchen for community meals, and private kitchens in individual homes for personal use. This picture shows the communal kitchen at Fjordvang in Thy, Denmark, with ecological architect Inger Klingenberg. Inger was the architect in charge of redesigning and retrofitting the farm building. Photo: Hildur Jackson.

the community. The social sphere, with its emphasis upon rights and equality, could be represented by a structure encouraging members to meet in a circle to discuss communal issues. This community center could also be used for cultural and educational purposes and might best be located within, or adjacent to, the residential areas. The practical side of life involving economics, ecology, and working in fellowship, could take shape as a series of offices for specialized functions, where there would be meeting spaces for management groups and other responsible bodies. Such a building or complex might be easily accessible from the farms, factories or workshops, in order to be linked physically to working life in the ecovillage.

A third principle for community design would be that the dispersion of the various elements within the village creates its own dynamic. In modern planning theory, it has become a rule that we separate residential, industrial and farming activities. Many small communities also do this, but we might want to think differently, and consider that work is part of life, following Christopher Alexander's advice in 'A Pattern Language': we can create a mix of living and working situations, with small productive market gardens in between. Whether integrated or segregated, it would in any case stimulate a greater sense of community to have a strong, clear and well-defined communal area which is centrally located, so that everyone has easy access to it.

A fourth principle of community design involves considerations of transport and access. Nothing divides and alienates as effectively as a busy road! Most of us would agree that motorized traffic should be kept out of residential areas, but access is still vital, and of course even more so for workplaces if there are materials and products, which require transportation.

Graham Bell once described Permaculture as a series of questions, leading us to answers. So our questions would begin with the social dimension:

How do you see your community? A tight group or a loose association of individuals?

How much do you want to share, and in what areas?

How much privacy or independence does each person or household want?

How can this be reflected in residential planning?

Will the community provide work for its members, or work space for rent for small businesses, or will it be up to each individual to organize his or her own workspace?

How self-sufficient does the community want to be in terms of food production (look at vegetables, main crops, orchards or animals)? What percentage of the members will create their income from this? Are there collective ventures, or is it up to private initiative?

How much childcare will there be? Kindergarten, school, further education? A children's farm and organized adventure playground?

What kinds of facilities will be made available for non-residents? Camping site, hotel, healthcare, educational or conference facilities? Will these require temporary accommodation, and what about access?

This planning and design process might well provide the glue that a group needs in order to acquire a collective sense of identity.

Let design be a tool for community building!

brobygg@start.no

The Eclectic Toolbox:
Conflict Resolution in Huehuecoyotl

by Beatrice Briggs

Beatrice Briggs is a specialist in facilitation and consensus process. She has lived in Huehuecoyotl ecovillage (Mexico, see page 124) since 1997.

In Huehuecoyotl, an ecovillage near Tepoztlan, Mexico, the community's 20-year history has exposed its members to many processes for resolving conflicts. A profound respect for individual differences and an equally deep resistance to "shoulds" and "musts", combined with a genuine commitment to confronting difficulties and an openness to trying new things, has produced an eclectic toolbox of methods.

One of our greatest assets for conflict resolution is the mountain at whose base we live. When people get upset, they tend to seek out a quiet place high above the community to get some perspective on the situation. Many times, this is enough.

Another tool, which has proved reliable, is the community's strong commitment to consensus decision-making. While not a panacea, our meeting structure provides a relatively safe place for airing ideas and feelings, identifying differences and seeking constructive solutions, while preventing personal attacks.

Interest in group processes has led some members to seek additional training as conflict facilitators, principally in the process-oriented methodology of Arnold Mindell. Others have studied Marshall Rosenberg's ideas on non-violent communication. New learning is shared, experimented with, and, if it proves useful, added to our toolbox.

Another rich source of information and inspiration is the global ecovillage movement. For the past two years, we have invited trainers from Findhorn and Zegg to help us reflect on our group dynamics and practice new communication techniques. This outside support has brought us closer as a group and given us new perspectives and tools.

New learning is shared, experimented with, and, if it proves useful, added to our toolbox.

Consistent with our "no one way" approach, individuals follow a variety of spiritual paths, including Tibetan Buddhism, shamanism and yoga. This situation promotes an attitude of tolerance and respect, while avoiding the pitfalls of dogmatism and guru-ism.

Several of the adult residents (the total number of which varies from 15 to 25) practice Re-evaluation Counseling, a peer counseling technique which involves compassionate listening as a tool for understanding what in our personal history causes us to react so strongly to other's behavior. Those who use this resource tend to be less quick to blame others for their feelings and more able to develop strategies for changing their own patterns.

Another resource is the circle of elders. Our ever-increasing number of members over the age of 52 (the age at which one becomes an elder, according to Meshica/Maya tradition) is learning how to use their wisdom for the benefit of all.

A chronic difficulty we face is that some of the members no longer live here, while others come and go for business or personal reasons, sometimes leaving for months at a time. This drains the community of the human resources needed to sustain group processes of all kinds, including those related to conflict. On the other hand, going away sometimes serves as a useful safety valve, providing time for tempers to cool and circumstances to change.

And then, there is always the mountain ...

briggsbea@aol.com   www.laneta.apc.org/rem/huehue

Bea Briggs leading a consensus workshop during a seminar in Poland.

Consensus

is a
decision-making process
which strives for
non-violent resolution
of conflicts
and
the cooperative
development of
decisions which everyone
can support.

Photo: Agni Komoch

Above, from left: the building site where Sieben Linden's "purists" build their ecological homes, entirely without modern technology: no machines are being used. This lifestyle can demand a certain level of sacrifice: Silke Hagmayer (middle and far right, with Ross Jackson) lives in a trailer while building her home. Far right: solar cooker. Photos: Hildur Jackson.

Conflict Resolution and Community at Sieben Linden

by Silke Hagmayer

Silke Hagmayer is a founding member of Sieben Linden. She is building a home there without the help of modern equipment, based solely on human and horse power. Silke is a co-editor of the Eurotopia Community Guide.

History

The creation of the Sieben Linden ecovillage in Germany was initiated in the late 1980s. The core group purchased 23 hectares (57.5 acres) of land in 1997 for the establishment of the actual ecovillage, a 300-resident socio-ecological model settlement. New construction in a geographically independent settlement is nearly impossible in Germany, as in many European countries, and it took the initiators many years of preparation and lobbying to legalize a project of this size. It was essential for them in that period to learn to communicate their ideas to the public and to politicians at all levels, in order to secure the smooth process of legalization that culminated in getting building permission. To create a well-adapted village design, plans and models were developed with architecture- and design students, integrating the opinions of 100 aspiring ecovillagers and including permaculture principles, pattern language methods, expert advice from existing ecovillages, as well as biological and geological studies of the building site. Twenty-one different administrative officials were asked to express their wishes, fears and conditions. The core group took four seasons to just watch and experience the site before starting to build the village. The early plans are used as inspiration today, as the settlers decide themselves how their autonomous neighborhoods should look.

It is important to know that a project this size needs many years of gathering an endless flow of opinions. It is worth taking the time to do this if the ecovillage is to become a creative expression of a new and diverse culture.

Democratic Structure

At Sieben Linden we have a genuinely democratic structure. We have no interest in and no need for leaders, but have respect for competence. We use the knowledge of professionals of all kinds to find our own ways and opinions. A spirit of inclusion supports the process of creation. The core decision-making group is constantly aware of people wanting to join in with the flow. The power of decision-making has to be connected with taking over responsibility and work. Taking over responsibility is seen as an act of serving the group. Our hierarchies are clearly reversible at any time; they function through the principle of delegation. Each person has one vote.

Legal Structure

We spend a lot of time on finding the right legal structures and contracts to secure our land and the money flow between the members. In these tough economical matters we use the worst-case scenario to find the most suitable legal body or contract to prevent disasters, in case everything should go wrong between us. Concern-

Sieben Linden Ecovillage, Germany

Sieben Linden near Poppau, is located on 22 hectares of land, at one hour's drive west of Berlin. The ecovillage construction phase started in 1997, after eight years of planning. The design below shows a variety of clusters, each following different paths of ecological development. The initiating group includes architecture students and teachers from universities in their planning process. The first years were spent establishing community-based facilities, such as the ecovillage's infrastructure, community rooms and buildings, shops, workshops, and a lake for swimming. In 2000, residential houses were built for more than 20 members. Sieben Linden is actively involved in networking and international cooperation, and co-produces Eurotopia, a directory of ecovillages in Europe.

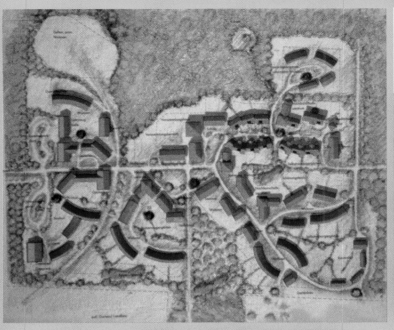

Top, from left: plan of Sieben Linden (used as a flexible guideline). Silke Hagmayer and her work horse, with whom she has developed a form of tacit cooperation. Right: The lake, which is necessary as water supply in case of fire, is filled with water from the well and from roof catchment. It is a self-cleaning swimming pool and a beautiful biotope. Below: Wooden frame for a house, built without the use of machinery. Below right: The "regiozentrum", community house, provides a communal kitchen, bathrooms, offices, children's room, library and guest/seminar spaces that are also used communally. Photos: Courtesy Silke Hagmayer.

ing the smaller, less essential structures, we are creative rather than correct, trusting rather than controlling, and believe in the sense of responsibility and honesty of our members, unless they prove otherwise.

Consensus Decision-Making and Delegation

The basis for all of our decision-making processes is a model of consensus decision-making that we apply in all our meetings, groups, subgroups and legal bodies like our cooperative (which holds the land).

We have a complex structure of all kinds of groups and subgroups that deal with different levels and different parts of our communal life. They all interact and work a good deal with delegating responsibility into smaller circles. The community as a whole meets once a week for the smaller everyday decisions and the cooperative as a whole meets four times a year for the more important decisions. When a new topic of importance comes up, we like to create space for opinion making and exchange through methods like "fish-pools" and "talking stick circles". When all ideas have been made transparent, we form a smaller group that ideally includes the extreme positions, and the people in it try to reach a consensus, before the subject comes back to the plenary.

To make the process of consensus decision-making efficient, we follow some rules that reduce power-games, veto-abuse etc.:

1. Members who are not concerned by the results of a decision, or members who are not ready to carry out the outcome of a decision, have no right to a veto.

2. Members who do not attend the plenary meetings that prepare a decision have no right to a veto.

3. If a veto has been exercised, the person must be ready to help find a new compromise – the veto is never the end of a discussion, but rather the beginning of a new process.

4. The community may ignore a veto in important issues if, after one week, no other member is found to support this extreme position ("Consensus minus one", which we learned from Crystal Waters in Australia).

Another principle that we work with to create peace between us is looking for unity in diversity ("Einheit in der Vielfalt"). We try to avoid decisions on anything, if there is not an obvious need for a common agreement. We believe that there are different paths of ecological living. One of the key secrets to real tolerance is the idea of creating spaces for every individual to express him/herself through individual projects alone, or together with others. If everybody receives this kind of latitude, it is very easy to respect one's neighbor's space, even if the neighbor does something completely different. Why reach a consensus on building with machines or without? Some build houses with and others without. Consensus should not stop the initiative of an individual or a subgroup, as long as no direct or clear damage is caused.

Our neighborhood model creates a great diversity of lifestyles in subgroups, and guarantees social contact to a certain extent through the communal planning and building process. No families or people build alone: our ecovillage is a village of communities. In the areas where we do seek a consensus, we are hard on our principles and soft on their application.

Another step toward successful and peaceful communication is separating the "emotional stuff" from the pragmatic decision-making process. Members need a safe space where they can truthfully and fearlessly express their most hidden thoughts and emotion. Otherwise these energies will disturb decisions that need to be taken on a pragmatic level.

We have tried out many types of supervision, self-therapy etc. to deal with the question of transparency, conflicts and inner growth. Finally, we are happy to have learned a very humorous and good way to deal with these topics: the 'Forum'* that has been developed by Zegg (a befriended community).

We follow the path of joy. We are looking for a way of living that can be continued indefinitely into the future. But no structure is sustainable (or will be continued by anyone) unless it is fun and nourishes the soul.

* The Forum is a communication form through which individual community members, placing themselves in the middle of a circle of other community members, engage in exchanges, share their thoughts, or show and portray themselves and their questions. The circle of community members trains itself in the holistic perception of this person, preserving an inner calm and giving feedback that is supportive and free of judgement. A good Forum is one where the portrayer doesn't confuse him- or herself with the problem at hand, where the human quality of the issue can be felt, and where a truthful contribution gives rise to a new insight, an opening up, or a moment of healing.

silke@oekodorf7linden.de

The Eurotopia guide to communities in Europe is edited at Sieben Linden, with Silke Hagmayer as a co-editor.

Healthy Lifestyle, Preventive Healthcare and Complementary Medicine

Introduction

by Hildur Jackson

Living a healthy lifestyle and practicing preventive healthcare, reducing stress and taking full responsibility for your own life and that of the planet – all this greatly improves your health. At some point, we may hope that societies can start investing in the creation of healthy lifestyles, as opposed to supporting the continued expansion of hospitals and other healthcare facilities, which are based on the fact that, today, ill health is economically beneficial for certain institutions (such as private hospitals) and specialized practitioners.

Many of the problems caused by the medical system are due to the fact that medical solutions are sought in inappropriate situations, where lifestyle, emotional, social or spiritual solutions would be much more effective. Simple activities can enhance our health, some of which are: daily meditation, prayer, singing, and dancing; yoga and other forms of physical exercise; connecting with nature (walks, earth restoration activities); a low meat (or no meat) diet, combined with locally grown and minimally processed food (the diet Peter Harper recommends on page 33); communicating and living in harmony with others; expressing oneself through arts, crafts and other creative avenues; building one's own house, and supplying one's own energy.

The ecovillage lifestyle incorporates many of these activities. All the elements of ecovillage living carry with them the potential to establish a healthier lifestyle for people. One of the main ideas behind ecovillages is actually to make a healthier existence more easily accessible, and visible.

Many ecovillages are experimenting with ways of healing 'dis-orders' and 'dis-eases', and restoring health through complementary medicine, healing therapies, massage, herbal and flower remedies. The following articles will give you some examples of how people at different ecovillages are practicing combinations of complementary and traditional healthcare in communities.

Complementary Health Services and Care in the Community

by Cornelia Featherstone, M.D.

Cornelia Featherstone lives in Findhorn, Scotland, where she practises complementary medicine. She is the author of 'Medical Marriage – Partnership between Orthodox and Complementary Medicine', 1997.

A person's engagement in community, a functional social network, is a central aspect of health. Many scientific studies have shown that being part of a community improves an individual's abilities to face challenges in life – for example, cancer survival rates are higher in those with a supportive network. At Findhorn we coined the slogan "A loving community improves your immunity".

Healthcare

When people in mainstream society talks about healthcare, they are actually referring to medical care. That "healthcare" is delivered within a hierarchy of experts (doctors) and recipients (patients). It consists largely of 'fixing' symptoms with a drug or a surgical procedure. The huge limitations of this system are widely acknowledged, by both patients and doctors alike. It is often stated that many things have contributed to improved health and longevity in the developed world – including housing, education, and water sanitation. Medicine hasn't played a significant role in that. Despite the exorbitant sums of money invested in healthcare worldwide, the orthodox medical system hasn't been able to address the large-scale health problems in modern society. In certain ways it actually contributes to these problems (e.g. pharmaceuticals contributing to pollution of the environment, the medical

Findhorn Scotland

The Findhorn Foundation started as a caravan park in 1962. Today it has become one of the largest community projects in Europe, with 450 residents and numerous activity centers and businesses. Findhorn attracts 14,000 visitors per year to its courses in personal development, alternative health practices, ecovillage design and much more. Guest facilities are plentiful and comfortable, including community, meditation and seminar buildings of a high standard, and a hotel, Cluny Hill. Findhorn is made up of diverse living and working clusters, which include wood and stone constructions, whisky barrel houses, caravans, and lately also an ecovillage settlement. According to a chart drawn up by Peter Dawkins, the placement of these areas corresponds to chakral systems (see page 14). Findhorn has been a leader in reintroducing a multifaceted spiritual worldview which embraces elements such as nature spirits, Christian mysticism and Buddhism, personal development, complementary healthcare, the restoration of nature, and artistic expression. The teaching of all these topics is a major focus and income for the community. Experience weeks and week-long large-scale seminars alternate with smaller workshops and extensive ecovillage training programs. In 1997, The Findhorn Charity was recognized for its work by the UN. Findhorn's Earth Restoration work, headed by Alan Watson Featherstone (see page 27), is also a multi-award-winning endeavor. Web: **www.findhorn.org**

Top: Findhorn members at the community house. Far left: guest house with grass roof. Left: Inspecting cabbage in the fields during an ecovillage training course. Below, from left: The Universal Hall has space for 500 people. The Living Machine cleans waste water using the John Todd model. Bottom, from left: Gardening. Whisky Barrel houses.

system disempowering people). On the other hand, the importance of medicine in saving individual lives is undisputed. Anyone who has been rushed into hospital and had their life saved by emergency interventions can attest to the significance of that service. Within the given ethos of our world today, no one suggests removing this service of saving individual lives. Instead, we strive to expand the access to this service to people in those areas who don't have the 'privilege' yet.

This is the area where the ecovillage movement and complementary therapies can contribute significantly to healthcare. In a healthcare system where those elements are fully integrated, medical solutions would only be sought when really necessary, ideally as a last resort.

Most ecovillages are not large enough to provide their own medical services. There-fore, a good rela-tionship to the local medical care providers is help-ful to ensure that integrated and con-gruent care is avail-able when required. However, it is important for an ecovillage to provide two main elements of health-care:

1. Natural healing methods, which encourage balance, prevent disease and

Cornelia Featherstone with her husband Alan and their son. Alan Featherstone founded the "Trees for Life Project" and received multiple awards for his efforts in Earth Restoration (see page 27) Cornelia is a health practitioner who runs her clinic from Findhorn in Scotland. Photo: courtesy Alan Featherstone.

give support when dealing with long-term illness. As natural healing is an integral part of daily life – how we eat, work, play, relax, celebrate, and care for ourselves – it is important that there are local resources to support individuals in finding their own way of creating balance in their life. Complementary or alternative healing prac-tices also provide significant opportunities for sustain-able employment within an ecovillage.

2. Neighborhood help – Care in the community when individuals need additional care. Neighborhood help is that aspect which makes community so attractive to many of us – that sense of belonging, of caring and being cared for. And the magic in it all is that care in the community not only supports individuals but is actually a powerful community-building gift.

Ina May Gaskin, from The Farm (USA), once said at a conference at Findhorn: "Only once a community has reclaimed birth and death can it realize the potential of self-determination and sovereignty." Care in the com-munity is an essential step in allowing birth and death to

be integrated into the fabric of community life. Once a community can provide the care needed for individuals, it gains the confidence that it can also provide for the big transitions in life – birth and death. When the circle is complete then a community is a truly safe place for life.

How to do it?

1. Volunteering is an important aspect of care in the community. Being a volunteer will ideally nourish the volunteer as much as the person they are there to help, only then is such a service sustainable.

2. Considering care in the community as *community service*, as much as washing the dishes, doing the rotas or any other communal tasks. Care in the commu-nity could become a recognized work shift. This would allow busy com-munity members to serve in that way without wearing themselves out.

3. Having *comple-mentary health* practitioners as entrepreneurs in the community – setting up their practice as an income earning business that earns them a living.

4. Utilizing the services of practitioners from outside the com-munity, either visi-ting ones or those from the local area.

Most ecovillages will find that a combination of all of these options may well serve them best in providing for their needs in community care.

Care in the community strengthens the heart of a com-munity. It builds relationships, fosters a sense of safety and allows joyful service where the nurturing is tangible to all involved.

healthcare@findhorn.org

Gesundheit!
Health in Community

Interview with Kathy Blomquist
by Karen Svensson

Gesundheit! Community in West Virginia is the brainchild of Patch Adams, M.D., and a group of dedicated friends and colleagues. It is the emerging microcosm of an envisioned healthier world. By introducing a compassionate, fun-spirited 'community-cum-hospital', Gesundheit! may grow into a subcultural model for healing which can inspire changes in the dominant medical culture. The following article explains how the founders of Gesundheit! see community contributing to health, and how their ecovillage is designed to integrate healthcare.

Gesundheit! Community started in 1973 as a home-based, free medical clinic in West Virginia. "We lived together under one roof, virtually forgoing our private lives ..." says Patch Adams. "Each staff person played many roles: farmer, cook, mechanic, clerk, nurse, doctor, artist". In 1979, the group called themselves The Gesundheit! Institute. "We chose the name because it makes people laugh, and thus become open to healing, and because literally translated, Gesundheit means good health," says Patch. Gesundheit! introduced overnight stays at the home-clinic, and eventually integrated the lives of those giving and those receiving care. It inspired the idea of a community-based hospital founded on sustaining joyful service.

In 1980, Gesundheit! purchased 310 acres of land in Pocahontas County, West Virginia. A small farmhouse, a large barn and several outbuildings came with the property. Today, Gesundheit! community consists of a "courtyard village" in progress, with the restored farmhouse in its center, and a wooden "Dacha". The Dacha was completed recently to house six of the staff. There is also a four-level, 6500 square foot, multipurpose workshop; a two-mile woodland trail; tool sheds; a three-season dwelling for long-term volunteers; preliminary landscaping; and organic gardening. Four people live on the premises permanently, augmented a lot of the time by groups of volunteers who stay from one week to several months.

> *"Love and intimacy are at the heart of why we become sick or well, sad or happy, why we suffer and why we heal; feeling isolated leads to illness and suffering; experiencing love and intimacy, connection and community, leads to healing."*
>
> David Ornish, "Love and Survival"

Q: How is healing connected to community?
Kathy: Community provides a safe, purposeful avenue to reclaim wholeness. So many people come through the door hurt, broken, depressed, and are overwhelmed when caring people welcome them into our home. Community can validate the parts of us that were dismissed or discouraged. In community, we notice each other, identifying patterns of behavior that bring us down, or up. Through the intimacy of living together, others are able to see and put words on one's underlying beliefs, to encourage a clear perspective of oneself, and suggest other patterns. A question like: "Have you thought of trying things this way?" can lead to a person changing behavioral patterns, and finding new, healthier templates.

More than anything, it is people's will to live their lives fully that can determine a healing process. Community encourages the will to live fully by creating a sense of belonging, and providing a place where one can let out one's "grittiness" and get a cuddle afterwards. Community is an astounding place to do that. You don't get permission to let it out in the main culture. But here, you're allowed to say "whoops!"; to be scared; to say 'I don't know'. In community we are able to be disharmonious and still stick with it, and to help each other through helplessness. The intention to stay present to each other is the main task in a community. When it's a safe place, it allows one to get the courage to speak up, say out loud what one thinks. The ego is put out there, in public. You can acknowledge it, be obvious about it, and then you can explore it, put it under careful assessment. Finding your voice is healing, there's no constipation of mind, it's all fluid. Health is about flow.

Q: How is Gesundheit's Community forming the basis for the future Gesundheit! Hospital?

Kathy: The Gesundheit! Hospital is unique precisely because it will be embedded in a community setting. The Hospital village will be adjacent to the courtyard village where healthcare professionals live together. In mainstream society, healthcare providers are lonely, isolated and tired of doing medicine in a competitive, greedy environment. Our present medical culture thwarts the people working in it. Complexities of technology and legality overshadow the simplicity of promoting a human connection at the core of health. Rachel Naomi Remen says: "The imbalance in the medical system, the emphasis on masculine-principle approaches and perceptions that pervades our entire culture, diminishes everybody ... When someone relates to you from the feminine side of themselves, what you see reflected is your own strength, your own capacity, your own uniqueness."

Intentional community is a safe laboratory where we

can bring the feminine features back into our social and healthcare design.

Q: In other words, The Gesundheit! setup primarily changes the medical structure from a masculine, authoritarian power, which takes over the patient's responsibility, to a culture of feminine joyful service, which empowers patients to become the main players in their own healing, and fosters human relations.

Kathy: Exactly. At Gesundheit! the hospital is the "gimmick" to create human connection. The doctor will meet the patient, and say: "Come, let's take a walk in the garden." There, the patient talks with the gardener. In between, doctor and patient get to know each other. Next day, maybe the patient will be with the gardener. He may find he's interested in gardening. The purpose that he came for (disease) is diminished by rediscovering an old passion, gardening. The goal here is authentic human relations through which you are reminded of something you really love to do. The pill becomes incidental to the full medicine. It's the soul regaining passion that promotes healing.

The medical community needs what intentional communities value: active engagement by all participants (i.e. patients and healthcare professionals together) for the health of the whole. At Gesundheit!, we want to model this: to create a new healthcare culture with other like minds. Quoting Rachel again, "You heal a dominant culture by forming a subculture of credible people in the middle of it who value something new, who reinforce something that the dominant culture represses."

At Gesundheit!, we do this by modeling. By modeling Joy. Ultimately, here, Joy is at the seat of healing. This doesn't mean we're always happy. But everything comes from a place of Joy, an emotional knowing, which is infectious. It looks like fun, and then it doesn't take long to foster a culture of Joy, when you can always see a glimmer of the Fool creeping in. A group of people living in a community according to this principle, to study the part of themselves that always remains hopeful and joyful, creates a culture of Joy.

Q: How do you build a healing community?

Kathy: With fun and play, because they are the quickest way to make authentic connections. Play makes us happy, enhances flexibility and the ability to deal with crisis due to release of tension, and increases creativity, which increases play, which increases creativity. It promotes health and healing. (To sum it up:) Wit, Mirth and Laughter. With Friendship, because we need each other to keep connected to ourselves. Listening and helping each other find new belief/behavior patterns. Intentional relationships as in intentional communities are the backbone of effective medicine. With Joyful Service, because this dissolves a greedy, hoarding, selfish society. To feel good, do good.

Q: What about the three ways of making a healthy, healing community written in your volunteer program description?

Kathy: That's right, those are really good guidelines:

1. Working with the land, the physical tasks of maintaining and consciously designing the natural and built environments

2. Working with ourselves, sustaining one's dynamic level of fitness – body, mind, heart and soul

3. Working with each other, creating a cooperative process in unity and diversity.

We use these to make community on a daily basis, to contribute to the physical, mental, emotional and spiritual foundation of Gesundheit! and to generate an extended community committed to perpetuating joyful service.

Top row, third picture from left, Kathy Blomquist. Far right, Patch Adams. Photos: courtesy Kathy Blomquist; Albert Bates; Hildur Jackson; Karen Svensson

LUMEN University of Natural Medicine in Italy:

Food is Medicine

Lumen University for Natural Medicine is located in a 17th-century mansion near Piacenza and Cremona in Italy. The community offers courses in natural therapy and related disciplines. Guest facilities include a swimming pool, communal spaces for meditation and exercise, and overnight accommodation. Within the community, health is seen as related to a satisfying lifestyle and good, wholesome food intake. Particular care is given to nutrition and diet. Lumen is open for visitors all year round. Elena Soldi has worked at Lumen for over seven years, and is a naturopathic therapist. She also teaches Bach flower remedies and nutrition at Lumen. Elena has been Editor of "Il Giornala della Natura" since September 2001,

by Elena Soldi

Photo: Lumen

LUMEN (Libera Universitá di Medicina Naturale) was founded with the goal of fostering a "natural health system" capable of returning energy and the joy of living to people and the environment. The LUMEN group has grown quite a bit over time, and today we have a fairly large nucleus of people who share ideals, work, friendship and daily life.

After ten years of work, we are now an accredited Natural Health Center, and practice natural therapies (such as reflexology, Bach flower remedies, crystal therapy, Qui Gong and massage). Working and living together are intertwined and set the tone for everything we do: our lifestyle, the therapies we offer, the creation of more sincere human relations, the search for the personal growth of every individual.

Nutrition is a very important factor for recovering and maintaining good health. The Ancients already knew that food is our primary medicine, and with food we can introduce useful substances in our body to activate and support all our functions. Not only that, but food also has more subtle components which carry important information for our emotional and mental levels.

At LUMEN, we follow a strictly vegan diet, which means we almost exclusively eat vegetables and food derived from vegetables. Good organic or biodynamic quality is important, since these methods respect the chemical and physical properties of the products. We like to eat our food as intact as possible: all wholewheat cereals (available in an amazing number of varieties, much more than we normally think), preferably in grain form to respect its original characteristics, raw fruit and vegetables, the former between meals and the latter as an appetizer to help the digestion of the enzymes they contain.

Good sources of protein are: soy products (milk, tofu, tempe), seitan (the gluten part of wheat flour), dried fruit (25 almonds per day can cover an adult's daily protein intake); legumes, and cereals also contain a fair share of proteins. We sometimes make use of oriental food like miso (a salty fermented soy paste, which enhances intestinal function) and seaweeds, which are important suppliers of minerals and vitamins, scarce in normal "modern" food.

We normally consume locally grown food according to the season. Our environment and climate can give us what we need: we only have to find a connection with our internal focus, a sense of respect for nature and a capacity to "tune in". These are important steps toward identifying the best and most appropriate food for each of us, as each human being is unique and has different basic needs.

Some of the crew at Lumen in front of the main building. Photo: Lumen

Designing for Teaching and Communication

Introduction

by Hildur Jackson

Teaching and communication are lifelines for ecovillages. Almost all ecovillages teach courses, and cooperation between ecovillages for setting up a sustainability curriculum under way (see Spring 2001 issue of Ecovillage Living *on the theme of sustainability education at ecovillages, www.gaia.org). Visiting or following a course at an ecovillage is an experience which provides people with knowledge of sustainability principles through immersion in the ecovillage lifestyle. It has the power to change people's lives.*

Living and Learning Centers at ecovillages are centers for experiential education, where students can learn the ecological, social and cultural aspects of ecovillage living hands-on. GEN's Living and Learning concept is based on utilizing the knowledge which resides in ecovillages for sustainability education, in partnership with universities, schools and individual students. The creation of Living and Learning Centers supports ecovillages by creating income-generating activity, increasing exposure, and creating relationships between ecovillages and established mainstream institutions. Many of the more mature ecovillages are, or are developing into, Living and Learning Centers. In the articles below you will find a description of the basic requirements for becoming a Living and Learning Center, as well as tips for establishing partnerships with universities and other educational institutions. You can find more information on educational programs on page 24, where Hanne Marstrand-Strong explains the principles of the Earth Restoration Corps. This Interview is very relevant to this section, as ERC ideally takes place in ecovillages.

Teaching and Education

Building a Living and Learning Center

by Philip Snyder

Philip Snyder, Ph.D., is the former Director of the International Secretariat of GEN (The Global Ecovillage Network). An anthropologist with a specialization in people and place, he is now based in Sedona, Arizona and is a consultant in program & organizational development and integrated land use.

To varying degrees, ecovillages reflect conscious design appropriate to both local and planetary realities. By marrying community with ecology, ecovillages attempt to address the profound challenges that face humanity: to live meaningfully in a manner that respects people and the Earth. Ecovillages can become key building blocks in the sustainable society of the future. This sense of wider responsibility is one of the defining hallmarks of an Ecovillage. Some ecovillages have taken this to another level – that of developing into Living and Learning centers. Previous issues of *Ecovillage Living* have explored some of the GEN Living and Learning Centers in the South and the North. All are 'works in progress', evolving as places that reflect sustainable living practices and more integrative learning models.

GEN recently approved three Living and Learning

Center (L&L) projects in the southern hemisphere (in Brazil, Senegal, and Sri Lanka), with whom a partnership for sustainability education has been established. There are many existing and emerging Living and Learning centers in ecovillages around the world, including places such as The Farm (USA) and Crystal Waters (Australia). These centers are living experiments in sustainable community that provide demonstration and hands-on training in developing green technologies and regenerative living systems that are also integrated with traditional culture and wisdom, creating an interactive learning community rich in experiential opportunities. The pedagogy is based on a partnership model in which instructors and students learn mutually from one another. Students come from local communities and may be resident at the center for varying lengths of time, integrating the experience of living there with the specific educational programs. This is an immersion, 'learn by doing' approach, as students join with instructors and staff to build, plant and create this new future on site. By integrating permaculture methodologies and related appropriate technologies with traditional culture, each center strives for workable solutions to the challenges of creating a sustainable way of living.

To build an L&L center in an Ecovillage is a serious, long-term enterprise that merits careful planning and community-based decision-making. It calls for a broad-based process of objective evaluation of the strengths, weaknesses and actual readiness of the ecovillage to undertake this mission. Environment and physical infrastructure, social conditions and economic capability all need assessment. With regard to the physical conditions, a very basic question is the actual location of the community. Is it near public transportation? An airport? A city? Is there medical assistance nearby if this is needed? Are there any defining or unique features of the site, which will enhance its attractiveness as a center? To what degree is the community self-sufficient with regard to energy, food, building materials, waste recycling, etc.? How much land is available for the work of the center? Are there functioning appropriate technologies that can demonstrate sustainable systems? Many of these basic parameters will determine the scope and type of center that might develop.

Demba Mansaré, founder of Colufifa in Senegal, discussing Living and Learning prospects with Philip Snyder in Denmark. Colufifa, together with Ecoyoff in Dakar, Senegal, are partners with GEN in the Living and Learning venture. Photo: Hildur Jackson.

The built environment is critical for success. Are there examples of natural building appropriate to the local environmental conditions? Is there indoor classroom space available? Associated resources such as computers, phones, fax, A/V equipment, and the like? Are there facilities for day or overnight guests/students? For how long and at what level of comfort? For instance, tents may be adequate for late spring, summer and early autumn workshops, but, if the climate is cold in winter, they would likely be inappropriate. Kitchen facilities, good food and clean water resources are critical elements. Are there suitable hands-on projects that provide good learning opportunities for students?

For an L&L Center to flourish, it needs to harmonize well with the rest of the life of the community in which it is embedded. Is there a community consensus to go forward with such a center? Are people ready for an influx of new people passing through? What degree of privacy is needed for community members to feel comfortable? A core of members needs to be firmly committed to such an endeavor, for it will require intensive work and energy commitment over years. Is there a responsive, participatory decision-making process in place? Who will be the instructional and support staff, and might this include outside people? What are the backgrounds, motivation, and time availabilities of this team? Do they have the level of experience and skills that others will regard as credible for the types of programs being envisioned? What are the strengths of the program envisioned? How will this be presented in a manner that can give very concrete and practical experiences an integrated context?

To thrive and attract people, it will be very helpful if a new center has active partnerships with allied groups, businesses, educational institutions, both locally and, ideally, nationally and beyond. Such partnerships and relationships will be key for marketing programs and harnessing needed resources. Indeed, depending upon the scale of the prospective center, significant financial resources will need to be mobilized in advance, along with personnel, infrastructure and other resources. Are there community funds to invest? Are there potential sources such as foundations and local government which may be approached? Careful financial planning with realistic projections of income and expenses is essential. A well-operated center can provide important livelihood for the community, but before it can begin to generate revenue, in the start-up phase there will need to be significant investment of work, money, and space to make such a center viable.

Many ecovillages have the potential to develop exciting partnership learning programs and perhaps even evolve into full-featured Living and Learning Centers. Many factors, including timing, need to be aligned for success. But there is no question about the need in the world for such centers, given the deep structural changes required for a truly viable future for all people.

philip@gaia.org

Academic Partnerships Through Living Routes

by Daniel Greenberg

Ecovillage education initiators. Second from left, Daniel Greenberg.

Photo: Hildur Jackson

Daniel Greenberg, Ph.D. is the head of Living Routes Ecovillage Education Consortium, which brings students to ecovillages around the world to study sustainability hands-on. He lives at the Sirius community in the USA.

At a time when academia's relevancy to the real world is being increasingly questioned, ecovillages are stepping forward to provide ideal "campuses" for students to experience and learn about sustainable living. Ecovillages are truly living laboratories for a sustainable future, and are now creating new models of education that can train leaders capable of addressing and transforming today's environmental and social challenges. Living Routes is helping build one new model by creating accredited, college-level educational programs that are based in ecovillages around the world. On these programs, students and faculty create "learning communities" within "living communities" and apply critical reflection and academic studies to their immersion experiences within ecovillages.

Living Routes works because it is based upon mutually beneficial relationships for students, ecovillages, Living Routes, and for affiliated colleges and universities.

Students benefit by being able to study and learn within ecovillages as part of their academic career;
Ecovillages benefit from the tuition, labor, and research that dedicated students and universities provide;
Living Routes benefits by gaining access to academia's resources, expertise, and large student population, and by being able to fulfill its mission of educating for sustainability;
Colleges and universities benefit by being able to expand their home-campus curricula with high-quality off-campus programs while avoiding associated administrative, financial, and logistical burdens.

While Living Routes is still a young organization and we are learning as we go, here are a few insights we have gained about developing relationships with academic institutions:

Prepare yourself. Call a series of meetings with all interested persons to develop a proposal for your community and, eventually, a potential academic partner.
Consider the following questions: Who in your community and local area has advanced skills and degrees in topics you would like to teach? Create an inventory of these resource persons and include CVs when available. What opportunities are available within and around your community for internships, service-learning projects, and independent research? What activities might students engage in during their stay (i.e. how "full-featured" is your community)? Are adequate accommodation, meeting spaces, and health facilities available? Would students have access to the Internet? Might language be a problem for international students? What financial arrangements would work for you?

Choose your potential partner(s) wisely. How well respected are they as an institution? Is sustainability a part of their mission? Do you know potentially supportive faculty and administrators? How flexible are they regarding the creation and control of new courses and off-campus study? It is also helpful to collect and study current materials such as mission statements, course catalogs, "State of the Campus" and Strategic Planning documents, and organizational charts of administrative and decision making structures.

Get to know key players. Talk with people in a wide variety of offices including Study Abroad, Admissions, Accounting, Publications, Registration, and Communications. Secretaries can often suggest who to approach and how. Ask questions such as "Who makes decisions?", "How are off-campus programs structured and financed?", "What would be required of ecovillages to maintain academic standards?", "What is the best way to approach people in power (e.g. email, letter, appointment, chat in hallway)?".

Consider your options. There are many ways to build bridges between an ecovillage and an academic institution, particularly if you are near each other. Here are a few ideas to get you started:
Thematic ecovillage tours (e.g., Appropriate Technology, Social Structure, Sustainable Agriculture, Ecological Design)
Collaborative research projects at both ecovillage and campus sites that can be monitored and studied by students and thesis candidates
Ecovillage-based courses (residential or non-residential), taught by both university and ecovillage faculty
Opportunities to pursue internships and independent study
Joint educational and service programs for youth and others in the surrounding community
A set of ecovillage-based programs forming the basis of a "major" or "minor" in Sustainable Development & Living

If it takes a village to raise a child, then perhaps it takes an ecovillage to educate an adult. If we work together, I believe that ecovillages will play a key role in transforming our current educational system and in training a new generation of leaders. Let's do it!

daniel@ic.org

Education at Ecovillages	Cultural - Spiritual					Social					Ecological				
	Creativity, Personal Development	Spirituality	Cultural Diversity	Holistic Worldview	Localization, Bio-regionalism	Communication, Education	Preventive Healthcare. Compl. Medicine	Building Community, Conflict Resolution	Modernizing Welfare	Localizing Economy	Green Businesses	Eco-building, Renewable Energy, Watercare	Local Organic Foods and Recirculation	Ecovillage Design, Permaculture	Earth Restoration
Auroville, India	•	•	•	•		•	•				•	•	•		•
Damanhur, Italy	•	•	•	•		•	•			•	•	•	•		•
Findhorn, Scotland	•	•	•	•	•	•	•				•	•	•	•	•
Gaia Argentina, Argentina						•	•				•	•	•		•
Growth Highschool, Denmark	•	•		•											
HueHuecoyotl, Mexico	•			•	•										
Ladakh, Kashmir		•	•	•				•					•		•
Lebensgarten, Germany	•	•		•						•	•	•	•		•
Sieben Linden, Germany						•		•		•	•	•	•	•	•
Sarvodaya, Sri Lanka	•	•		•				•				•	•		•
Snabegård, Vrads Sande, DK	•	•		•				•				•	•		•
Sirius, USA		•		•				•			•	•	•		•
Tamera, Portugal		•		•									•		•
The Nest of the Tiger, Denmark	•	•	•	•									•		•
Zegg, Germany	•	•	•	•									•		•
Bridge-Building School, Norway						•						•			
Colufifa, Senegal					•	•		•	•	•	•	•	•		•
Ecovillage Ithaca, USA				•								•		•	
Ecoyoff, Senegal			•		•	•						•	•		
Hertha, Denmark								•	•	•	•	•	•	•	•
IPEC, Brazil					•	•						•	•	•	•
Solheimar, Iceland											•	•	•	•	•
Torri Superiore, Italy	•		•		•							•	•	•	•
CAT, Wales, United Kingdom					•			•			•	•	•	•	•
Crystal Waters, Australia					•	•					•	•	•	•	•
Dyssekilde/Torup, Denmark					•	•						•	•	•	•
Folkecenter, Thy, Denmark					•	•						•	•	•	•
Hjortshøj, Denmark									•			•	•	•	•
L.A.Ecovillage, USA						•		•		•		•	•	•	
Svanholm, Denmark						•		•	•			•	•	•	•
The Farm, USA	•				•						•	•	•	•	•

Most ecovillages teach. The chart (drawn up by Hildur Jackson; design: Rolf Jackson) gives an idea of the possibilities for creating a global ecovillage education in (say) 10 modules. All the different modules may be easily covered in many different ecovillages. The first horizontal group is the mainly spiritual ecovillages, the second the social and the third the ecological ecovillages. The chart is probably not quite correct but shows but reflects the variety and richness of education in existing ecovillages.

The following European villages teach but are not in the chart (contact Lucilla Borio for more information: info@gen-europe.org): Czech Republic: Perma Lot. Finland: Keuuru, Katayamäki. France: Bio Lopin, Carapa. Germany: Kommune Niederkaufungen. Wales: Tinker´s Bubble, Britdir Mawr, Hockerton. Hungary: Gyürüfü. Israel: Kibbutz Lotan. Norway: Vallersund Gaard. Poland: Dambrowka, Wolimierz. Russia: Grishino, Kitesh. South Africa: Tlholego, Kuthumba. Spain: Selba (former Carrucha Cultural), Lakabe. Sweden: EKBO Gebers. Switzerland: Ecovillage Clos du Doubs (former Epidaure). Turkey: Harman Ecological Society.

A similar list could be made for American ecovillages and for the rest of the world.

Communication

Ecovillages may be rather independent microcosms with a high level of self-sufficiency, but this does not mean that they are cut off from the rest of the world. Indeed, most ecovillages want to share their message. Contact and exchange with others is vital for their survival, in order to: maintain a support network, which strengthens each individual ecovillage; develop outlets for their courses and business activities; stay abreast of developments; and inform (both within the network and externally). Most ecovillages have become quite good at communicating. The www.gaia.org website provides many examples of ecovillages which have set up functional communications systems (websites, newsletters, books and videos, etc.). Some of the most developed sites are Crystal Waters, Findhorn, Svanholm, The Farm, Damanhur, and Auroville.

GEN's Communication Infrastructure

by Lucilla Borio

Lucilla Borio is the Secretary of GEN Europe and Africa. She is also in charge of coordinating GEN's International communications activities. Lucilla lives and works at the ecovillage of Torri Superiore, Italy.

Communication as a word refers to how we, as human beings, transmit information to other humans, and how we react to the information received. In the information society, communication is basically everything. It can determine the survival or death of organizations, and sadly often of individuals too. As the GEN "Secretary for Communications", I will outline below some of the principles and tools we use for communicating within our organization and with the outer world.

Internet

Website

In total, the www.gaia.org site has over 2000 pages about ecovillages and related projects. Among others, the site features databases for searching ecovillages, news, resources and events.

Home page of www.gaia.org, which offers over 2000 pages about sustainability and ecovillages and related projects around the world.

Mailing Lists

We presently have 43 mailing lists. Most lists have the sole purpose of circulating information and news, while some directly refer to decision-making bodies with international or regional authority.

Email

Each person with a full-time computer job knows what enormous amounts of email messages we have to process every day. Especially in the US and Europe, the trend of having one computer per house is multiplying potential correspondents with no limit. Each person has the potential to flood everybody else's mailbox with his/her own messages alone. It is therefore of the highest importance that we remember that our brains are not computers, and that there is no way we can absorb the huge quantity of information passing through our PCs/Macs every day. Important messages and trivia enter our attention frame at the same time, and it is not always easy to tell the two apart.

Marti Mueller from Auroville (India) proposed we adopt "email ethics", which I summarize below:

An email address is a home base that should be respected and not given to a third person without permission.

Email is for rapid interpersonal communication, not for marketing, making money from contacts, obliging people to pass on chain letters to other addresses. All messages should state the sender's name.

Email is about logistical rapidity. People's personal lives should not be inundated with information overload or obligations to respond to messages that don't concern them directly.

Email use requires integrity and should not be a vehicle for discrediting people's reputations or involving third parties in personal quarrels.

Computers shall be kept up to date with the latest anti-virus programs. Attached files should not be sent without ensuring they are virus-free, or even better pasted into the body of the message.

As most of the world does not have regular access to email, *hard copies of important messages* shall be sent to African, South American and Asian partners to keep them informed.

Printed Material

Our graphic style has evolved over the years since the original sand-colored, simple-but-elegant brochures and "The Earth is our Habitat" booklet into a plethora of layouts and styles in independent publications. Our logo – a 'world-map' butterfly with the name Global Ecovillage Network – remains a distinctive sign and is present in most GEN publications, both international and regional. The use of recycled paper and ecological ink is also a unifying feature in most of our material, but not always explicitly referred to in the text.

Books

GEN Ecovillage Directory 2000 (by GEN Oceania)
Directory of Ecovillages in Europe 1998
Ecovillages and Communities in Australia and New Zealand, 2000
Eurotopia Directory 2001
"And We Are Doing It", Ross Jackson
Kali Yuga Odyssey, Ross Jackson
Creating Harmony, edited by Hildur Jackson

Regional offices have their own supplies of important books for sale, including the Communities Directory published by the Fellowship for Intentional Communities in the USA.

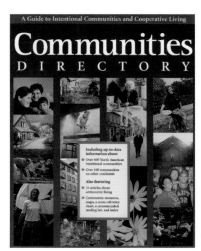

Communities Directory can be ordered at the GEN regional offices and via the Fellowship for International Communities, www.ic.org

Newsletters and magazines

The GaiaVillages/GEN Communications office in Denmark has released two International magazines in the years 2000 and 2001: *Ecovillage Millennium* (January 2000), 5000 copies; and *Ecovillage Living* (spring 2001), 6000 copies. Both issues of the magazine (edited by Hildur Jackson and Karen Svensson) were met with

Ecovillage Living was issued in Spring 2001, with a circulation of 6,000 copies.

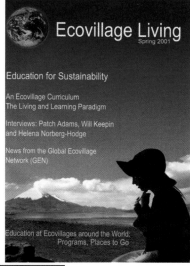

Creating Harmony, edited by Hildur Jackson, is full of first-hand knowledge, practical experiences, and stories about overcoming humanity's greatest stumbling block, conflict.

The book helps us explore new, holistic ways of living and working together.

The Earth is Our Habitat brochure was issued for the Habitat II conference in Istanbul, in 1996

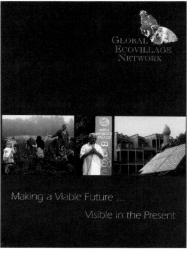

The GEN folio provides text and picture information on the network and its goals. It is being used as a jacket for information material to be handed out at conferences and meetings.

remarkably positive feedback, and proved to be effective communications tools about ecovillages and related projects, especially for fundraising and in public contexts such as conferences, seminars, speeches and festivals.
The GEN regions publish regional newsletters:

GEN-Europe continues to work with seven national language editions in partnership with magazines in Italy, Spain, Poland, Turkey, Denmark, Portugal and France. They produce a three-page English version twice a year.

ENA prints and distributes the four-language newsletter *Ecovillages* in English, Spanish, Portuguese and French, and has ongoing co-operation with the Fellowship of Intentional Communities.

GENOA regularly publishes its GEN-Oceania newsletter *Ecovillage News*, plus the recent special four-color edition on the Ecovillage Training Center.

All regional newsletters are also available in electronic format.

Flyers / brochures

Via the communications office in Denmark, GEN has produced an International flier. GEN Europe invested time and funds to produce versions of the GEN-International flyer in a few languages during 1999 and 2000, and has produced a new GEn-Europe flyer in ten languages.

Folders

These folios were produced in 2000 by the communications office in Denmark, presenting GEN on four colorful pages with pictures from ecovillages and related initiatives around the world. It provides useful background information on GEN while constituting a good-looking press package jacket.

Audio-visual tools
Videos and musical CDs

GEN produced the Habitat Revolution video, which presents the movement through interviews and film from ecovillages. GEN-Europe has produced a video on the Summer 2001 GEN Europe meeting in Poland. Agnieszka Komoch produced an educational CD ROM on ecovillages and European networks for GEN-Europe in June 2001.

Slides and pictures

The GEN slide show consists of 81 images from five continents, sorted by topic. Slides can be very time-consuming, but in my experience they can be extremely supportive in low-tech venues where computers and projectors (an excellent solution, especially at conferences) are not available for power-point presentations.

GEN has an international photo exhibit, which consists of 50 enlarged, plasticized pictures of ecovillages around the world (produced at the communications office in Denmark). This format is very flexible and allows for easy transportation and setup. GEN-Europe has a regional photo exhibit (50 pictures, 30 x 45 cm) which has been displayed in a number of occasions (Italy, Spain, Poland, Germany etc.) and was used for the 2002 UNESCO "Planet'ERE" Conference in Paris. A new exhibit (21 pictures in poster format) was created with EU funds from the Environment DG, and translated into French, Spanish and Turkish.

Power-point presentations

Albert Bates, ENA (Ecovillage Network of the Americas) International Secretary at The Farm, has developed a high-quality power-point presentation designed to present GEN at major events and conferences.

info@gen-europe.org

The GEN Europe Council at a meeting in Lakabe, Spain. Lucilla Borio is number two from left, second row. Agnieszka Komoch is standing, third from right. beside her, Lepre Viola from Damanhur, Italy (see article page 78).
Photo: GEN Europe.

Torri Superiore, Italy

Torri Superiore is located in Ventimiglia, Italy, near the French border. The ecovillage is built into a medieval stone village perched on a steep hillside between the Riviera's Mediterranean coast and the mountains. Since 1989, its inhabitants have been restoring the 166 rooms of the labyrinth-like settlement. The surrounding nature features an abundance of terraces now being recultivated, a river with a natural swimming pool and a waterfall, and mountains for climbing. The neighboring village has close ties to this culturally motivated project. Torri Superiore receives large numbers of guests all through the year, and provides comfortable accommodation for them. In 2001, Torri Superiore started an ecovillage tourism project under the auspices of GEN Europe. They hold permaculture courses, and organize meetings with local agriculturalists to promote ecological practices. The ecovillage has recently started a restaurant where visitors can enjoy fresh local food and wines, while looking out over the valley below. Torri holds summer camps for young people who want to help build up the ecovillage and experience daily life with its residents. Torri residents have Italian and international backgrounds. All generations are represented, the latest additions being two young children born in 2002.
www.ecovillages.org/Italy/torrisup *Photos: Torri Superiore*

The Cultural-Spiritual Dimension

Introduction

by Hildur Jackson

Over the past millennia, humans have become co-creative in the planet's evolutionary process through expressing a succession of different worldviews. These worldviews, from which our various cultures originate, have defined themselves largely by the way in which they have integrated individuals, society and nature; and by the degree to which they have infused these dimensions with a sense of spirit.

In today's world, tribal cultures still live by a deep knowledge of natural cycles, combined with spiritual practices that honour a higher unifying force. Eastern cultures have developed and refined spiritual knowledge and ancient wisdom, and are now teaching this to the whole world.

Western culture integrated spirituality until around 1600, when a break was established between spirituality and science, religion and politics, the soul and the rational mind. This schism still prevails today. On the one hand, it has allowed unprecedented control over nature through technological advancement, which has benefited mankind immensely in the material sense; on the other, it has made it easier for materialism and consumerism to define the lifestyle of millions in an expansionist economic system and worldview, which has become an intolerable ecological burden for the planet.

In ecovillages, people are trying to heal the fragmented aspect of the prevailing culture by living a holistic worldview. They have tried to formulate – and live – an alternative to the mainstream path, aiming at "restoring whole circulatory systems in people and nature on all levels". This was the formulation which ecovillages in Denmark adopted as the purpose of the Danish Association of Ecovillages ten years ago. It represents a way of unifying cultural/spiritual, social and ecological movements in a new worldview, analogous to the integration of different levels of the Chakra system in the human body, and the four elements (Earth, Water, Air, Fire).

A recent attempt at formulating a new worldview which may once again unite science and spirituality in a new cultural stream, has been expressed by Ken Wilber in his book A Theory of Everything. *Wilber includes culture and nature, spirit and science in a "four quadrant, all level model", symbolizing the integral vision into which the next worldview is to evolve out of the current age of modernity. He sees the emerging culture as one which transcends modernity, holding on to the beneficial aspects of today's rational industrial worldview while also integrating the self, society and nature with a pervasive sense of spirit in all dimensions, and reaching out towards a new level of consciousness.*

Left: the multi-religious meditation room in Lebensgarten, Germany, has pictures of spiritual leaders whom people feel close to, from all over the world. Photo: Agnieszka Komoch. Middle: some of the old American Indian tribal rituals are still observed in the USA. Here, the Chief of the Bella Coola Nation from Alaska, in traditional dress. The Bella Coola tribe members try to preserve their cultural heritage. Photo: © Peter Engberg, from the film: "Coming Back Home". Right: Asia presents cultures rich in diverse religious and spiritual beliefs. Here a Buddhist stupa in Colorado, USA (supported by the Manitou Foundation). Photo: GEN.

Creativity in Ecovillages

Art and Culture at Damanhur, Italy

Excerpts from www.damanhur.org

Founded in 1977, Damanhur (northern Italy) is an internationally renowned center for spiritual research. Damanhur is a Federation of Communities and Regions with about 1000 citizens, a social and political structure, a Constitution, about 50 economic activities, its own currency, schools and a daily paper.

According to Damanhur's philosophy, every human being is an active part of a spiritual eco-system, which includes larger and larger forces. Every individual shares an original divine nature that expresses itself as potentialities to be re-awakened through the expansion of awareness. This process is repeated through several incarnations towards enlightenment.

Art and aesthetic research are at the heart of Damanhur's spiritual path. They are tools capable of giving substance to the hallowing of time and space that now finds concrete expression in the Temples of Humankind. The result of over twenty years of work, these form a hidden underground temple of 6,000 cubic meters, carved by hand out of the rock. They are rich in mosaics, glass, paintings and sculptures, with the largest Tiffany cupola in the world. The Temples of Humankind, built in the heart of the mountain, are a series of underground Halls where art and beauty become a means of communication with the Divine. The rooms are connected to each other on different levels in a pathway that is likened to the journey that every human being undertakes from birth to death and again at rebirth: the Temples of Humankind, for those who enter them, represent a real initiation path. The Temples of Humankind are a living being, nourished by the artistic expression and actions of all those who build decorate and use them. Since their conception the Temples have been designed to gather and celebrate all the human arts. The spaces are the perfect stage for dance, song, music and theater. Each Hall has its own specific acoustics where sounds multiply and turn into pure energy. The sacred in Damanhur is a concrete reality, created by sharing, by the offering of everybody's creativity, and by the strength of the realization of common ideals.

Esoteric Physics and Time Traveling

The Federation of Damanhur is noted all over the world for its extraordinary experiments in time traveling, which border on Science Fiction. By uniting spirituality, art and technology, Damanhur's research groups often succeed in carrying out experiments that contemporary science considers impossible.

A few years ago a prestigious English magazine, *Kindred Spirit*, published an exclusive article on some of our experiments with time travel and since then the news has spread all over the world. Most people think it is just fantasy, others keep an open mind and wonder about the nature of time and reality as we experience it through the senses. Theories supporting these experiments are connected to the discipline of Esoteric Physics that has been studied and developed by the Olami Damanhur University for many years. Seminars are open to all those who wish to study with us and deepen their knowledge of the great mysteries of the universe.

Meditation

Meditation in Damanhur signifies more than just a technique. Meditation is a way of conducting our own existence according to spiritual principles. Everyone therefore works on their inner self thanks to the help of others, to overcome their limitations and reawaken their own divine part, the dormant senses and the consciousness. For us 'Meditation' is the pathway Damanhurians choose to follow in their own lives. Meditation represents the fundamental principles that human beings constantly search for; to find, discover, study and constantly verify by experimentation and practical application, day by day. The principles of Meditation can be applied 24 hours a day.

For us Meditation is a wide and illuminated road on which every individual discovers his own way to move in harmony with the universal laws. It is therefore an interior discipline, a continuous field of exploration, a never-ending source of enrichment and density. Through the School of Meditation it is also possible to learn to utilize rituals and techniques, which step by step can be applied to spiritual growth, but the various disciplines proposed along the way are only the means and not the end. One of the goals we are working towards is the re-awakening of the human being as a spiritual, material, divine being, free of the patterns that reduce his/her essence.

The "Ways"

In Damanhur every citizen chooses one of seven spiritual paths, called 'Ways', to experiment with their spiritual growth, according to their own aspirations, preferences and skills. In Damanhur the most significant aspects of the day and year are marked by ritual moments in which the meaning and the awareness of existence is celebrated.

At this point in time when more and more peoples and races are disappearing, reducing the culture and diversity of all Mankind, Damanhur is creating a new human group with its own artistic, philosophical and cultural expression; a new People based on the exaltation of the differences among individuals, differences made precious and irreplaceable in the pursuit of a common goal.

Damanhur

Italy

Damanhur was inspired by Oberto Airaudi, called Falco (his Damanhurian name), in 1977; it now has 500 residents and 300 members-at-large. It is situated in the Italian foothills of the Alps, where Damanhurians have (in secret for the first 18 years) excavated their underground Temple of Humankind. The Temple consists of seven halls, all artistically decorated with murals, statues and Tiffany glass mosaics. Damanhurians value variety and change, and alternately choose one out of seven spiritual-creative paths. They live in communities belonging to five major groups (Tentyris, Etulte, Damil, Rama and Pan), which make up the Federation of Damanhur. They choose two leaders every six months. Damanhur has developed 40 businesses, its own currency, schools, a university, research projects (esoteric physics) and a daily newspaper. An Australian town planner described it as the most fascinating of the European projects which he visited. There are eight affiliated communities in Italy, Berlin, Sweden and the US. Web: **www.damanhur.org** Email: **welcome@damanhur.org**

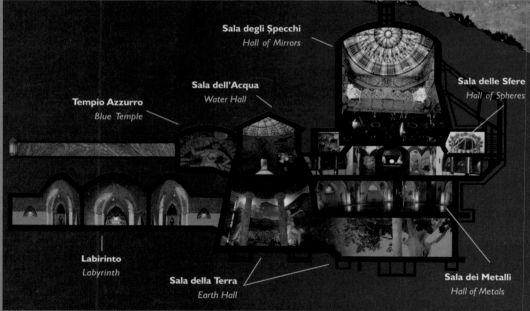

Sala degli Ṣpecchi
Hall of Mirrors

Sala dell'Acqua
Water Hall

Sala delle Sfere
Hall of Spheres

Tempio Azzurro
Blue Temple

Labirinto
Labyrinth

Sala della Terra
Earth Hall

Sala dei Metalli
Hall of Metals

Top: Tiffany glass ceiling in the Temple. Above Left: Falco's blue room in the Temple. Above right: View of the Temple of Mankind. Right: Fountain near the outdoor temple. Far right: Damanhur has its own currency, the Credito. Below left: Empirical testing of Damanhur's own cheese. Below center: Damanhur has built a mall which houses everything from a café to a jewelry store, a woollen goods store selling Damanhur's woven shawls, and a handmade glass store. This is where people meet in between classes, or after work, and where visitors get an impression of daily life at Damanhur. Below right: House decorated in Damanhur's typical style (there is an art workshop in the basement).

Spirituality

Learning to Live a Spiritual Worldview

by Hildur Jackson

The longing for a spiritual life

Many people have experienced glimpses of the divine in their lives, and develop a thirst for a more spiritual existence. They may start with a vague idea of how to pursue this longing, which then becomes a constant companion. They long for daily meditations, prayers, chanting or dancing in a group where everybody is on the same quest. They long for a quiet, simple life in beautiful surroundings, and in harmony with the cosmos. Some try to fulfill their aspirations by creating spiritual communities or ecovillages. A spiritual teacher may be the attraction for some people, while others hope to create a group that can support the development of each of its members. Ecovillages in the North have accepted many new spiritual paths, including esoteric Christian practices. Will Keepin, of the Satyana Institute (USA) states that for him, the purpose of an ecovillage is to help each other realize our divine nature (see 'Ecovillage Living', page 20). Will is a scientist who has worked with spirituality for many years (see page 127).

The process of creating an ecovillage, added to a spiritual practice, seems to me a "highway" to personal development in itself. Other people in the community help you hold a mirror to your personality, your strengths and weaknesses. You have many opportunities to learn who you are, and what you need to change in yourself to improve your life. You can leave the old patterns behind, and try to adopt a new worldview as you go. For many, this kind of process has happened over many years before manifesting in physical structures such as the spiritual ecovillages we see today. Spiritual ecovillages are still in an experimental phase. Twenty years from now, our collective spiritual level in the North will hopefully be more elevated, allowing for this spiritual evolution to establish itself. In places like Ladakh (Kashmir), Sri Lanka, India and Africa, local cultures still allow spirituality to play an important role. This spirituality, when honored, often makes it easier for them to choose a sustainable path.

Spiritual leadership

Many communities were started to manifest a spiritual life on Earth, such as Findhorn (Scotland), Auroville (India), The Farm (USA), Damanhur (Italy), Lebensgarten (Germany), Snabegård (Denmark), Tamera (Portugal) and Plum Village (France). When people live together, it is easier for them to gather for meditation and prayer, and to create a simple, "mindful" lifestyle cooperatively.

Cultural Focus

Other ecovillages were started with a cultural focus, such as Torri Superiore (Italy) and Huehuecoyotl (Mexico), with a desire to maintain local culture and heritage, and an impulse to create one's own culture. In Ladakh (Kashmir), Sarvodaya (Sri Lanka), and Colufifa and EcoYoff in Senegal, the cultural and spiritual dimensions are intertwined.

Many spiritual communities have a spiritual guide (or a couple), or an inspirator who helps the community develop their relationship to the divine. Damanhur has a 'king and queen' team, two persons elected as guides for a period of time. Falco, Damanhur's spiritual guide, lectures once a week and his lectures are taped, written down, copied and then discussed. These lectures seem to be the central spiritual inspiration of the community. Falco is a researcher and a visionary, who believes in the law of change. He is not so much a leader as a gentle, multi-talented person who shares his visionary ideas with the community, and whom the community recognizes as a valuable guide.

Tamera and Zegg (pages 15; 83-85) have Dieter Duhm and Sabina Lichtenfels as a couple inspiring the others in person and through writings. The community also has other supporting leadership structures.

Findhorn (p. 92) had three core persons guiding the community in its beginning phase. Later in Findhorn's development, Eileen Caddy was the only remaining spiritual leader, then she renounced spiritual leadership, as described in her book, *Builders of the Dawn*. Since then Findhorn has been experimenting to find its way forward. There currently is a 12-person leadership group in place.

At The Farm, Steve and Ina Gaskin were initiators.

In Sarvodaya (Sri Lanka) Ari Ariyaratne was the spiritual and practical head of the movement for 40 years. Now his son Vinya, a member of the GEN Board, has taken over the leadership of the organization while Ari is concentrating on spiritual and peace work (see pages 117-119; 134-137).

In Denmark, The Folkhighschool for Human Growth and Vrads Sande/Snabegård (p. 114), The Golden Circle (Asger Lorentzen), Munach and The Center for Growth (Jes Bertelsen) each have one spiritual leader.

Lebensgarten in Germany (p. 69) has chosen a different spiritual structure. It has a small chapel with pictures of many spiritual leaders from Jesus, Buddha, Sri Aurobindo/Mother, Yogananda and Maharishi to living persons like Mother Meera, representing many different spiritual and religious practices. They have several meditation halls for different meditation techniques. Dancing and chanting are everyday expressions of harmony.

How spiritual leadership interacts with the daily worldly decision-making structure is an interesting research project

Above: three hand-carved crosses carved in burr oak by Richard Brockbank at Findhorn, Scotland. © Richard Brockbank, Bay Cottage, Findhorn, Moray, Scotland.

for the future, and it will be exciting to watch how this develops in the years to come. It would be interesting to tell the full spiritual story of Findhorn, Auroville, Damanhur, Lebensgarten, Zegg and many other communities. However, due to practical limitations, we have had to keep the number of articles down. We have chosen to interview Vinya Ariyaratne about the significance of Spirituality for the Sarvodaya Movement for Peace. Marti Mueller has written an article about Auroville, in India, which is by far the biggest spiritual ecovillage we know. This account is followed by an article about a relatively new Danish project, Vrads Sande/ Snabegård, linked to a global organization around the raja yoga system of Sahag Marg. We also present stories about the Muslim faith and traditional Spirituality in Western Africa.

To open this section, we offer you a Celtic Prayer to pay tribute to the Christian tradition, which is not represented in the following articles:

*Christ! King of the Elements
Hear Me
Earth, Bear me
Water, Quicken me
Air, Lift me
Fire, Cleanse me
Christ! King of the elements
Hear me*

*I will cleanse my desire through love of Thee
I will lift my heart through the air to Thee
I will offer my life renewed to Thee
I will bear the burden of earth with Thee
Christ! King of the Elements
Fire, Water, Air and Earth
Weave within my heart this day
A cradle for Thy birth*

*Chapel built around a rock which forms its altar.
Architect: Christopher Day. Photo: Martin Voss-J.*

Spirituality in Auroville, India

by Marti Mueller

Marti Mueller has been a resident of Auroville since 1983, and lives in Paris, France, part of the time. She is a founder of the 'Children and Trees' educational project and the Nada Brahma Resonance Center. She is also on the steering committee of the Auroville Tamil Heritage Center for honoring indigenous peoples. She is the Chair of the Advisory Board of GEN. Her latest book is The Spirit of Community.

The 34-year-old community of Auroville in South India is not an ecovillage *per se*. It is rather a cluster of ecovillages on the verge of being a city of the future, imbued with values that make intentional communities exciting and relevant. Located on the Bay of Bengal, Auroville was first conceived by the Mother as a center for human unity. It was given a special status as an international community by the Indian Government through an act of parliament more than ten years ago. Auroville has also been recognized by UNESCO.

Auroville: The First Step Was Spiritual

If Auroville had not been founded on spiritual ideas, it is unlikely that it would have survived at all. The early pioneers lived on a barren eroded plateau where the hot sun showed no mercy, water was sometimes nonexistent, and the surrounding inhabitants were largely poor subsistence farmers with great heart but little in the belly. And yet, no sooner had the Mother's vision of Auroville, "the city the earth needs", been pronounced, than it captivated the minds and hearts of those who heard about it. And so in 1968, a year that heralded turbulent cries for change throughout the world, Auroville was born near Pondicherry in South India. Youth from throughout the world came to lay soil from their countries in a giant urn in what would later become the Matrimandir (The House of the Mother) peace garden.

The dream of Auroville emerged from the ideas of the French visionary, Mirra Alfassa, commonly referred to as "the Mother". She was deeply inspired by the Indian philosopher Sri Aurobindo, who believed that man is simply a transitory being and that a great evolution in our collective consciousness would inevitably occur. The Mother envisioned a center for human unity where people from cultures throughout the world could gather to create a new world. She saw Auroville as a living laboratory of evolution, a bridge between past and future where children's souls could be nourished and where youth would never age, but remain poised to bring divine consciousness into matter. This was to be a place where the evolution in human consciousness was not only possible, but also a prerequisite to the next stage in our history. And the invitation was extended to everyone. "Auroville belongs to no one in particular but to humanity as a whole," she said.

From Ecovillage to Ecoville

From a small pioneering community, Auroville has grown into a burgeoning international settlement. While we sometimes fall far short of the founding aspirations, the community is well on its way to becoming a unique place in the world. Today, nearly 2000 Aurovillians live in some 90 settlements. They steward some 3000 acres of land. Nearly 2 million trees have been planted. There are more than a dozen farms, two dozen experimental schools, and more than a hundred small handicraft businesses. There's a center for research in appropriate energy systems and experimental architecture, including low-cost eco-housing. There's a large healing center, complete with watsu (aqua massage), an impressive program in martial arts, and a center for Indian studies. There's a laboratory for research on the transformation of consciousness, a linguistics center (including living Sanskrit) and the Matrimandir, a large dome-shaped building in the center of the city that looks like it could take off into space. It is a place for contemplation and inner work.

Auroville was planned with four distinct zones: international, cultural, residential and industrial. In the international zone, different nations have been invited to contribute cultural centers. The Bharat Nivas Indian cultural center and the Tibetan Pavilion are already living realities. Auroville gets funding from institutions throughout the world. A recent Asian Urbs grant was given by the European Commission for a town hall annex. We now have an urban planning department that not only takes Auroville into consideration, but the entire Pondicherry biosphere as well.

marti@auroville.org.in avguest@auroville.org.in
www.auroville.org

Auroville, India

The Auroville township, located south of Chennai on the Tamil Nadu coastline, was founded in 1968. It was inspired by the vision of The Mother, the spiritual collaborator of the Indian philosopher Sri Aurobindo, as a center for human unity. It has around 1,500 inhabitants from about 40 different nations. There are nearly 100 communities of varying sizes. Auroville has nearly two dozen schools, a number of research institutes, cultural centers, a seed bank, forests and sanctuaries, appropriate technology and renewable energy centers, and many commercial units. Nearly three million trees have been planted in the past 30 years. Guest facilities exist and Auroville hosts a number of student exchange programs.

www.auroville.org

Photo: © Ireno Guerci

Top right: Matrimandir at the center of Auroville, with a center for 'concentration' and 12 buildings (under construction) in petal formation around it. ***Below left:*** *Research building built out of compressed earth blocks.* ***Middle:*** *Auroville's mandala.* ***Right:*** *house.* ***Middle row left:*** *Tree nursery.* ***Right:*** *Bonfire in front of Matrimandir.* ***Bottom:*** *Solar dish for cooking, on top of the community kitchen and dining hall. It can provide heat for the cooking of two meals for 1000 persons a day.*

Photo: Philip Snyder

Courtesy Marti Mueller

Photo: Philip Snyder

Photo: Philip Snyder

Photo: Auroville

Photo: © Ireno Guerci

What Makes Auroville a Success

Building a center for human unity in a country where bullock carts are used to transport computers, and human numbers surpass all imagination, brings a certain type of challenge with it. Auroville's strength lies in that it is a crossroads of North, South, East and West, of urban programs and rural traditions, of Western invention and Eastern wisdom. It heralds unity though diversity and is home to people from all walks of life.

Essential to Auroville's future as a community is the fact that it is located in India, a country with a remarkable sense of welcoming openness to the rest of the world. India is a nation with a long tradition of spiritual teachers and many of the keys to "being" in a world that is focused more and more on "becoming."

Looking back on it, I would say that the essential ingredients that made and make Auroville evolve and grow are:

1. A strong clear set of founding principles given by the Mother in the Auroville Charter (see box).

2. A group of tough pioneers who believed in the transformation of consciousness and saw Auroville as a living laboratory for evolution.

3. A real environmental focus on building a sustainable eco-system, which led to creative experimentation in reforestation, seed banks, and appropriate energy systems.

4. An intense commitment to art, music, dance and culture. (Honoring beauty and the inner being nourishes the imagination and brings extraordinary joy).

5. A deep commitment to new forms of experimental education and the development of the psychic being. (Auroville undoubtedly has its share of indigo children, as kids born here have the opportunity to focus on the integral being).

6. A firm commitment to being willing servitors of the divine (in a philosophical rather than a religious sense).

7. A sheer stubbornness, an absolute persistence and a refusal to believe in impossibilities.

8. A sense of humor that usually manifests in bizarre forms of self-criticism.

9. The courage to laugh at ourselves and acknowledge our mistakes.

10. A commitment to higher collective goals: being part of solutions for our Planet rather than part of the problems.

This is the essence of Auroville and of any community's success today.

And of course in Auroville's case, there has been a lot of crucial cross-pollination. We have received many people from all over the world (Findhorn, Damanhur, the Baca, the GeoCommons etc.) and we often go visiting to learn from others (this is why networks like the GEN are so important). Whether it's to grow organic carrots, or to manifest the coming of a new spiritual age, communities emerge out of a deep and often radical need for change. As we face the worldwide destruction of our natural resources, the rapid erosion of traditional cultures and the globalization of our economies, communities that stand apart and empower people to live sustainably are crucial. They are the foundation stones for our children and a meaningful future.

Auroville's Charter:

1. Auroville belongs to nobody in particular. Auroville belongs to humanity as a whole. But to live in Auroville, one must be the willing servitor of the Divine Consciousness.

2. Auroville will be the place of an unending education, of constant progress, and a youth that never ages.

3. Auroville wants to be the bridge between the past and the future. Taking advantage of all discoveries from without and from within, Auroville will boldly spring towards future realizations.

4. Auroville will be a site of material and spiritual researches for a living embodiment of an actual Human Unity.

Snabegaard Community

and the Vrads Sande Ashram

by Susan Marcia Klaus

Susan is a journalist and lives at the ashram of Vrads Sande in Denmark. She is the author of Welcome to the Future, *a description of 53 ecovillage projects, which competed for the title of "Best ecovillage project in Denmark" in a competition arranged by the Danish Association of Ecovillages (LØS) and supported by the Danish Ministry of the Environment.*

Formerly a popular holiday center, Vrads Sande Ashram in Denmark is today a well-attended meditation center for people from all over the world to practice the raja yoga system of Sahaj Marg. Since the establishment of the ashram in 1992 about sixty practitioners of Sahaj Marg have settled nearby. Twelve of these families form the small living community cohousing of Snabegaard – a member of the Danish Association of Ecovillages (LØS), with a purely spiritual basis.

Vrads Sande Ashram is the main common facility in Northern Europe of Shri Ram Chandra Mission (SCRM), the organization embracing Sahaj Marg. The World Headquarters is located in Chennai in India, where also resides the present president of SRCM and master of Sahaj Marg, Shri Parthasarathi Rajagopalachari, affectionately called Chari.

Vrads Sande is located 20 kilometers south-west of Silkeborg, in the heart of Jutland. The property spreads over 30 acres, including a big meditation hall, a main house with a common kitchen, two dining rooms, a meditation room and two dormitories, a café, and more than 30 guest apartments. Because of the location in a unique and highly preserved natural environment, the authorities don't permit new buildings, which sets a limit to the number of permanent residents. Presently three families live at and put as much work into the ashram as their daily lives allow them. Most important they serve as coordinators of the work, since Vrads Sande is becoming an increasingly active place. All work in the mission is voluntary, so the local members share the everyday responsibilities to make it run. But the life, work and community of Vrads Sande Ashram involve the whole international network of SRCM, not least abhyasis – as the practitioners of Sahaj Marg are called – from Germany, Holland and Sweden.

Snabegaard

In 1993 a group of SRCM members bought the Snabegaard farm in Vrads together, with the intention to settle close to the ashram to support its development. The farm made this possible, as there was permission to build new houses on twelve plots around it. Two of the community's residents were carpenters; they started a building company and built most of the (currently) nine new houses, most of them with a focus on sustainability, all in wood and with Finnish mass stoves and solar systems for heating. A few of the members have started organic farming, though only as a spare time job, since none are farmers as such. All have other educational backgrounds and jobs, but many hope to be able to earn their livelihood more locally in the future.

Snabegaard plays another important role: when seminars at Vrads Sande exceed the number of 400 people for accommodation. In summer 1995 the 50th anniversary of the world organization took place in Vrads, with 2000 participants from Europe, Asia, Africa and America. On this occasion – the biggest common work task for SRCM Denmark so far – large tents for meditation, dining and sleeping were put up at Snabegaard. Since then, dormitory tents have been put up on the farm fields for a few seminars.

Community life in the village

With the other abhyasis who settled in single-family houses and apartments in and around Vrads, the inhabitants of Snabegaard mix with the 170 villagers of Vrads in many different ways. Many participate in a quite active village community life, for instance in the co-op shop which started out shortly before the ashram. Placed in the middle of Vrads, the local co-op store has become a social center. Besides selling an increasing number of organic products and handicrafts made by locals, it serves as an important meeting place. News ideas are exchanged around its little café table. There's a small library, and a gallery with various exhibitions of mainly local arts and crafts, and 16 voluntary shopkeepers run a small campsite for the many tourists who pass through Vrads every summer. A quarterly newsletter also stems from the shop cooperative.

Snabegaard Community - Vrads Sande Ashram:
Since 1992, 60 people have moved to the community of Snabegaard, in Vrads, Denmark, and to the Vrads Sande Ashram. Here they have built a spiritual Community based on the practice of Sahaj Marg Raja Yoga in the middle of Jutland. On the painting (right, by Hildur Jackson), you see the meditation center; Vrads Sande (15 ha) with 34 apartments, a dining hall and other buildings; and at the bottom of the picture, the meditation hall. From Vrads Sande, the road winds its way through a hilly landscape to the Snabegård Community (20 ha with 12 houses, top left on the picture) and to the village of Vrads (top right). They are all situated on the high ridge ('højderyg') of Jutland and surrounded by forests, heather hills and agricultural lands. A bicycle path which runs through Denmark passes through the area and brings thousands of visitors to the co-op store in the middle of Vrads, just opposite the old village church.

Photos: Below: A house at the Snabegaard community; middle: Inside the house, the kitchen with a mass stove (left) for cooking and heating; right: celebration.
Middle row: Left: Children playing; middle: Chari, The Spiritual Master of Sahaj Marg; right: The Master's house at the Ashram. Bottom left and right: Opening celebration of the co-op in Vrads; middle: the coop offers free coffee and tea to visitors.

Photos are courtesy of Hildur Jackson, Eric Klitgaard and Susan Marcia Klaus for Vrads Sande SRCM.

Snabegaard
Vrads Sande
Denmark

© Eric Klitgaard

VRADS KØBMANDSHANDEL

Different activities take place in the village hall, such as monthly common meals during the winter season. The village hall is owned by most of the citizens in common. In the old smith's place just opposite the village hall another common room was recently inaugurated, after having being restored with ecological techniques by nine villagers who bought it together in 1998. In addition, this property contains two work halls – one for one of the Snabegaard carpenters, who apart from building wooden houses also opened a store for ecological building materials here, and the other for two artisans who build Finnish mass stoves and strawbale houses.

Many activities in the village come and go, but a coninuing one is the Vrads choir that meets every winter on the initiative of a local composer and conductor. Keeping the choir open to everybody who likes to sing, he knows that the best music includes many different voices with each having its part to play.

The spiritual practice of Sahaj Marg

Sahaj Marg – meaning the Simple or Natural Way in Sanskrit – is a raja yoga system of spiritual training based on heart-centered meditation. The practice is founded on the principle that God pervades the heart of each and every person. The goal of the practice is explicitly spiritual: attaining the ultimate goal of human existence, which is oneness with God. Just as a bird needs two wings to fly, a human being needs to attend to both material and spiritual aspects of life to rediscover his or her true essence. Ordinary life with its demands of family, relationships and work is a perfect environment for spiritual growth. Sahaj Marg blends spiritual practice with managing our everyday lives.

Meditation is continuous thought on one thing, and according to Sahaj Marg "we meditate on that which we want to become". Thus, with the guidance and support of the spiritual teacher, the abhyasis meditate on the Divine Presence in the heart as the most direct means of realizing the goal.

Two aspects distinguish Sahaj Marg from other meditation practices: transmission and cleaning. Transmission is the offering of the subtlest divine current directed by the spiritual teacher to the heart of an abhyasi.

"As power can be transmitted, as thought can be transmitted, as speech can be transmitted, so also spirituality can be transmitted. When the transmission is made into the heart of the practitioner, he is filled with a force higher than himself and therefore his evolution or progress becomes not only very much speedier, but

President of SRCM and master of Sahaj Marg, Shri Parthasarathi Rajagopalachari, also called Chari, in front of the meditation hall at Vrads Sande. Photo: Eric Klitgaard.

also becomes in essence independent of his own capacity for progress. This transmission gives the practitioner the possibility of growing without limitations," as Chari explained in one of his many speeches.

According to Sahaj Marg, everything we do and think leaves impressions on our minds and hearts. These impressions deepen into tendencies, which condition our behavior and prevent us from realizing our potential for spiritual growth. If they are not removed, they remain as seeds, which can come out and flower when the appropriate environment is created for them. The cleaning of Sahaj Marg removes the tendencies and prepares the abhyasi to receive transmission.

"The meditation and cleaning processes balance each other, support each other, for our evolution. Meditation in itself, without cleaning, is to my mind useless. It would be like having a powerful car bogged down in slime and mud. And cleaning by itself is like being on a beautiful road in a car without any engine," Chari once said.

The spiritual teacher

The spiritual journey within is of a scale beyond our conception. Sahaj Marg states that alone and unguided, it is almost impossible to avoid our own self-delusions beyond a certain stage. The role of a spiritual teacher is to serve humanity by helping sincere seekers to become masters of themselves. Acceptance of a spiritual guide requires discrimination and scrupulous care based on personal experience with the practice.

"Spirituality is like climbing a mountain. In the beginning is very easy. But if you are really trying for the high ranges, to reach the peak very soon there is hardly a way. You have to find it. That is why mountaineers have guides. The guide knows the way, though there is no visible way," Chari said in this connection.

Preceptors are abhyasis prepared and permitted by the living Master to introduce people to the Sahaj Marg system, and to conduct both group and individual meditations (sittings). During a sitting the preceptor cleans and directs the transmission to the abhyasi's heart.

Training in Sahaj Marg is open to all over eighteen years of age. The only qualification is a genuine and abiding interest in spiritual growth and the willingness to participate. To start the practice, a minimum of three introductory sittings with a preceptor is required.

susan@marcia.dk
Literature on Sahag Marg: *www.srcm.org*

Spirituality in the Sarvodaya Movement for Peace, Sri Lanka

Interview with Vinya Ariyaratne, leader of Sarvodaya

by Karen Svensson and Hildur Jackson

The Sarvodaya Shramadana Movement for Peace has engaged in participatory community development for the last four decades, now working in about 12,000 villages out of a total of 30,000 in Sri Lanka. This village-based development corresponds to the vision of GEN and is an alternative path to directly involving people in the market. Sarvodaya is the biggest member of GEN and has brought us invaluable inspiration. The movement's philosophy was summed up by Vinya Ariyaratne, who followed in his father's footsteps as leader of Sarvodaya:

"The Sarvodaya model of development is envisaged as encompassing six dimensions: spiritual, moral, cultural, social, economic and political. When these dimensions are balanced, there will be an awakened society."

Q: What is the role of spirituality in the Sarvodaya movement for peace? You have a Buddhist background, but you work with many different religions. Does Sarvodaya have its own special practice?

Vinya: The Sarvodaya Philosophy, though derived from Buddhism, has a universal application, because it has brought out the essence of spirituality (the spiritual component of Buddhism). It is combined with all the religions that exist in the Sri Lankan villages, among which are Christianity and Hinduism.

The spiritual dimension of Sarvodaya brings out an understanding of your inner self in relation to the outside world. Service and development within Sarvodaya always have spiritual guidance as their source of inspiration. Our spiritual practice motivates hundreds of thousands of people to serve others, to bring happiness to other people through helping them satisfy their basic needs. We have brought about volunteerism in people. We start with spiritual development (which impacts on the moral and cultural levels), followed by social development, economic development and finally political development. We help people to understand themselves and the situation they are in first (spiritual). In a new village, we start with a Shramadana camp, meaning the voluntary sharing of labor to fulfill a basic community need (for example cleaning the village). A camp can last for two to three days, or even a week. It's an initial mobilization. We start the camp with meditation, combined with traditional cultural activities and indigenous practices. In a Hindu community, we bring out the Hindu philosophy to awaken the inner personality. We train people from all ethnic groups in this work, so our entry point is development, not a particular religion, and spiritual development is brought in as part of the development process. Every day a couple of hours are spent on spiritual and cultural activities, where meditation is the common activity. The basic meditation technique we follow concentrates on breathing in and out. Ana BaNa SaBhi (mindful breathing). A person belonging to any religion can practice it. We meditate together, and then each religion is given five minutes for their practices, Hindu chants followed by Christian prayers, and so on. This promotes interreligious harmony in our country in a big way. We have never had any problems integrating spiritual development for people from different religions. The media are promoting misconceptions about religions. We are now trying to bring about better understanding for religions, also at an early stage (children's books, understanding the basic values of different religions).

Q: How is spirituality integrated in practice in your five phases of development?

Vinya: In the higher stages of development we retain the meditation, the common spiritual practice. Our spiritual practice affects the activities people are involved in. In the economic dimension, for example, we give out loans for activities, and we know that people will never use them for anything harmful to human beings or animals. That is a result of the spiritual dimension of our development: applying spiritual awareness in the economic dimension. This is also true in the village society, in issues related to governing society: people in Sarvodaya will be influenced by the mental balance they achieve as a result of the spiritual awakening. They reach decisions by consensus, resolve conflict without resorting to any violence.

Q: What can you say to other networks and movements of communities about the inclusion of spirituality in the community's work?

Vinya: The spiritual dimension is important as an integral part of an ecovillage/community. Don't separate it out from what is happening, it needs to be integrated in everything that we do. At the same time, it will not happen automatically, there has to be a conscious effort to retain this high level of spirituality (activities which are bringing the community together, keep spirituality integrated). In our villages we try to get people to meet together in the evening to meditate and discuss with each other (even if only half an hour). Spirituality can take different forms. It's a matter of at least a few people realizing the importance of a spiritual practice, and the rest of the community will catch up. Really feel the energy, and the others around you will be converted and will start as well.

To recognize the need for spirituality is the first step. We have built a Peace Center where people come from all walks of life to meditate. It's remarkable the change you see in these people, when they experience it. Some come reluctantly (it's their company that sent them) but they go through something so rewarding that they are convinced. We've heard from the companies that people who go through our very defined meditation program find that they can function much better in their professional environment after this. They have shared this with management, after which more people were sent. They say they've noticed a tremendous impact in the workings of their companies. The human relation improved between senior managers and subordinates, they understood each other better, management listened better to workers' needs, workers were not antagonistic any more, but tried to resolve issues instead. This resulted in improved productivity, the whole atmosphere changed,

Left: Sarvodaya organizes community meetings and meditations as a part of village development in Sri Lanka. Photo: GEN.

Above: Sarvodaya's founder Ari Ariyaratne (far left) guides visitors through the Sarvodaya Peace Center. In the foreground, the Lotus pond with its Path of Mindfulness. The Peace Center offers accommodation and educational facilities. Photo: courtesy Agnieszka Komoch.

people felt inspired and the working environment improved. They used to send people to management courses. With us, it's about trying to harmonize with nature, greenery, understanding yourself, connecting, bringing in inner peace and outer peace. Teachers at the Peace Center are Sarvodaya founder Ari Ariyaratne, and four other trained teachers, who allocate their time and conduct the meditation program. Through the center we also offer alternatives to the very violent political process in Sri Lanka. In our Living and Learning curriculum we also have a module called: "The Spiritual Dimension of Awakening".

Q: How do you define spirituality?

Vinya: The connection I have with my own self. An understanding of the outer world is a result of how you relate to your inner self and your inner process. Through spirituality you get very balanced in your thinking. It inspires us to have compassion, understanding for other people, to get joy out of what we do, to feel equanimity (so we don't feel disturbed by negative things that happen). In my life I never wanted to have lot of fame or money, I wanted to serve people as a medical doctor. I now devote my time to creating healthy lifestyles for people so they don't get sick (mentally and physically), working on prevention. I'm able to shoulder a lot of stress thanks to my spiritual conviction. I believe in Buddhism. Other religions also help. Belief in God helps bring these values forward.

Peace Meditations

Sri Lanka has suffered from its violent ethnic conflict for over 19 years. As opposed to the logic of the "war for peace," Sarvodaya has initiated a new people's peace initiative: peace meditations. The first peace meditation took place in August 1999, gathering 200,000 people of various ethnic and religious backgrounds. This is now a regular event. During peace meditations, people sit in silence, and engage in a one-hour meditation for peace. During the meditation, participants are invited to erase from their minds all the divisive elements in their society, and instead to look at humanity and nature as interconnected. Everybody extends their loving kindness to all living beings and directs the spiritual energies towards raising their spiritual consciousness, praying for the unity of all people so that an end to the war can be brought about. Peace will not come about if only symptomatic approaches are taken. Gun control and the dispersion of violent groups will not work if there still is a war in people's minds. Building peace in people's minds is Sarvodaya's approach to peace (see also p. 134).

gensa@sri.lanka.net

www.sarvodaya.org

Colufifa and Spirituality

Interview with Demba Mansaré and his wife Elise Guldagger

by Hildur Jackson

Danish Elise was married to Guinean Demba Mansaré in 1999, as his fourth wife, a status that she accepted as part of Demba's cultural tradition. Thirty years ago, Demba initiated the Colufifa village movement for ending hunger (in Faoune, Senegal). Elise grew up at the Nordic Folk highschool at Kungsselv in Sweden, which her parents started. In this spirit, she started the "Bicycles to Senegal" project in Denmark, which ships used bicycles and other appliances to Senegal in empty return containers. She arranged a West African network meeting in Denmark in Winter 2001, gathering 15 NGO leaders from Africa. During the meeting, all were invited to join with her, her husband and the NGO leaders in one of their five daily prayers, as part of their Muslim religious practice.

Q: Can you tell us about Elise's conversion to Islam, when you married?

Elise: For me, it was one more door opening towards God. I pray five times a day. I pray in many ways. My far closest relation to God is when I sing. I sing in the way God makes me sing. I follow the Francis of Assisi prayer: "Make me an instrument of your peace." It has been my guideline for many years. And just before I met Demba, I was about to decide to become a Franciscan sister.

Demba: Being a Muslim is a fundamental element in my work. Without that, I could not maintain the work with poor farmers for a sustainable future in the heart of Africa. You meet lots of disappointments in this work. Without the Muslim faith, which permits me to be in a position to understand the other person and serve without conditions, I could not persist. Many people in the network are Muslims, but there are also Christians and animists. It does not create problems, quite the opposite.

Q: How is it, Elise, to be married to an African Muslim husband?

Elise: I think it is God who has created our love. Our very first meeting was during a prayer, and it opened my heart and all my being towards a life of working for the poorest of the poor. Coming to the small villages in Africa, I realize they have so much to give and they give so much back. They live their spirituality in everyday life and their social life is so strong and rich. Since I am a nurse, I am learning much from the traditional ways of healing, praying, taking care of the dying and respect for the elders. I have learned that the only way to become whole is by sharing. I met the Dalai Lama some years ago, and he advised me to work with the elderly and the poor, and to sing. I hope that I am creating bridges between cultures, religions and traditions. For the third time now I am following the fast of the month of Ramadan, which started on November 17th. It is a spiritual training and a deepening of my prayers especially relating to gratitude, forgiveness and reconciliation.

When I visited the small mountain village in Guinea Conakry, where Demba was born, and his 90 year-old father is the head of the village elders, we went to pray at the grave of his mother. As a woman, I was not allowed to enter the sacred site. I had then already decided to be buried at Demba's side in Africa, together with the other wife, but when my five Danish children heard that I was not allowed to enter the site, they said that they would not allow this. We discussed this with Demba. Coming back last year, he brought me to the grave and after the prayer, more women entered and Demba told me that the council of the elders had decided to open it up for women.

Left: Elise Terena Guldagger-Mansaré praying with her husband Demba Mansaré, founder of Colufifa in Senegal. Photo: Courtesy Elise Guldagger.

Colufifa and EcoYoff, Senegal

In January 2002, Senegal adopted ecovillages as the building blocks for an official sustainable development strategy, and a national network of ecovillages was founded. Two of the important members of this network are Colufifa and EcoYoff. Colufifa is a network of villages which started 30 years ago in Senegal, under the leadership of Demba Mansaré. Colufifa promotes village-based development in Senegal and Guinea primarily, with their main basis in Faoune, Senegal. EcoYoff is an ecological community program based in Yoff-Dakar, Senegal. It was started in 1996, after the Ecocity conference (held at Yoff) created tremendous enthusiasm for sustainable development in Yoff's inhabitants and government. EcoYoff has developed a highly successful internet business based on an in-house government information system (SIUP), and has initiated the building of an ecocity. They host education and international exchange programs. EcoYoff and Colufifa network within Senegal, with Guinea, Mali and other African countries, and intercontinentally. *Photos: Elise Guldagger, Kolja Hejgaard and Lucilla Borio.*   EcoYoff: mzeitlin@refer.sn   Colufifa: ajaae-colufifa@sentoo.sn

Top, from left: Clay huts in Madina, Guinea, built for participants of the Permaculture course held in 2000 by Colufifa. Demba's family. Above, from left: Demba and his fourth wife, Elise Terena Mansaré-Guldagger from Denmark, building a dam in Madina. Elise and Demba planting. Praying. Right: Sesame paste production plant, manned by women in Faoune, Senegal. Packing the sesame, and preparing sesame cakes. Hot air dryer for fruit, installed at Madina by members of the Torri Superiore Ecovillage in Italy (Madina's twin village). Below, from left: Mango tree at Madina. Compost toilet at Yoff, Dakar, installed for demonstration purposes at the home of an Imam, a local leader. Ronald Diop, at Yoff's EcoCenter, explains waste treatment systems.

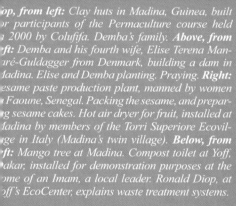

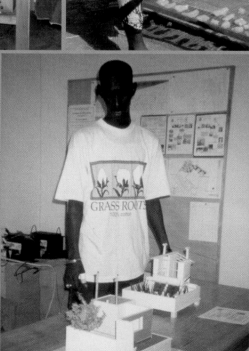

Spirituality at EcoYoff, Dakar

by Karen Svensson

The spiritual protection of the village of Yoff, Dakar, in Senegal is entrusted to a particular combination of traditional spirituality and Muslim faith. The villagers observe a spiritual practice which mixes the worship of the Ocean Genie, Mame 'NDiaré, and the observance of the Muslim faith through the Layène brotherhood, whose mosque and prayer field occupy a central place in the village, alongside the sea.

Mame 'N Diaré and the Priestess:

The village protector is Mame 'NDiaré, the feminine Ocean spirit who appeared for the first time to a fisherman named Gallu Samba in 1558. She came over a pathway from the Yoff Island off the beach, and told the fisherman that her name was the very name of the woman who would be the fisherman's first wife: Mame 'NDiaré. This is also why the spirit is believed to be a feminine spirit.

Mame 'N Diaré's cult is tended by a Priestess who goes by the name Thioum Laye (the family from which all the Ocean Spirit's priestesses are descended), and lives in the Tonghor quarter of Yoff. The Thioum Laye Priestess is assisted by her older sister during the healing ceremonies, and she travels with her when she is called outside the village. The Priestess is the relay between the

The Mosque of the Layène Brotherhood, built where it is said that Seydina Limamou Laye planted a tree stub behind which the sea retreated, and where a well srpung forth. Photo: Kolja Hejgaard.

people of Yoff and the "Genie"; she is the moral guardian of the village and responsible for its inhabitants. She performs healing ceremonies and traditional rituals to placate Mame 'N Diaré and call for her assistance. Ritual ceremonies involve the slaughter of animals or the gushing of "lait caillé", curdled milk, over stones and bones. According to the gravity of the situation, it will command the slaughter of a chicken, a goat, or an ox (usually for matters involving the whole village).

The Muslim Faith: The Layène Brotherhood

The Muslim part of the village's spiritual life is tended to by the followers of Seydina Limamou Laye, who had a divine revelation in 1884. No one believed in his vision at first, nor did they want to grant him land to build a mosque. But then he performed a miracle: he planted a tree stub in the sea, and the sea retreated beyond it to expose a large piece of land on which the mosque now stands. The he stamped with his foot on the ground, and a well sprung forth. These miracles marked the start of the "confrérie Layène", the Layène Brotherhood.

In Yoff, to allow for the social levelling of the classes and the families, everyone is allowed to substitute his last name with 'Laye', if he so desires. The philosophy behind this is that everyone should have a shot at equality in this world. There is a weekly Friday meeting at the Mosque. There are two prayers a day, and weekend celebrations. The grandson of the Brotherhood's founder, Hussein Limamou Laye, still lives behind the mosque.

Most of the inhabitants of Yoff are of Muslim faith and also worship Mame 'N Diaré, which becomes most visible during healing ceremonies and festivals for the Ocean Genie. There is great respect for both streams of spirituality, and both are kept alive.

Celebrating Life, Honoring Cultures and Natural Cycles

Recovering the Sacred in Nature

by Philip Snyder

Philip Snyder, Ph.D., is the former Director of the International Secretariat of GEN in Copenhagen. An anthropologist with a specialization in people and place, he is now based in Sedona, Arizona and is a consultant in program & organizational development and integrated land use.

The great sea
Has sent me adrift
It moves me
As the weed in a great river
Earth and the great weather
Move me
Have carried me away
And move my inward parts with joy.

– Song of Uvavnuk, Inuit woman shaman

The consciousness of the modern world is almost unimaginably different from that of humans in the millennia of our deep past, that vast sweep of time that stretches back through the Ice Ages into the birthing of humanity. In those days we lived in a profound intimacy with nature, and we knew the Earth for what it was – the source of our sustenance, of our very lives. Earth-based spiritualities were the primordial religion of humanity: the shamanic drawings on the caves and rocks of Europe, Australia, Africa, the Americas, Asia are all testament to that earlier awareness. The emergence of agriculture signaled a deep change in how we were to live with this Earth, and the civilizations that arose from intensive farming developed new religions that began to shift away from the earlier intimacy with the primal forces of Nature.

Industrialism shattered our connection with the living Earth far further, giving rise to a post-modern consciousness in which Nature became an abstraction, something 'out there', to be viewed through a window or on a video screen. Now, with so many people living in cities, encased in a world of buildings, roads, cement, asphalt – entirely produced by industrial culture – are we surprised to discover that 'the environment' is now a 'problem'?

Amazingly, the earlier sense of the sacredness of Nature has survived these changes in our collective cultural evolutionary journey, as seen among the many native and indigenous peoples around the world. The Aboriginal 'Dreaming' coexists with contemporary urban Australian society; traditional American Indian spiritualities persist and even thrive amid the busy technocratic world of the United States, and this is so in all the continents. Traditional societies worldwide tend to have a much more integral connection with surrounding Nature, which provides directly for much of their needs for food, shelter, clothing, etc. Their spiritualities often reflect the depth of this relationship, and abound with ceremonies whereby the people can express their gratitude for the abundance of this nurturing Earth.

As Thomas Berry makes clear in *The Dream of the Earth,* one of the imperatives of the coming 'Ecological Age' is for modern humanity to awaken our 're-enchantment' with the Earth, to recover a sense of the surrounding world as filled with the sacredness of life. We must break through the numbing sense that has developed that the Earth is merely a non-sentient 'it', a kind of utilitarian storehouse there to fulfill our desires. We must begin to respect and, yes, love the living wonder of this planet. Ecovillages can create ideal conditions whereby this re-enchantment of the world can flourish, especially for the children who are raised in a context which instills in them the sense that the Earth and life are sacred, to be treated with care and even reverence.

People need plentiful opportunities for direct engagement with Nature. The creation and care of gardens is one obvious way that communities can co-creatively work with life, building humus, growing plants for food and beauty, encouraging bees and birds and other life. The garden can become a kind of sanctuary, a place of both work and repose, with perhaps a water feature and place to sit and contemplate the splendor and peace of life as it unfolds through the seasons. Ecovillage land use can reflect and honor the twin poles of our human nature – for both solitude and communion. Are there places set aside which are quiet, with some measure of privacy and tranquility? Can such a contemplative oasis be developed? What better retreat from the busy-ness of the world than in a special place out in the air and light and growth of the world, perhaps with a view or sheltered by trees and flower-covered stone walls? *(Continued p. 126)*

HueHueCoyotl   Mexico

In 1982, after 10 years of traveling as nomads all over t[he] planet, a group of artists found their home base near Tepo[zt]lan in Mexico. Here, they started the art and culture e[co] village of Huehuecoyotl. At Huehue, as it is often called[, a] mixed group of 20 full-time and many part-time reside[nts] from various countries blend in with local culture in a co[lor]ful way. Some of the HueHue crew still move around, with [the] Caravana, a traveling theater which has toured South Am[er]ica since 1998, and whose members also provide Permac[ul]ture courses and other useful education modules. The Hueh[ue] people work as writers, poets, painters, healers, photog[ra]phers, filmmakers, gardeners, merchants, architects and c[on]sultants in a wide array of professional fields. *Photos:* Hueh[ue] Philip Snyder, Agni Komoch.   **huehue@laneta.apr.o[rg]**

*Top left: Preparing a play at HueHue's theater. **1st r[ow] down, from left:** Traditional Indian ritual; view over Hu[e] HueCoyotl from the mountain. **2nd row down, from le[ft:]** Inside the theater/meeting room; HueHue residents und[er] their sacred tree, to which they retire to meditate or f[ind] answers to important questions. **3rd row down, from le[ft:]** typical house; bathroom with mosaics; street at HueHue.*

© Art Ludw[ig]

A Holistic Worldview in Practice

Findhorn's Statement of Common Ground

Findhorn's Statement of Common Ground establishes ways for Findhorn residents to put their holistic world-view into practice in their daily life. They are the result of 40 years of experience in living a spiritual life:

1. **Spiritual practice.** I commit myself to achieve spiritual practice and align myself with spirit to work for the greatest good.

2. **Service.** I commit myself to service of others and to our planet, recognising that I must also serve myself in order to practise this effectively.

3. **Personal growth.** I commit myself to the expansion of human consciousness, including my own, and I recognise and change any of my personal attitudes or behaviour patterns which do not serve this aim. I take full responsibility for the spiritual, environmental and human effects of all my activities.

4. **Personal integrity.** I commit myself to maintain high standards of personal integrity, embodying congruence of thought, word and action.

5. **Respecting others.** I commit myself wholeheartedly to respect other people (their differences their views, their origins, backgrounds and issues), other people's and the community's property and all forms of life, holding these all to be sacred to the divine.

6. **Direct communication.** I commit myself to using clear and honest communication with open listening, heart-felt responses, loving acceptance and straightforwardness. In public and in private I will not speak in a way that maligns or demeans others. I will talk to people rather than about them. I may seek helpful advice, but will not seek to collude.

7. **Reflection.** I recognise that anything I see outside myself - any criticisms, irritations or appreciations - may also be reflections of what is inside me. I commit myself to looking at these within myself, before reflecting them to others.

8. **Responsibility.** I take responsibility for my actions and for my mistakes. I feed back to others in a caring   and appropriate fashion, to challenge and support each other to grow.

9. **Non-violence.** I agree not to inflict my attitudes or desires (including sexual) on others. I agree to step in and stop, or at least say that I would like stopped, actions (including manipulation or intimidation) that I feel may be abusive to myself and others in the community.

10. **Perspective.** I take responsibility to work through and put aside my personal issues for the benefit of the whole community. I will resolve all personal and business conflicts as soon as possible. I acknowledge that there may be wider perspectives than my own and deeper issues than those that immediately concern me.

11. **Co-operation.** I recognize that I live in a spiritual community and that it functions only through my co-operation and my good communication. I agree to communicate clearly my decisions. I agree to communicate with others who may be affected by my decisions and to consider their views carefully and respectfully. I recognize that others may make decisions which affect me and I agree to respect the care, integrity and wisdom that they have put into their decision-making process.

12. **Resolution.** I commit myself to every effort to resolve disputes. At any time in a dispute I may call for an advocate, friend, independent observer or mediator to be present. In the event of a dispute continuing unresolved I will have access to the grievance procedure. I commit to following this procedure (to be decided by the community).

13. **Agreements.** I commit myself to keeping agreements I have made and not to break or try to evade any laws, rules or guidelines, to have honest dealings with all bodies and to pay all charges and dues owing.

14. **Commitment.** I commit myself to exercise the spirit of this Statement of Common Ground in all my dealings.

The Findhorn Foundation – A holistic Worldview in Practice: *Findhorn is a place which has proved, over the years, that it is conducive to new thinking, decision-making, and synergies between people. There is a sense of surplus for the rest of the world: Findhorn hosts large-scale conferences, which are attended by many International leaders in the world of ecological restoration and related fields. They hosted the first International conference on Intentional Communities in 1995, which laid the foundation for the Global Ecovillage Network. In Easter of 2002, they organized a conference on Earth Restoration as a preparation for the Earth Summit, Rio +10 in Johannesburg, August 2002.* **Below right:** *Attending the Earth Restoration conference, Hanne Marstrand Strong of the Earth Restoration Corps (USA); Helena Norberg-Hodge from ISEC/The Ladakh Project (Kashmir) and the Community Supported Agriculture program in the UK; and Vandana Shiva of the School for Education for Earth Citizenship (Bija Vidyapeeth) at the Navdanya farm in Northern India (Uttaranchal). They came up with a proposal for a Women's Earth Restoration Fund there. Photo: Daniel Greenberg.* **Below left:** *Lizzie Mead and her daughter Manlon Bentley man the reception during the Earth Restoration conference (Photo: Daniel Greenberg). The community also offers a wide variety of courses for visitors, which are well attended. Findhorn residents experiment with new ways of looking at the world, as well as with a wide variety of the elements of ecovillage living (such as ecological building,* **Bottom left** *on this page, a new strawbale house, on a 40 cm stone fascine to keep humidity at bay – its roof was finished during the conference). Photo: Hildur Jackson.* **Bottom right:** *Findhorn residents looking down through an opening in the roof of the Great Hall before it was finished. Photo: © Findhorn Visuals.*

Continued from page 123

Likewise, space can be consecrated to community celebration and communion, with one another and the surrounding world. Here the seasonal junctures – summer turning to autumn, winter turning to spring – can be acknowledged and experienced deeply together. Life passages such as the coming of age for adolescents, marriage, death and birth, can all find grounding in the special spaces that a community sets aside and cultivates for these important rituals of our collective and individual lives. Indeed, the power of community to fashion and transform a landscape in ways that enhance both living processes and the life of people is very great indeed. Depending upon the scale of the land, ecological restoration can become an integral part of the way a community works with Nature, returning greater diversity to the local habitat, conserving and building soil and water, nurturing the abundance of life. Restoration work parties are vehicles for communal joy and connection. Going deeper, the whole property of a community can quite explicitly become consecrated as a kind of large, living mandala of sacred intent, with altars towards the edges of the four quarters of the land, and a centerpoint defined. Communal prayer and meditative energy can create an overall space for living in which the community will feel more aware, more at peace, more connected.

To engage and nurture the Earth is to renew ourselves and help re-awaken our gratitude for the preciousness of all life.

philip@gaia.org

Satyana's Principles of Spiritual Activism

by Will Keepin

Will Keepin is the director of the Satyana Institute, Colorado, USA. Originally a scientist, he now teaches spiritual leadership and gender reconciliation.

The following principles emerged from several years' work with social change leaders in the Shavano Institute's (also founded by Will Keepin) "Leading with Spirit" program. Any attempt to articulate such principles is clearly fraught with peril. We offer these not as definitive truths, but rather as key learnings and guidelines that, taken together, comprise a useful framework for "spiritual activism."

1. Transformation of motivation from anger/fear/ despair to compassion/love/purpose. This is a vital challenge for today's social change movement. This is not to deny the noble emotion of appropriate anger or outrage in the face of social injustice. Rather, this entails a crucial shift from fighting against evil to working for love, and the long-term results are very different, even if the outer activities appear virtually identical. Action follows Being, as the Sufi saying goes. Thus "a positive future cannot emerge from the mind of anger and despair" (Dalai Lama).

Photo: Hildur Jackson

2. Non-attachment to outcome. This is difficult to put into practice, yet to the extent that we are attached to the results of our work, we rise and fall with our successes and failures – a sure path to burnout. Hold a clear intention, and let go of the outcome, recognizing that a larger wisdom is always operating. As Gandhi said, "the victory is in the doing," not the results. Also, remain flexible in the face of changing circumstances: "Planning is invaluable, but plans are useless." (Churchill)

3. Integrity is your protection. If your work has integrity, this will tend to protect you from negative energy and circumstances. You can often sidestep negative energy from others by becoming "transparent" to it, allowing it to pass through you with no adverse effect upon you. This is a consciousness practice that might be called "psychic aikido."

4. Integrity in means and ends. Integrity in means cultivates integrity in the fruit of one's work. A noble goal cannot be achieved utilizing ignoble means.

5. Don't demonize your adversaries. It makes them more defensive and less receptive to your views. People respond to arrogance with their own arrogance, creating rigid polarization. Be a perpetual learner, and constantly challenge your own views.

6. You are unique. Find and fulfill your true calling. "It is better to tread your own path, however humbly, than that of another, however successfully." (Bhagavad Gita)

7. Love thy enemy. Or at least, have compassion for them. This is a vital challenge for our times. This does not mean indulging falsehood or corruption. It means moving from "us/them" thinking to "we" consciousness, from separation to cooperation, recognizing that we human beings are ultimately far more alike than we are different. This is challenging in situations with people whose views are radically opposed to yours. Be hard on the issues, soft on the people.

8. Your work is for the world, not for you. In doing service work, you are working for others. The full harvest of your work may not take place in your lifetime, yet your efforts now are making possible a better life for future generations. Let your fulfillment come in gratitude for being called to do this work, and from doing it with as much compassion, authenticity, fortitude, and forgiveness as you can muster.

9. Selfless service is a myth. *In serving others, we serve our true selves. "It is in giving that we receive." We are sustained by those we serve, just as we are blessed when we forgive others. As Gandhi says, the practice of Satyagraha ("clinging to truth") confers a "matchless and universal power" upon those who practice it. Service work is enlightened self-interest, because it cultivates an expanded sense of self that includes all others.*

10. Do not insulate yourself from the pain of the world. *Shielding yourself from heartbreak prevents transformation. Let your heart break open, and learn to move in the world with a broken heart. As Gibran says, "Your pain is the medicine by which the physician within heals thyself." When we open ourselves to the pain of the world, we become the medicine that heals the world. This is what Gandhi understood so deeply in his principles of ahimsa and Satyagraha. A broken heart becomes an open heart, and genuine transformation begins.*

11. What you attend to, you become. *Your essence is pliable, and ultimately you become that which you most deeply focus your attention upon. You reap what you sow, so choose your actions carefully. If you constantly engage in battles, you become embattled yourself. If you constantly give love, you become love itself.*

12. Rely on faith, and let go of having to figure it all out. *There are larger 'divine' forces at work that we can trust completely without knowing their precise workings or agendas. Faith means trusting the unknown, and offering yourself as a vehicle for the intrinsic benevolence of the cosmos. "The first step to wisdom is silence. The second is listening." If you genuinely ask inwardly and listen for guidance, and then follow it carefully, you are working in accord with these larger forces, and you become the instrument for their music.*

13. Love creates the form. *Not the other way around. The heart crosses the abyss that the mind creates, and operates at depths unknown to the mind. Don't get trapped by "pessimism concerning human nature that is not balanced by an optimism concerning divine nature, or you will overlook the cure of grace." (Martin Luther King) Let your heart's love infuse your work and you cannot fail, though your dreams may manifest in ways different from what you imagine.*

Satyana's Principles of Spiritual Activism
©2002 Satyana Institute
mail@satyana.org

Photo: © Peter Engberg

Localization, Bioregionalism, Resisting Economic Globalization: A New Culture Emerges

Introduction

by Hildur Jackson

Globalization, as a concept, harbors wonderful and exciting possibilities for us: opportunities for global communication and exchange can allow us to create a global culture and lifestyle built on respect, equality and justice. Ideally, it can gradually make a good standard of living possible for everybody everywhere. However, today the dominant form of commercial globalization protects a few large stakeholders who cultivate the free market as their exclusive field. This type of commercial globalization is to be resisted if we want to bring about a truly harmonious and equitable world. Instead, we can focus on globalizing a satisfying lifestyle, which maintains and builds up local resources everywhere. Ecovillages exemplify a way of life which can be implemented all over the world using people's local resources. The political directions for creating an environment where such a lifestyle can evolve, are localization and bioregionalism. On the surface, the existing commercial globalization may look very tempting: advertisements, glamorous soap operas and TV series present a life of abundant material wealth and ease. These media manifestations are found even in remote villages in the southern hemisphere. The glamorous picture is not often shown to be linked with all the problems it creates. To resist it, one needs knowledge about its true implications, and the will to make a conscious choice and stick with it through hard times. One also needs some strong political arguments to support one's stance, and make its realization possible. This section will provide you with some arguments in favor of localization and 'integral society'.

Quileute Indians in traditional dress rowing their canoe toward the high-rises of modern-day Seattle. Photo: © Peter Engberg, from the film 'Coming Back Home'. The Quileute Nation is from Washington State. Its members attempt to preserve their cultural heritage and traditions, and those of the native peoples of the Earth. The photographer's title for this picture is: "Coming Back Home ... 200 years later."

Why the Ecovillage Movement is of Political Importance

by Ross and Hildur Jackson

Ross and Hildur Jackson are co-founders of Gaia Trust (Denmark), as well as initiators and funders of the Global Ecovillage Network.

Most people today would accept the view that "globalization is inevitable". Indeed the positive aspects of globalization – cultural exchange, electronic communications, increasing transparency – are inevitable. However the negative aspects are not: whether we base our trade rules upon the interests of commercial corporations, or upon the needs of the citizens of our world, is something which we can influence. There is an alternative to commercial, corporate-led globalization, though you will hear little of it in the commercially controlled media. The ecovillage movement has a historic significance in this respect, directly addressing the threefold need for resourcing people and their living environment, and providing concrete examples of alternatives to commercial globalization. Such alternatives will eventually win out, since the current system is not meeting the needs of a large percentage of the world's population. The global society of the 21st Century is in crisis – spiritually, socially and environmentally, though Western media mostly do not reflect this view. This is not surprising, since the crisis is most visible in the other 90% of the world population.

1. The Political Dimension

The West is in denial mode. The Western belief that economic growth is the solution rather than the cause of the crisis is a major stumbling block to understanding. This view has driven recent trade policies, forcing the developing countries of the world into an insoluble dilemma, as the economic system which exclusively benefits the wealthy sectors of society creates more poverty, greater disparity in income, ever-increasing debt, disintegrating local communities and growing big-city slums in the developing countries. The global South is angry and wants justice, independence, and a fairer share of the economic pie. The global North needs to reconsider its role in the planetary system and "sweep in front of their own door" i.e. create global justice, and seriously consider whether the acquisition of even greater consumption is in their own long-term interest.

The current situation is politically unstable and untenable. The current global disparities of living standards cannot persist. They are building up the pressure for an explosive reaction. Historically, such disparities have inevitably led to war. The NGOs of the world have demonstrated against Western policies (Seattle, Nice, Gothenburg, Quebec City, Genoa), but they are up against the powerful union of commercial, media and government cooperation, which are all promoting the policies which are destroying our communities worldwide in the name of a misplaced commercialism. But the NGOs lack a common vision that would make their actions more intelligible to the general public and give renewed hope to the destitute. The situation is especially devastating for the young generation of the poor countries, who experience that they are being left with no future. Their desperation is the basis for fundamentalism and terrorism. The ecovillage movement is also a reaction to the crisis, but in a positive and constructive mode, based on personal action in changing lifestyle in keeping with the longer term needs of a global society in ecological balance. They may well be the models for the rest of the world to turn to, when the reality of the current crisis is finally acknowledged.

Let us summarize the three problem areas which are motivating ecovillagers to experiment with alternative solutions.

Social Problems In the South: terrorism, social upheaval and disintegration, poverty, global inequality, wars, instability, slums, social refugees, population growth out of control, uncontrolled urbanization, disease, illiteracy, destruction of small farms, loss of rural jobs. In the North: isolation, rising criminality, family disintegration, loss of social networks, rising health costs without improvement of health, stress, unemployment, marginalization of weak groups, increasing drug use, insecurity, fear of terrorists.

Ecological Problems In the South: loss of species and biodiversity, desertification, salination, chemical and particle pollution. In the North: over-consumption, destruction of the soil, genetically manipulated foods, diseases among cattle, loss of natural animal habitats, chemical pollution, synthetic building materials causing allergies and poor health, and endocrine disrupters threatening fertility. All over the planet: water shortages and groundwater disappearance, global warming, fear of nuclear catastrophes, ecological refugees, depletion of non-replaceable natural resources.

Cultural/ Spiritual Problems In the South: fundamentalism, loss of historic cultural values, resistance to Western materialism, anger and frustration with their hopeless situation. In the North: barren materialism, loss of contact with nature, compartmentalized, mechanistic fragmented worldview, fear, lack of purpose, lack of love, lack of deeper meaning of life.

Ecovillages offer a whole systems approach to sustainable development, which can be created anywhere. Here, we can see directly how the ecological, social and spiritual issues fit together in a holistic unity, and manifest a new culture. Ecovillagers, Agenda 21 activists, the Voluntary Simplicity movement, Earth Charter groups, the People's Assembly, Jubilee 2000, and many other NGOs should work together to realize an alternative solution based on economic localization and cultural and spiritual globalization.

As a political strategy, this goes beyond the traditional right/ left compartmentalization and deals with the very heart of the problem. While most NGOs created to form alternatives to the status quo have focused on single issues, it is now time for them to get together in a single global movement. NGOs and ecovillages, unified, may become the new agents for localization in this century, taking over as major actors in the movement for global justice, just like the unions stood for fair play in the industrial world during the 20th Century.

Why should sustainable communities be the way forward? Because an individual can only fully express his or her individuality and divinity in a well functioning local community with a social network. Here, everybody can have the freedom to create the kind of life they want, grow their own food, establish businesses with friends and loved ones, increase their security, and build roots. Expressions of integral society are the very foundation of human culture, and we are losing them all over the world. We must consciously re-establish viable local communities as our first priority rather than try to satisfy our needs by an ever-growing consumption of goods and services. In the global South the ecovillage strategy has been recognized by many as the basis for fighting poverty and a prerequisite to redemption of debts. The knowledge necessary to create such communities and societies is readily available, as this book demonstrates.

2. We have to live sustainably everywhere

Wolfgang Sachs, of the Wuppertal Institute in Germany, illustrates the required solution to the crisis this way: we need to reduce the consumption in the northern hemisphere by 90% if we want all people on this planet to have an equal share, and if we want to live sustainably.

Let us look at the existing Western pattern of human settlements for a moment, to better understand the level of consumption and the need for change. We have big cities, suburbs and the countryside (villages). We have large-scale agribusiness, weekend houses and nature reservations. Many people in the West take part in a double or triple ecological overload – an office that is heated, a house that is heated and sometimes a weekend house to get away from everything. One or two cars transport families between the three places in ever-greater distances on ever-faster highways. Europe loses an average surface of eight football fields a day to highways.

Food is produced far away in vulnerable monoculture systems on ever fewer but larger farms, in increasingly artificial ways, and then transported in gigantic lorries and containers to the cities where it is consumed. Waste is transported away by truck or train, and dumped in landfills or into the ocean.

Children, the elderly, the handicapped and the unemployed are handled at expensive institutions away from their natural social network and marginalized, with

The future of our Earth lies in our hands, and in those of our children. They need to grow up with values which will enable them to improve on the conditions which we bequeath them. Photo: Helle N.-Rasmussen

growing social problems as a result. Nature reservations are created where we can experience the nature that we ruin by our lifestyle. It is our lifestyle that is ecologically wasteful and socially damaging.

A new lifestyle is emerging, where work, living, and leisure/nature are combined in one place in much less wasteful ways - in ecovillages. In an ecovillage future, we may hopefully end up reducing our pressure on the planet by the required 90%, so that the global North does not use more than its share of the planet's resources. Instead of using the resources of three planets if everybody should adopt our Western lifestyle, we could build ecovillages and be able to face our grandchildren and great-grandchildren saying: we give the planet to you in a better condition than the one it was in when we received it from our ancestors, with space for us all to develop sustainably.

3. Localization: The Economic Dimension

What is the kind of economic system that we have to create to support this vision? Is it at all possible? Former Greenpeace economist Colin Hines has written an important book, *Localization: A Global Manifesto*, showing how a policy of localization can be introduced at all levels, from local and national to international levels. This is a policy which places the actual power in the hands of the

Hildur and Ross Jackson

people in local communities, rather than in those of foreign commercial players. He proposes a WLO - a World Localization Organization to replace the WTO (World Trade Organization.) National and local administration would decrease, as people themselves increasingly make decisions affecting them.

Health systems would change drastically with the introduction of preventive healthcare, a healthier lifestyle, and responsibility for people's wellbeing at the local level. Such a setup could be tried out immediately, for example by making experiments eligible for tax breaks. In the long run, administrative reform and laws supporting localization would be needed.

The introduction of local complementary currencies could be encouraged. Over 2000 such systems have been started up during the last 20 years, with great success. From historical experience, we know that they work, especially in times of great unemployment. They create wealth and jobs locally. There is no scarcity with these "feminine" currencies.

Any new system of national and international economics, if it is to be sustainable, must be based on the protection of local cultures and local economic life as a basic human right.

Is an Ecovillage World Possible?

Could the ecovillage concept be extended to the entire world, including the mega-cities? Many people who are new to the ecovillage movement conclude quickly that it could not happen. Ecovillages are seen as strictly rural models. Twelve billion people cannot all live in the countryside, after all. Right? Therefore the movement is of marginal importance. End of discussion.

But they are missing an important point. The ecovillage vision is far more than establishing a cohousing in the countryside and growing your own food. It is about a new lifestyle that incorporates ecological, social and spiritual/cultural dimensions, a lifestyle that reestablished the local networks that have always been a part of human existence, but which have been disintegrating in more recent history for a variety of reasons. That lifestyle can in principle be established in a mega-city or a suburb as well as in the countryside. However, it is easier in the current environment to start with some virgin land to get some convincing models established. The reasons are not hard to find. And we need some full-scale models to demonstrate how all the elements of sustainability fit together. It can then be replicated in full or in parts in all local neighborhoods. In the South it very much fits with existing community values and will be easier to implement as the existing alternative is so hopeless.

One factor which will accelerate the development of ecovillages is the increasing cost and decreasing quality observable in the welfare state's institutionalized care of individual citizens from cradle to grave, and their corresponding health care. With an increasing number of elderly in the population, it will become even more obvious that the current system is simply too expensive. In the future, it will be discovered that these same tasks can be solved at much greater cost-effectiveness and more satisfactorily for all by using the resources of local ecovillage communities and by putting far greater emphasis of preventative medicine and healthy home-grown food.

The biggest challenge will be the megalopolises of the South like Mexico City, Mumbai, Calcutta …The first step has been taken by Senegal by making ecovillages official national policy. It is close to traditional village life. When people are asked what they really want out of life, they invariably respond that, besides a personally satisfying workday, they want to live harmoniously with their families and friends in safe, attractive surroundings with access to clean air, clean water, clean soil and to nature. The ecovillage future described in these pages comes far closer to this ideal than the current society, where these conditions are a rare exception rather than the rule.

Ecovillages in the Southern Hemisphere

Introduction

by Hildur Jackson

As mentioned at the beginning of this book, 50 to 75% of the population in the global South is still living in villages whose social, cultural and spiritual fabric remains intact, and whose inhabitants largely survive on subsistence economies supported by self-sufficient agricultural production.

The survival of these villages is threatened by globalization and urbanization, as villagers want or are forced to adopt a more modern, Western lifestyle. Global politics, from that of the World Bank to aid agencies, are to integrate them into the flux of commercial globalization as fast as possible. Often countries in the southern hemisphere see no alternative, especially since most of their leaders and elite groups have been trained at Western Universities. Hordes of villagers migrate to large cities, while those remaining, following global consumer demand, are under pressure to shift from polycultures to monocultures on the land. A new policy of development is needed to keep people in the villages, and to have people in cities move back to the land – to resist globalization, and maintain the social fabric of the villages, while allowing for improvements and modernization.

Networks like Sarvodaya in Sri Lanka, NAAM and Colufifa in Africa, and The Ladakh Project in Kashmir are establishing new alternatives. They seek to achieve a form of village-based sustainable development which is rooted in the use of local resources and the maintenance of a solid social-economic structure before venturing into the globalized economy. They are defining programs that combine their own culture and spiritual traditions with a reorganization of social, political and economic structures, which help people meet their basic needs while adapting to modern requirements. They are seizing the opportunity to build a modern life on traditional village structures and cultures, and step into an ecovillage future while avoiding the mistakes of the West. The programs introduced by these networks integrate the following elements:

Education and literacy programs for children and adults, based on a living and learning pedagogy
Earth restoration
Health programs (including herbal medicine and preventive healthcare)
Building schools (local ecological building style)
Renewable energy systems
Water and sanitation program/ recirculation
Local food production; storage of grain
Roads and transportation
Microcredits; creating local currencies and local abundance
Spiritual practices and traditional values

Ecovillage networks in the global South can support much of their own development with local resources (see page 134); their need for support decreasing as they build up local ways of meeting people's basic needs. Once villages are able to meet people's basic needs, they can start thinking about finding ways of trading on the global market, through village cooperation and fair trade.

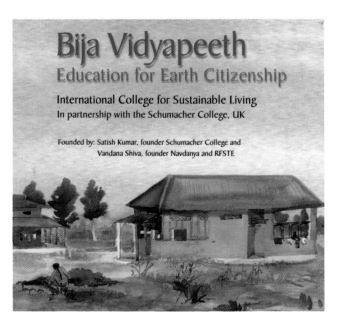

Right: the International College for Sustainable Living was founded by Vandana Shiva and Satish Kumar at the Navdanya organic farm in northern India. Activities include courses on biodiversity, organic farming, ecological building, ecological living, and Earth Democracy. Email: vshiva@vsnl.com

Village-Based Development in Sri Lanka

The Sarvodaya Movement for Peace in Sri Lanka started in the 1950s when a young teacher, Ari Ariyaratne, moved into underprivileged villages and started working with the most downtrodden communities there, "to dispel ignorance, inequality and powerlessness" through village development. Ariyaratne says: 'The development of a country depends on personality awakening based on labor and installing this awakening in the individual and the group ... Labor includes not only physical work but also sharing of time, resources, thoughts and energy ... Awakening happens through loving kindness (Metta), which Mahatma Gandhi valued and adopted as his main strategy." This includes respect for life and extending friendly thoughts towards all, and transforming these thoughts into action. "From the beginning, I had faith in the common faith and small-scale activities," says Ariyaratne. His faith has been rewarded by the achievements of the Sarvodaya Movement, which established a model for village development currently extending to over 13,000 villages (of a total of 30,000) in Sri Lanka. With the help of Sarvodaya, these village communities build strong social economic infrastructures to meet their basic needs and eventually expand to become surplus-generating entities, a formidable result in a country torn by civil war.

Vinya Ariyaratne, son of Ari and a medical doctor, is now the Director of the Sarvodaya Movement for Peace. He also heads the South Asia subregional office of the Global Ecovillage Network. Sarvodaya is the home of one of the Living and Learning Centers affiliated with GEN in the southern hemisphere. Here, people can learn about sustainability hands-on.

Below: Children perform a play in a Sarvodaya village. Creative activity is one tool for building community. Photo: Agni Komoch/GEN.

Right: some of Sarvodaya's voluntary staff members gathered around Sarvodaya founder Ari Ariyaratne. Photo: GEN.

The Sarvodaya Movement for Peace

by Vinya Ariyaratne

"Sarvodaya Shramadana" means "awakening of all through sharing of one's labor, time, and energy." For Sarvodaya, development is a process of ongoing personal and social awakening of the individual, the family, the community, the national and global societies. Since its inception, Sarvodaya has tried to offer an alternative to top-down development.

The Sarvodaya model of development is envisaged as encompassing six dimensions: spiritual, moral, cultural, social, economic, and political. When these dimensions are balanced, there will be an awakened society.

Buddhist principles such as loving-kindness, compassion, equanimity, truth, non-violence, and self-denial are observed and nurtured through community development activities. Protecting and nurturing the natural environment is one of the outward expressions of loving concern, compassionate action, non-violence, cooperation, and social unity for both people and living creatures.

Sarvodaya's ongoing development activities strive for some of the basic ecovillage goals: self-sufficiency in food, energy, production, and services and a lifestyle in harmony with fellow beings and with nature.

Sarvodaya and Villages

As a general rule, Sarvodaya starts facilitating village development programs upon request from the individual villages. Sarvodaya does not intend to force development top-down, but invites villagers to become active participants in their own development, and to foster an approach to development, which starts at the bottom, at the roots. According to Sarvodaya's Five-Stage Development Program, villages are sorted into five groups according to their developmental progress.

Stages One to Three mainly evolve around psycho-infrastructure and community capacity building. Simultaneously, Sarvodaya's Social Empowerment Division gradually establishes an organizational basis for sustainable development in a village. The process results in the formation of preschool, mothers', youth, farmers', and elders' groups which come together in an apex organization: the Village Shramadana Society. These groups function to initiate, plan and implement village development programs within their designated areas of responsibility. In Stages Three to Four, Sarvodaya's Rural Technical Services (SRTS) focus on building the social infrastructure of the village, introducing projects to ensure adequate housing, latrines, domestic water supply, roads, culverts, and foot bridges. In Stages Four to Five, Sarvodaya's Economic Enterprises Development Services (SEEDS) assist a village in the achievement of financial self-sufficiency through a carefully designed, step-by-step program. SEEDS activities include a credit and savings program for starting and improving small businesses; business counseling; leadership training; management and vocational skills training, and the development of agricultural enterprises. In 1995, Sarvodaya launched the Pioneering Villages Program, in which the villages that have reached Stage Five embark on helping neighboring Intermediary and Periphery villages.

Development Is a Process
of Ongoing Personal and Social Awakening

by Vinya Ariyaratne

Q: Can you give us some examples of how you start up the different phases of development in a village?

Vinya: I'd rather talk in terms of the three foundations we lay in a village. The first is the psychological infrastructure in the community, which consists in bringing villagers together through voluntary community action. This is essential to build the social infrastructure, which brings a bit more organization to the community. Initially we make people understand their own situation, and have them participate in a community activity.

The social infrastructure is based on organizing villagers in groups (mothers, youth, farmers, elders, preschool), where people can come and discuss their problems. Then we get the whole community together in a village society and get them legal recognition: they become a small democratic unit for village self-government. We introduce basic elements of community organization: rules, election process (officers), the keeping of accounts. The third foundation, based on the psychological and social infrastructures, is the economic infrastructure: we develop a banking scheme, a credit scheme, and such.

The spiritual dimension runs through all these parts of the development. People get together and meditate, and follow this spiritual practice all the way through. It's an integrated process.

Q: What is a typical activity started within one of the groups?

Vinya: Activities within the groups are based on meeting village needs. The Youth group organizes and follows courses in biodiversity; they are also interested in information technology, do training in information skills. Youth learn technical skills so they can find employment. We have set up telecenters (a computer, internet access) serving several villages at a time; we are planning one telecenter for 20-30 villages. One district groups 300 to 400 villages.

Q: How do Sarvodaya villages integrate into today's globalized marketplace?

Vinya: We don't have to link directly to the global marketplace to survive. In Sri Lanka, 3500 villages have started their own economic program; they produce things required by the community, satisfying their basic needs. We don't believe the global system can help the people. We want village communities to create their own wealth, using their resources (instead of letting the global community taking their resources out of the villages), so they can develop as economic blocks.

We try to improve things at the village level. To help establish this, we plan a national bank, the Sarvodaya Bank.

Below left: Sarvodaya meeting. Photo: Agnieszka Komoch. Right: working in the plant nursery at the rapidly expanding Tanamalwila Living and Learning Center. Photo: Max Lindegger.

Q: Would you recommend this for African Networks, who try to produce for sale?

Vinya: No, there's nothing wrong with producing something for sale in the global marketplace. We also produce things for the global market. But we take care not to become dominated by the world economic system. There are many things we can do to meet our needs at a local level, and that is what we focus on first of all. It's a difficult balance to achieve. Most of our villages can produce more than they require. This is possible if you strengthen your own micro-level economic system first.

Q: What are some surplus businesses?

Vinya: At the village level, we mostly have agriculture for self-sufficiency. But we have local crafts, batik, which we collect and export. We have started a relatively new business in ornamental fish.

At the village level we also produce household items such as brooms and brushes, and bricks for construction. We have a printing shop which works at a national level. Wood crafts (wooden toys) are actually exported both to Europe and North America. Our metal (welding) workshop produces wheelchairs at low cost, and office furniture. We also have training centers where we offer educational programs (we teach government people and other NGO topics such as community health, biodiversity, information technology, and much more: altogether about 30 programs), and we rent out facilities.

Q: What changes have happened in Sarvodaya since you took over after your father, Ari Ariyaratne?

Vinya: I have spent a considerable amount of time strengthening the next level of leadership, empowering them. It's a difficult transition, as it is a movement, and you can't totally convert into a professionalized organization. But we need to professionalize, because we have very limited resources, not the same kind of donor funding as we received 20 years ago. So I had to bring in changes: we rely more on internal income now. I have worked on long term financial and staff projections.

We've seen lots of positive results. We have entered into new programs as a response to needs: information technology; in the environmental area, a biodiversity program, training youth on environmental methods; the community health program has expanded; our population is rapidly ageing, so we work out how to look after the elderly. Reproductive health issues are not addressed by the government, so we set up programs in this area.

Q: What can you tell us about funding?

Vinya: We cover 40 to 50 percent of our costs ourselves, through business and local production. For 50%

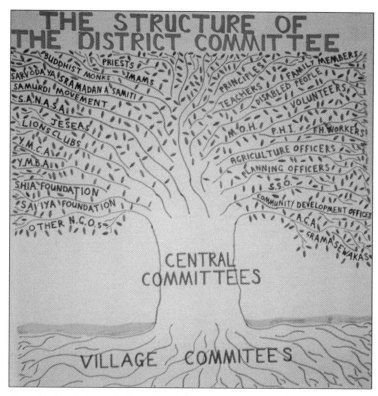

Organizational chart of village-based development at Sarvodaya. Photo: GEN

of our operational costs, we are dependent on external donors. But we cover the rest with our business income. We are a big organization, we need $800,000 to run on a yearly basis, which is a small budget for all those villages (around 13,000 villages at present). Three times more than our cash budget we generate in terms of labor contribution, and supplying resources at the village level.

Our largest funders to date are the Nippon Foundation in Japan and Novartis in Switzerland. Then there are SIDA (Sweden), NORAD (Norway) and USAID. Our government does not allocate us money, but gives us tax concessions. Then there are some more private foundations. We have 30 small and big donors.

gensa@sri.lanka.net

Dr. Vinya Ariyaratne is the son of Sarvodaya founder Ari Ariyaratne, and a medical doctor. He is now, like his father before him, a brave and innovative Director to the Sarvodaya Movement for Peace. Photo: Hildur Jackson.

The First Government-Supported Ecovillage Network

Interview with Souleye 'NDiaye by Karen Svensson

Souleye 'NDiaye is an advisor at the Ministry of Youth and the Environment in Dakar, Senegal. The minister of the Environment in Senegal has appointed him to be the contact person for a Senegalese Network of Ecovillages, which was created in January 2002. Souleye was in Denmark in October 2001 for a meeting of West African and European NGO leaders and ecovillage initiators, organized by Elise Guldagger and Demba Mansaré of the Senegalese Colufifa organization (see pages 120-121). This article explains how a government can and should cooperate with ecovillage initiators to establish ecovillages as the best strategy for sustainable development.

Q: How does your government support the development of ecovillages in Senegal?

Souleye 'NDiaye: Marian Zeitlin of EcoYoff (see page 121-122) and Demba Mansaré from Colufifa came to see my minister (of the environment) and explained the concept of ecovillages to him. They wanted to build a network of ecovillages and the minister of the environment decided to help them. He appointed me as a contact person for the creation of this network. My staff and I meet twice a week for planning, and we meet with Marian and Demba once a month in Dakar. We also have network meetings with ecovillage candidates at EcoYoff. Our wish is to build not only a Senegalese network, but also an African network of ecovillages. We have six villages as candidates.

Q: Why are ecovillages important to your country?

Souleye: In the ecovillage concept, we find all the values of Senegalese society: family, friendship, culture, spirituality, and solidarity. In the North you have lost these values. Families have disintegrated … If we don't do anything at our end, we are going to lose everything like you already did. If we destroy our neighborhoods, our resources, our families, where are we going? Ecovillages are a model by which we can keep what we have, and live a modern life. We can have our computers and be connected to the Internet, but resist globalization. We can also resolve water and waste problems. For 20 years I have worked with local communities and land use. It's easy for me to understand the concept of ecovillages, because it's not so far from what we know – in Senegal, a lot of the ecovillage concept is already there – and it's close to what we want.

What Demba Mansaré did 25 years ago, when he started the COLUFIFA network of villages, was very important. Demba was right to say that the only way of development was ecovillage development. A few months ago, Demba was our ambassador for West Africa, in Mali, Burkina Faso, Ghana, Guinea and Gambia. We are going to build networks with colleagues in other countries.

Q: What is the role of EcoYoff in Senegal?

Souleye: Yoff is a little village in the big city of Dakar, which has 2 million inhabitants. EcoYoff (Yoff's ecovillage organization) resists globalization: they keep their culture, their solidarity, and spirituality, they maintain the village within the city (Dakar). The government has given EcoYoff a piece of land where they are building an Ecocity with hundreds of plots. People will have to sign agreements before being allowed to build: they will have to accept the ecovillage rules, live the ecovillage way of life. The Ecocity resolves the problems of waste and water. There is recycling, waste water treatment, water collection, and solid waste treatment; they will re-use waste for permaculture. They will be the first Living and Learning Center in Senegal, together with Colufifa. They show that the best way of development is ecovillage development, not globalization.

Q: What are you taking back with you after your meeting here in Denmark?

Souleye: I have seen that the movement of ecovillages was not built in one day. In the beginning, no one understood what you meant, but now everybody knows the need for change, the need to have another way of life, not to live in a spirit of waste, where one does not concern oneself with solidarity and wellbeing. We need to have patience, perseverance. To all diplomats in the South, I also take the message that we need more democracy. Democracy is important.

I have made a lot of friends here. We are building up relationships between ecovillages in the South and in the North (twinning), for close cooperation and exchange, and to spread the ecovillage concept to the other African countries and the world. We are twinning ecovillages, such as Torri Superiore in Italy with Madina in Guinea-Conakry, and we can twin with ecovillages in France and Denmark.

Q: If you met a government official in the South who had never heard of ecovillages, how would you explain to them that they should adopt the ecovillage concept?

Souleye: I would say:

1. Become aware of the degradation of your environment (take care of resources).

2. Know that resources and values of sharing, solidarity and spirituality should not be lost.

3. Those who have achieved their "development" while leaving these things behind, regret it today, and are going back to them because they are fundamental for a human being's life. They now want ecovillages, because that's what ecovillages are all about.

I am reading Ross Jackson's book: *And We Are Doing It! Building an Ecovillage Future*. I think this is the message: Do It! Don't just talk about it, do it.

Email: menv@sentoo.sn

The Colufifa Movement against hunger in Senegal was founded by Demba Mansaré in Senegal. The principles of sustainable development which the movement stands for are officially supported by the Senegalese government. Photo: Elise Guldagger.

*Exchange between countries is essential if we are to learn from each other. In October 2001, Colufifa organized a meeting of West African and European NGO leaders and ecovillage initiators in Denmark. Participants in the meeting visited Danish ecovillages, and looked at different building styles at Torup (here a cob house by Flemming Abrahamsen). Photo: Hildur Jackson. Below right: looking at Flemming Abrahamsen's cob house from the inside, and talking about building techniques.
Photo: Hildur Jackson*

Right and below: The January 2002 founding meeting of the government-supported Senegalese Ecovillage Network with representatives of EcoYoff, Colufifa, GEN and the ministry of the Environment in Dakar, Senegal. Photos: GEN.

A volunteer from the Farm Project working in the fields. Photo: ISEC.

Kashmir

The Ladakh Project

by Helena Norberg-Hodge

Set deep in the Indian Himalayas on the western edge of the Tibetan plateau, Ladakh, or 'Little Tibet', is one of the highest and driest inhabited places on earth. This is an extremely harsh environment, yet for centuries it was home to a rich and self-sustaining culture.

Then in the early 1970s, came 'development'. The first roads into the area brought heavily subsidized goods and idealized images of western consumer culture – undermining the local economy and eroding cultural self-esteem. The result has been increasing community and family breakdown, unemployment, sprawling urban slums and pollution.

Since 1975, The International Society for Ecology and Culture (ISEC) has been providing the people of Ladakh with information about the impact of conventional development in other parts of the world while exploring more sustainable patterns of development. We have helped establish several local organizations including the Women's Alliance of Ladakh (WAL).

Ladakhi women in traditional dress spin at a meeting. Photo: ISEC.

With over 6,000 members from virtually every part of Ladakh, WAL has become a formidable force in the region, giving women a collective voice that enables them to influence the policies of both village leadership and the government. Among their activities has been a campaign to ban plastic bags, a program to raise awareness about the importance of planting local seed varieties, and an effort to limit the impact of television on their children.

Every summer the Alliance holds an exhibition of local skills and knowledge, bringing together women from all over Ladakh to display their crafts, share the special cuisines of their villages, exchange seeds, and celebrate their culture with several days of music and dance.

For more than a decade we have also been running a program aimed at the Westerners who come to Ladakh – each summer reaching about 3,000 tourists. The focal point of this effort is a daily screening of our film Ancient Futures, followed by a discussion led by ISEC staff and volunteers. Ladakh is an ideal place to spur a basic rethinking of the direction of progress – from runaway economic growth to mega-technology. The film and discussions, as well as written materials we provide, help to peel away layers of propaganda about 'progress' and economic 'growth'.

Letters we have received - sometimes years later - from visitors to Ladakh who have been exposed to our work there, indicate that the effect is deep and long lasting.

Our Farm Project enables Western volunteers to live and work with Ladakhi farm families for a month or more during the agricultural season. Participants are given an opportunity to witness directly the impact of the global economy, and the consumer culture on localized economies. At the same time, participants are able to experience life in a culture where the sense of community remains strong and the connection to the land is still deep. During their stay in Ladakh, participants also attend 'Global-to-Local' workshops led by ISEC staff, which helps to put the summer's experience into a global perspective.

The program benefits the Ladakhis as well. Seeing Westerners working in the fields encourages Ladakhis to re-evaluate their belief that all Westerners look down upon 'dirty' manual labor, and shows them that many people from 'comfortable' urban societies actually yearn for a life closer to the land.

Western participants' interest in and enthusiasm for local cultural practices helps to reinstill a sense of pride in Ladakhis for their own way of life.

www.isec.org.uk

South Africa

The Tlholego Development Project

by Paul Cohen

Paul Cohen, one of the founder members of Tlholego, has played a significant role over the past twelve years as a learner/mentor, manager/fundraiser, designer/builder and catalyst for guiding this process forward. In 1997 Paul was awarded an Ashoka fellowship for his pioneering work in helping to establish the Tlholego project.

The Tlholego Ecovillage is located between the high-veld grasslands and bushveld savannah, on the Western side of the ancient Magaliesberg Mountain Range, about a two-hour drive west of Pretoria. There are vast lands surrounding Tlholego, consisting of grasses, trees and red clay soils. The climate is hot and dry most of the year, with summer rainfall between 350 and 650 millimeters. The altitude is 1200 meters above sea level, and there are light to medium frosts in winter.

During the early eighteen hundreds, people who had developed a sustainable economy based on cattle, iron and trade over many centuries were suddenly confronted by a series of devastating invasions. Within a single generation, the fabric of their society was completely destroyed and their chiefdoms were reduced to poverty and servitude. Some of our members are descendants of this ancient culture and our village is situated adjacent to Molokwane, a 300-acre iron-age site and one of the best remaining examples of early Tswana settlements in this region.

The 20th century has been a time of rapid economic growth in and around the Magaliesberg region. Irrigation, technology, and expanding markets have increased agricultural output, mining has brought widespread prosperity, and tourism has flourished.

But only in the past ten years has South Africa emerged from a lifetime of apartheid, and our great leaders like Nelson Mandela have been free to be fully appreciated in the world. This has created a unique environment for positive change. At the same time, we face widespread poverty as one of our biggest challenges.

In 1990, the founders of Tlholego (a Tswana word meaning 'creation from nature'), were drawn fortuitously towards preventing the Tshedimosong farm-school from closing. Our mission – to create an ecovillage model for poverty reduction – merged with the needs of the Tshedimosong School and we formed an organization, the Rural Educational Development Corporation (Rucore), to purchase this land, and create a nurturing environment for this process to unfold.

Tlholego has grown from a group of people, who were initially not driven by sustainable intentions. A small team of us, with some financial support from grants and gifts, began to introduce the practice of sustainable design to several farm worker families and some town people living in the area. For ten years, we created an experience of mutual learning. We employed people to practice and think about sustainable approaches to land tenure, building houses, managing waste, growing food, harvesting water, soil and plant resources, working through conflict, healing the past, making mistakes, building community and creating wealth.

We have sustained this learning experience long enough for people to build new skills, trust, and importantly, to begin to make a living from eco-friendly technologies. We can now also appreciate the tremendous value we have added to the natural resource base, through improvements to the soil, water and biological systems.

Today our village has around thirty-five long-term members. Our intention is to house between 10 to 15 families, approximately 65 to 100 people in the years to come. Through our community and educational process, we have impacted directly on the lives of our neighbors and our schoolchildren and their families, and we have trained many hundreds of people from South Africa and around the world in Permaculture design, sustainable building technologies and eco-village development. In our approach to poverty change, we have experienced that a single integrated strategy on the village scale has worked wonders to solve several challenging problems at once.

Tlholego is now entering a new phase of economic and social development. Our focus is tending more to commercialize around our tourism potential and building the value of a genuine eco-African experience. It is our ongoing intention that this model for rural sustainable development be continuously improved and widely replicated.

www.sustainable-futures.com

Tlholego, South Africa

PROPOSED HOUSING FOR TLHOLEGO VILLAGE

Tlholego (Tswana for 'creation from nature') in South Africa started in 1990, when its founders decided to help prevent the Tshedimosong farm-school from closing, by cooperatively creating an ecovillage model for poverty reduction. Some Tlholego members began introducing sustainable design to the area, an effort which resulted in new skills, trust, an ability to make a living from eco-friendly technologies, and great improvements in the natural resource base. Today the village has around thirty-five long-term members. The intention is to house approximately 65 to 100 people in the years to come. Tlholego not only has considerable outreach in the local community, but also trains people from all over South Africa. They are currently expanding their tourism potential. *Photos: courtesy Tlholego: **Top left:** Tlholego's managers. **Left:** Permaculture plan for the village. **Top right:** Some of the community members. **Right:** Child with freshly picked vegetables. **Below:** water well, house. **Two rows down left, bottom:** Strawbale houses, covered in a clay mixture. **Right:** Straw roof over the open community space, with ventilation shafts for cooling.*

www.sustainable-futures.com

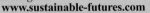

The Process of Creating an Ecovillage

Startup Groups: Organization and Process

How to get a Group Together and Organize the Process

by Hildur Jackson

Ecovillages are not developer-led. They are made by people, for themselves. If you want to start an ecovillage, you have to get a startup group together. The process of creation is what makes the glue that will turn the ecovillage into a functioning community. When you have a group, you start looking for land or buildings. It usually takes years and there is often quite a bit of participant turnover, as some people may get worn out by the hard work, decision-making process, or change their minds as to where they want to live.

So form a small, committed group. If you get too big a group together, the organization of the process may become difficult. On the other hand, if some members of the group disappear, when you get down to actually having to put money on the table, it may not be a bad thing to have some extra members in reserve. In Norway, the Kilden ecovillage group started a system of monthly contributions within the founding group early on in their process, and arranged courses and seminars for the group on topics like CSA (community supported agriculture) and permaculture.

During the brainstorming phase, a Future Workshop will help clarify goals (see page 146). A seminar on meeting techniques and conflict resolution is also a good investment. Part of this process is to have everyone write down a small number of requirements that they definitely do not want to deviate from (Patch Adams' suggestion is three for each person, with the advice for everyone to accept giving in on any other items which are not on their priority list). When the land has been found, a permaculture design course or ecovillage course is strongly recommended. It allows for the creation of a common vision and avoids unpleasant surprises in terms of unexpressed expectations and conflicting goals.

There are four major steps to take during the startup process:
1. Define your vision.
2. Make this vision concrete, e.g. as an ecovillage design.
3. Make sure that all participants in the founding group are able to take responsibility for their personal and family lives (work, children, partners and their emotional/ spiritual life).

4. Agree upon community processes for decision-making and conflict resolution.

1. Defining the Vision.

Find the words that express a common vision for the ecovillage/community. Clarify your goals, and find your identity as a group. The ecovillage curriculum may be helpful in this process (p. 4). You may decide to have integration of all 15 elements as your distant goal, but decide on one or more areas to start with. The description of ecovillages drawn up by David Kanaley, who researched ecovillages for his municipality in Australia, may also be a point of departure for identifying areas of focus (p. 159). Will Keepin, from the Satyana Institute in the USA (p. 127), expressed his vision for a future ecovillage as follows: "(A place where) each person would be supported in a deep surrender to their own divine guidance" (*Ecovillage Living Magazine*, Spring 2001). When creating the Danish ecovillage network in 1993, what united representatives from spiritual, ecological and social projects was a vision based on a circulatory worldview: the purpose of ecovillages was seen to be the restoration of whole circulatory systems in nature and in people, on all levels. It was represented as a circular drawing of the elements earth, water, fire, air, reflecting the Root, Hara, Solar Plexus, and Heart chakras in people.

2. Materializing the goals in a concrete form, such as a concrete ecovillage design – based on an ecovillage or permaculture course – is very helpful. Words can be interpreted in different ways, but translating concepts into a design forces people to think things through. A realistic time frame, as well as a financial projection for realizing the design and its subsequent implementation, are important factors for success. You need constant progress to keep the group together, but realistic expectations are key, to avoid disappointment. A brochure with your design and a description of the project will be beneficial when negotiating with authorities, and helpful for attracting more residents.

As an example of a statement of vision and goals, here is the Global Ecovillage Network's charter:

GEN Mission, Vision and Purposes:

Vision: We envision a planet of diverse cultures of all life united in creating communities in harmony with each other and the Earth, while meeting the needs of this and future generations.

Mission: We are creating a sustainable future by identifying, assisting and coordinating the efforts of communities to acquire social, spiritual, economic and ecological harmony. We encourage a culture of mutual acceptance and respect, solidarity and love, open communications, cross-cultural outreach, and education by example. We serve as a catalyst to bring the highest aspirations of humanity into a practical reality.

Some questions you may want to answer together:

Are there things you absolutely do not want in the ecovillage: meat, tobacco, alcohol, drugs? Or maybe cats and dogs (to protect fowls and birds)? Are there rules you want to set up? Like no smoking indoors or no meat in the community kitchen? Or that everybody has to accept engaging in a personal development process?

---

3. Finding the right core people to build an ecovillage is not easy. You have to be able to rely on each other, and share an equal burden. Core groups have to be constituted of people who are able to take responsibility for their own development. There is a lot of sustained work to be done, alongside having to provide for oneself and for one's family, and contributing to the wellbeing of the group. For the founder group, you want to attract strong, well functioning families and singles with a sound financial situation and good professional capabilities. The core group needs to be composed of people who can hold the distance and persevere under pressure. It needs to be well-functioning and gather good momentum before it can embrace other individuals or groups who may need special attention and care. Startup ecovillage and community groups easily attract people who have been unable to manage their lives in mainstream conditions, and who see the emerging community as a possible salvation from poor partnerships or emotional problems, isolation or a poor economy. You need to think this through. One or two troubled persons in a core group can significantly reduce a project's chances of materializing. Once the village is takes shape and there is enough surplus to go around, it can open up and welcome new residents who need presence and support.

Even with a core group of solid people, you may want to make sure that everyone is willing to engage in a personal development process, so that you have the best possible chances of handling human problems which may arise common practices such as meditation or yoga may help to clear and harmonize energies.

4. Group processes, decision-making processes and conflict resolution models should be adopted before conflicts arise. You can opt for decision by consensus, consensus minus one, respecting minority or majority decisions. Conflict resolution models could be third person intermediary, or calling on a certain system or person.

What kind of leadership do you want in the ecovillage? Do you want spiritual leadership? Or leadership coming from common meditations? Damanhur in Italy has two elected leaders (king and queen) for half a year, and a guide who inspires them by weekly talks. Or is the common meeting the highest forum, supported by leaders of subgroups? In this case you need to decide on the number and themes of subgroups and their relationship to common meetings.

Make the process become a purpose in itself. And have fun!

Remember that you have to:
-*Find land*
-*Get permissions; negotiate with many authorities*
-*Create a process where people have to serve on many subgroups*
-*Make a design*
-*Research ecological building, water systems, renewable energy systems, etc.*
-*Learn to solve conflicts*
-*Find financing*
-*Raise a family, cultivate a relationship, earn a living*

Preparing for meetings: stating how you all feel, possibly a meditation or moments of silence may help clear the mind. How do you set up an agenda together? Who will run the meeting? Do you prepare items beforehand? Set a time frame for the meetings. Sit in a circle so that everybody can see everybody. Use a talking stick or keepers of the heart. After each session listen to their experiences of how the group functioned. Call a "forum" if needed to clear personal things. Make meetings fun. Take moments of silence before new sessions. Accept that we think with the whole body and that all parts of the body must be nourished during meetings. Move, dance, sing, massage the shoulders. Write decisions down in a book open to everybody. Specify who is doing what before when and start the next meeting by reading this out.

As inspiration for your vision work, you may want to look at the vision statements of other ecovillages and related projects. The Mother expressed the dream about Auroville, in India, as follows:

"There should be somewhere upon earth a place that no nation could claim as its sole property, a place where all human beings of good will, sincere in their aspiration, could live freely as citizens of the world, obeying one single authority, that of the supreme Truth; a place of peace, concord, harmony, where all the fighting instincts of man would be used exclusively to conquer the causes of his suffering and misery, to surmount his weakness and ignorance, to triumph over his limitations and incapacities; a place where the needs of the spirit and the care for progress would get precedence over the satisfaction of desires and passions, the seeking for pleasures and material enjoyment."

"In this place, children would be able to grow and develop integrally without losing contact with their soul. Education would be given, not with a view to passing examinations and getting certificates and posts, but for enriching the existing faculties and bringing forth new ones. In this place, titles and positions would be supplanted by opportunities to serve and organize.

The needs for the body will be provided for equally in the case of each and every one. In the general organization, intellectual, moral and spiritual superiority will find expression not in the enhancement of the pleasures and powers of life but in the increase of duties and responsibilities. Artistic beauty in all forms, painting, sculpture, music, literature will be available equally to all, the opportunity to share in the joys they bring being limited solely to each one's capacities and not by one's social or financial position.

For in the ideal place money would be no more the sovereign lord. Individual merit will have a greater importance than the value due to material wealth and social position. Work would not be there as the means of gaining one's livelihood, it would be the means whereby to express oneself, develop one's capacities and possibilities, while doing at the same time service to the whole group, which on its side would provide for each one's subsistence and for the field of his work.

In brief, it would be a place where relations between human beings, usually based almost exclusively upon competition and strife, would be replaced by relations of emulation for doing better, for collaboration, relations of real brotherhood.

The earth is certainly not ready to realize such an ideal, for mankind does not yet possess the necessary knowledge to understand and accept it or the indispensable conscious force to execute it. That is why I call it a dream.

Yet this dream is on the way to becoming a reality…."

The Mother, A dream (1954)

Meeting at Auroville, in the shade of the luxuriant greenery which replaced the arid landscape of the past.
Photo: courtesy Agnieszka Komoch.

Future Workshops

Renewal through Play

by Ditlev Nissen

Translated by Karen Svensson

Ditlev Nissen has studied and taught conflict resolution and Future Workshops for many years. He lives and works in Christiania, Denmark, where he also started his consultancy firm, "Utopian Horizons".

Robert Jungk (1913-1994) developed Future Workshops, through which people envisioned desirable futures and the means of achieving them, as a way of regaining power over their own lives, and fighting tirelessly for sane alternatives and ecological awareness. He felt that the important thing was to create contexts for social innovation; places where people could create ideas. "From these seedbeds emerge the projects, the real practical changes that over time move our civilization away from its present self-destructive course".

The Future Workshop is a meeting technique designed to help people find alternatives to lifestyles or living conditions with which they are not satisfied. It can revolve around housing, local community, work, network etc. Through the Future Workshop, groups work out solutions which can spark off a transformation in communal living conditions.

A group of people seeking to change their living conditions could choose to work on the theme of: "Our ecovillage five years from now". The workshop opens with the Criticism Phase, where we are consistently negative: we produce too much waste, we don't know our neighbors, there are no elderly people living with us, we are dependent on our individual cars, we have too many parking spaces, money has too much influence in our lives, etc. After a one- to two-hour brainstorm, where keywords are written down on wall posters, the keywords are grouped by criticism theme and the points of criticism are dramatized non-verbally.

The Utopia Phase is unplugged from the reality of the world out there: everything is possible. "If we could decide for ourselves ..." The Utopia phase starts with a brainstorm: one can for example imagine a large cohousing for the elderly, children and older people can enjoy each other's company, collectively organized workplaces, consensus decision-making, self-sufficient biodynamic food production, collective solar and bio-power systems, car share, sustainable community economics, and so on. Keywords are grouped in "Utopia

themes", which form the basis for a three- to four-hour group session where the utopia unfolds through words, drawings and models of various kinds. To finish, the various utopias are presented to the other participants in the workshop as a story, a game, illustrations, a tour through Ecotopia or news spots.

In the Realization Phase, we hold on to the criticism expressed, and take our wishes seriously. Through playing devil's advocate and through the loving expression of criticism, we ask ourselves: "Can we see ourselves living in the presented Utopias (is it a castle in the air or is it truly a possible solution to the things said during the Criticism Phase?)" and "Are our Utopias sufficiently appealing that we want to hold it up as the goal for our future actions?" After this we look at which of the Utopias can be realized here and now, and which can be carried out in reality in the long or short term. What are the hurdles, and what actions can we take that can help us get closer to the envisioned Utopia? The Utopia phase is rounded off with a "Who Does What?" session, where participants – if they have time and the desire to do so – tell each other what concrete actions they are going to undertake to continue working on elements of the Utopia. Finally, the transcription of the text on all the wall posters is delegated to a designated editor, who will include everything in the workshop minutes, and send them to all participants. A follow-up meeting is scheduled four to eight weeks after the workshop. Questions to be answered are: how far have we come with "Who Does What?", are there Utopias which need a bit of first aid assistance, and how should we continue to realize the most attractive Utopias.

The Future Workshop is a socio-ecological method which gives participants social experiences that can be significant for the transformation processes required for sustainable development. During the workshop, participants receive tools which help them look at the past, the present and the future in a constructive way. They experience fellowship in a spirit of respect and understanding, and can see the power of thinking in terms of opportunities rather than limitations.

A successful Future Workshop imbues participants with the desire, the courage and the necessary perspective to take action toward their expressed goals and desires for the future.

Group work originates in participants' experiences in daily life, and consequently brings with it an action and transformation potential which can influence their life-styles in a sustainable way. Based on my experience with dialogue-oriented processes, I believe that the above men-tioned potential for action and change can be stimulated even more, if the Future Workshop is supplemented with other dialogue-oriented and process-catalyzing methods as part of the total development process.

Robert Jungk's library has been donated to the Bank of Ideas in Norway. *www.idebanken.no* It is difficult to find English language literature about Future Workshops.

www.christiania.org/utopia
utopia@christiania.org

Christiania, Denmark.
Photo: Albert Bates

The three phases of Future Workshops:

Criticism Phase: expressing everything which we are dissatisfied with. We are consistently negative.
Utopia Phase: we look at things from the opposite angle, and express our wishes and dreams for the future. We unplug from reality – everything is possible. If we could decide for ourselves …
Realization Phase: we hold on to our wishes. How do we start realizing them?

Rules for the group:
Everything is taken seriously – but not necessarily solemnly
Everyone is welcome to speak his or her mind
We communicate with keywords
Keywords are written on the wall-journals
No discussion is allowed

Some pieces of advice:
Duration: two to three days
Number of participants: between 12 and 30 people. When there are over 30 people, the workshop needs to be split up into parallel workshops which meet at intervals, in order to ensure a unified group process.
Preparation: an introductory meeting should be held ahead of time, which allows participants to get answers to their preliminary questions about the process and to join in finding a theme for the workshop.

Practical Considerations

Working with Authorities

Max Lindegger

by Max Lindegger

Around the world, right now, there must be a thousand groups planning an ecovillage. This figure is not based on any evidence, and I have no statistics to back it up. It's a gut feeling, based on the numbers of people contacting our office in Australia and on my observations during travels around the world. My guess is that around 500 of these groups will get together for a couple of months or years to talk about, draw and dream of an ecovillage. Then they will split up, and some will regroup to start this cosy, feel-good and at times frustrating process again. Of the other 500, maybe one half will firm up their options and confirm their commitment, maybe look at land – and then probably disband because they can't agree on a suitable site or realize that you need money or collateral to buy land. Others will succeed in securing land, drawing up plans and need to go to the next stage: facing the authorities. Sadly, some, totally unnecessarily, fail at this stage.

Below are first a few points to ponder on the way to the local authority's chambers:

Public servants are not your enemies. They are actually there to help you.

It will be easier for them to help you if you are clear about what you would like to achieve.

Read the relevant Act. Get help if you can't understand it.

Be challenging with your aims, but stay realistic. Don't waste anybody's time.

If possible, attend pre-planning meetings with your local authority. Present your plans in well-developed draft format.

Be open to compromise.

Be 100% honest – even when it hurts.

Get to know the technical and political wings of your local authority.

Study election publicity: check what the local Councilors stand for. Find a supporter!

Developers (remember, you are about to become one!) rarely introduce more than one new idea in a new project.

Expect surprised looks, when you try to change the world in one clean sweep!

Lobbying for support is legal, paying for favors is bribery.

Learn from the mistakes of others and try to make as few as possible of your own.

Learn what you don't know.

Don't try to do it all on your own. Work with a team.

Have a front person. Make sure the local authority knows who to talk to and who is talking for you.

Getting an ecovillage project passed by your local authority may seem like a "life and death" struggle - but it's not. On the other hand, if it's not always fun, it's still worth doing.

When we (myself, Robert Tap and others) first approached the Town Planners of our local authority regarding Crystal Waters, we got a lot of sympathy but little support. According to the existing rules of the time, on the land area of Crystal Waters a maximum of 16 families were allowed to settle, and the mix of residential, commercial, light industrial and educational facilities (i.e. a village) was not permitted under legislation at the time. However, now we have 83 families living here, and the zoning we need for a true village to develop.

We persisted, we lobbied, we talked and we gained support. At the decisive meeting, when the proposal for Crystal Waters was on the agenda, every Councilor voted for the project.

Miracles are possible – they just take a little longer!

crystalwaters@hotkey.net.au

www.ecovillages.org/australia/crystalwaters

Financing Ecovillages

Overcoming the Financial Stumbling Block

by J.T. Ross Jackson

Ross Jackson, PhD., is the co-founder and Chair of Gaia Trust (Denmark), which has been the main funder of GEN so far. His background includes advising international financial institutions on investment strategies and financial planning.

Finance is a major stumbling block for many ecovillagers, who are often intimidated by money matters and need guidance.

One of the major barriers to the growth of the ecovillage movement is the financing of houses. Often this is because of the unusual clauses relating to joint ownership of land, rights of purchase when someone leaves, etc. In some cases, windmills, biological wastewater treatment and other ecological features complicate matters. These special factors are inconvenient for banks and credit unions because they require special risk evaluation. We had an interesting example of this recently in Denmark. The Danish Association of Ecovillages, one of the first national networks (formed in1993), lobbied the government successfully for a 30% state guarantee on credit union loans to ecological residences. In spite of this reduced risk, the credit unions continue to automatically reject applicants because of their unfamiliarity with such projects. Part of the problem is also the general unfamiliarity of ecovillagers with money and finance matters. However, some interesting initiatives from different parts of the world do offer encouragement.

In the USA, a group called Spirit Money in Boulder, Colorado has taken the initiative in forming a link between the financial institutions and the builders of ecovillages and cohousing projects. With their bank backgrounds, they can talk the language of the banks and put together saleable financial packages for new American initiatives (see www.spiritmoney.com).

Some European alternative banks and a few pension funds are leading the way in financing ecological building, taking an ethical investment approach. The anthroposophical banks, led by the Triodos group, have been particularly active.

A completely different approach was taken by Danish strawbale builder Steen Møller, who started a self-build project recently for 30 homes, based on the principle of no loans whatsoever and no waste! The idea is to start small (about 40 m²) and expand if and when you can. An interesting condition is that at least one person in each residence must work from home in order to avoid the traditional "dead" suburb syndrome. He has the full cooperation of the local municipality who sees it as a way to attract new life, and he has caught the attention of a national TV station, which is doing a documentary on the project, following the builders from day one (see page 159).

Another Danish initiative by the national ecovillage network is a proposal to the legislature to allocate 100 million Danish Kroner for land purchase or rental for 20 qualifying ecovillage projects. Having good models can be a quick way to get people to change lifestyle and cut down on the ecological footprint as sought by Agenda 21. This project also addresses another major problem for ecovillagers, namely finding a suitable site and getting permission for experiments in new lifestyles.

GEN is also working on a funding initiative, not for individual ecovillage projects but for the establishment of three Living and Learning Centers in the Global South. These are envisaged as places where education in sustainability would include both classroom and field work in collaboration with local ecovillages. GEN hopes to get funding from some combination of private funds, governments, and foreign aid programs. Sites have been found in Sri Lanka, Senegal, and Brazil (see page 98).

ross@gaia.org

www.ross-jackson.com

Don't be intimidated by money matters ...
Ross Jackson (right) with Patch Adams. Photo: Hildur Jackson

Fundraising is Friendraising

Interview with Jeff Grossberg

Agnieszka Komoch signing an EU grant, cheered by the GEN Europe Council, Summer 2001. Photo: GEN.

by Karen Svensson

Jeff Grossberg has created, managed and consulted with visionary organizations for 30 years. He has led visioning, strategic planning and organizational development efforts, and has raised tens of millions of dollars as Executive Director of a major American foundation, a nationwide spiritual organization, and of the largest holistic learning center in America, and – for the last 10 years – as a consultant to more than a hundred progressive organizations. Jeff lived at Sirius community (Mass., USA) for a few years before moving to Boulder, (CO) in 2001.

"Fundraising is not so different from building communities: you develop your vision, and you share it with others, whom you then develop a relationship with," says Jeff Grossberg. "Fundraising is a broader vision of how people are involved in your community. There are the people you live with in the immediate community, then the farmer down the road whom you share advice with, and then people who will support your vision in different ways, maybe from a distance."

Q: How do you inspire individuals to donate funds?

Jeff: "Many people will be inspired by what you're doing. Find out who they are, and communicate effectively with them. Understand that people (individuals) are giving away money, and are looking for those areas in their life that they are interested in. If they are the right people for you to approach, they could be longing for community – but maybe feel they can't leave their jobs, their houses – or they simply share the same values, caring about the Earth, wanting to change things."

Q: What about inspiring companies?

Jeff: "I remember one community I worked with, whose members felt aligned with the values of a local company. They had asked for money several times, but gotten nowhere. Now they were artists, musicians. They offered to put on an Easter party for the children of the employees with egg hunts, music, and costumes. Among the parents of these children was the wife of the company's CEO. She enjoyed the party and was invited to the community and they became friends. She invited some members of the community to her house, where they became acquainted with her husband, and talked about their values, their community. A few months later, they thought of asking him for advice on how to approach the board of the company for funding. He then offered to introduce the idea to the board." Now that the CEO of the company knew them, and what they were about, he could vouch for them and the community was approved for funding. "It's not rocket science, but it's about identifying the people you know, working to include them, creating vehicles for this."

Q: How do you connect with foundations?

Jeff: "Many people look at foundations for funding. It's the hardest money to raise: it takes most time, there are most strings attached, and there is most competition. For larger organizations, such as the EU, one key point is still to create relationships with critical people. The nature of the relationship has to be appropriate. You may meet on a committee, make contact with a staff person. It's good if you have a friend who can vouch for you to one of the program officers – we're still talking about people. Build a relationship over time (if you don't know anyone in the organization). If your application was rejected once, you can contact a staff person to ask what you should do better next time. You can place the organization on your mailing list for newsletters, let them know if you have raised money elsewhere (send them a news clipping). They build up a file on you, over a few years, and one day when your name comes up someone will say: 'Oh, yes, we've been following them for a while, they really follow through, they seem serious.'"

Q: How does one overcome one's blocks about fundraising and asking for money? What can one do to feel comfortable with this?

"You can think: 'I have a cause, I'm investing my life in it, it's so important to me that if I have to do something uncomfortable, I'm willing to do it.' I personally think that if I ask courteously, and based on a sense of vision, and they say no, that's fine, I don't feel devalued. The thing is to ask the other person: 'Are you in a position to help? Does this work for you?' A lot of people are going to say no. But it gets easier with time and practice. Anyway, you'll never know unless you ask. I once asked a person (whom I'd known for quite some time) for support, and he immediately said yes. When I wondered why he hadn't thought of giving us money before, he said: 'Nobody ever asked me.' You can also try to role-play, see what it sounds like. Also, remember that people and organizations are looking to give away funds, and if you can come up with something that matches their interests, you meet their needs as well as yours."

Basic Principles of Fundraising, by Jeff Grossberg

Fundraising is also called "development" to indicate the wider perspective needed when thinking about obtaining financial support for one's organization. Indeed, fundraising has to be built into the larger vision and strategic planning of the organization.

Visionary development (fundraising) is about:

Clarifying your vision (purpose, values and beliefs) and mission
Expressing it clearly, expressing your needs in terms of it
Finding people who share it (start with the inner circle and build out)
Defining these people's CIA (capacity, interest, access)
Building relationships with them (cultivate)
Soliciting

Money follows!

eastways@ic.org

Pitfalls to Avoid

What Not to Do by Declan Kennedy

Here is some good advice from a man who ought to know, an architect with many years' experience in building and designing ecological solutions. Declan was the first Chairman of GEN (1996-1999), and is co-founder of Lebensgarten Ecovillage in Germany (1985) see article pages 69-71, and pictures pages 70; 76; 170-171.

1. Avoid long discussions – do not talk too long about founding an ecovillage; get started on site as soon as possible. One tip that helped often was a regular meeting for an hour or so every Friday; however there should not be more than 12 months from the "start" to the moment of breaking ground for the first buildings.
2. Avoid a "green field" site; urban, suburban or existing village extensions make a "start" easier.
3. Avoid an empty site; a plot with even one old existing building on it allows all potential members to experience where they might live and can be temporary housing while building your home nearby.
4. Avoid weekend commuters who travel to the next town during the week, to their old homes or an apartment. This will make community building more difficult. Full commitment is necessary, especially at the start.

What to Remember by Max Lindegger

1. Minimize up front financial exposure before you have approval from local government authorities.
2. Avoid using financial incentives to attract the 'right' people.
3. Work with a smallish group of people to develop a vision and acceptable rules. Invite others to join your group when you are ready. Don't change the vision/rules simply to attract more people.
4. Don't promote your project too early. Promote when you have approval and security of title/tenure.

Demonstration Center or Ecovillage?

by Peter Harper

In this article, Peter Harper advises people to take a close look at the very different requirements posed by demonstration centers and ecovillages, and to evaluate the real-life implications of these two models before building the settlement. Though we know of several places in Denmark and Italy (for example Damanhur) where the combination of ecovillage and ecocenter seems to work, it is a real challenge. The potential problems exposed here need to be taken into account in the design and planning of the ecovillage/ecocenter.

At the 1995 ecovillages conference at Findhorn, I and several colleagues represented CAT (the Center for Alternative Technologies, Wales) which had started life as an ecovillage in 1974. It was great fun to compare notes with other communities of similar vintage to our own (like The Farm, Auroville, and Findhorn), to hear about the unfolding patterns of successes and failures, and how things now stood compared with the early years.

The parallels were often striking, yet there was something odd happening; something that didn't fit, which I couldn't figure out. I struggled with this for a few days, until a comment of Max Lindegger's suddenly clarified the problem. He remarked that visitors often walk around his community, Crystal Waters, and leave disappointed, saying: "Is this all?" Yet Crystal Waters is a carefully planned and highly complex settlement. In other words, what is important at Crystal Waters is not readily observable to the casual visitor. I have heard the same story told about Findhorn, and it seems largely true of all genuine communities. They do not exist to be casually observed, and if they did it would seriously compromise their true purpose.

I suddenly realized that CAT is an entirely different kind of animal, one, which is specifically designed for short-term visitors. In some ways it is the very opposite of an ecovillage. Over the years it has become more and more adept at communicating with visitors, and at the same time the significance of its residential community has declined almost to vanishing point.

There is something fundamental here. It reminds me of Tom Stoppard's observation in "Rosencrantz and Guildenstern are Dead", that actors are the opposite of people. An actor on stage, at the end of a passionate half-hour soliloquy, would be extremely disconcerted to discover that there had been nobody in the auditorium. In total contrast, a private person (possibly that very actor), imagining they were alone for half an hour, would be shocked and embarrassed to discover that they had in fact been watched.

This symbolizes the difference between ecovillages and eco-demonstration centers or eco-centers for short. Although both have wider purposes, they have a different balance of internal and external relationships. In an ecovillage the internal links are more important than the external links. In an eco-center it is the external links which are more important. The balance of links makes a surprising difference to almost everything.

How did this transformation happen at CAT?
All ecovillages need an economic base. The inevitable failure of CAT's original self-sufficiency program led within a year to an economic crisis. This was solved by reorganizing part of the site as an exhibition and opening it to paying visitors, who would also buy refreshments and other goods. Initially this was seen as a positive move in creating a full-featured settlement.

Meanwhile most of the staff continued living on the site, but there were constant tensions between "simply living" and "putting on a show". Our visitors were very keen to see how we lived. But the very act of strangers observing private life – or even the knowledge that they might – utterly changes it. Some members responded by finding homes outside the site and negotiating a strictly working relationship with the organization – already changing the balance. Others stayed on the site and tried to create visitor-free zones, but numbers dwindled; there were no children or retired people, no innovation or dynamism: the heart seemed to go out of the community. I must admit I found this puzzling: there is no strictly logical reason why a thriving residential community should not run a visitor center as part of its economic base. To a certain extent the Findhorn Foundation has managed this, but I can think of no other examples of organizations that survived for long on this razor-edge. It seems the psychological pressures force you to go one way or the other.

So now CAT relates more to other eco-centers than it does to most ecovillages, and is unusual in that most other ecocenters were specifically founded as such, not originally as communities. Examples include De Kleine Aarde in the Netherlands, Centre Terre Vivante in France, Folkecenter in Denmark, and Energie und Umweltcentrum in Germany. Rather slowly a parallel universe to GEN is developing, creating an international network of ecocenters. They are complementary. The role of ecocenters is rapid, standardized mass communication of knowledge and skills. In contrast, the results of ecovillage experiments and experience must be communicated in a softer, slower and more profound and personal way. Both are necessary.

Expanding the Ecovillage Concept

Ecovillages are demonstration models which show how the different elements of sustainability synergize when put together. The principles demonstrated by ecovillages can be applied as successful sustainable alternatives in urban planning, and can be integrated in existing neighborhoods and other types of communities. The ecovillage concept also provides viable solutions to emergency situations, which require the societal and practical reorganization of large groups of people who have been displaced. In this section, we show how the integration of the ecovillage concept can benefit "mainstream" residential configurations, and can solve problems posed by – among others – urbanization and the massive relocation of people due to natural disasters or civil war.

Ecovillages for Disaster Reconstruction

Ecovillages: A Planning Paradigm for Natural Disaster Areas

by Karen Svensson, based on an interview with Rashmi Mayur

Dr. Rashmi Mayur, Director of the International Institute for a Sustainable Future (IISF) in Bombay and a consultant with the United Nations, has visited natural disaster areas in Japan, China, Mozambique and India. His conclusion is, that ecological – as opposed to technical – reconstruction in these areas is the only viable option. "As disasters increase in the world, we are actually presented with equally increasing possibilities for ecological reconstruction," Mayur says. "The ecovillage principle encompasses everything needed to resettle refugees in the wake of natural disaster, and to prepare against such calamities in the future. We have to seize this opportunity to establish ecovillages as the planning paradigm in exposed areas."

Rashmi Mayur is one of the major spokespersons for the global South at the United Nations, and takes part in the planning of major UN conferences. He produces the magazine Eco Earth and has a weekly one-hour radio show in New York, for which he recently received an award. He has been linked to GEN since 1995. Rashmi is in the process of establishing a Living and Learning Center near Bombay.

Right: Rashmi Mayur speaking in front of a children's peace quilt. His dedication to the fate of children who have been left orphans after natural disasters has led him to start a project called "Hope for the Children Homes", which builds and organizes homes for orphans in Bhug Gujarat, India, where the January 2001 earthquake claimed over 65,000 lives. The "Hope" homes are based on principles of ecology and ecovillage living. One of their purposes is to teach the young residents about ecology and ecovillage principles, cooperative farming, and ecological disaster preparation.

"We are moving into the century of disasters," says Rashmi Mayur, with a frown on his forehead. "In the past decade, we have suffered more losses due to cyclones, floods, droughts, earthquakes and fires than in any other given decade. And it's only getting worse. Due to the greenhouse effect, of which the main culprit is CO_2 release in the atmosphere, we will be seeing dramatic increases in these kinds of phenomena all over the world."

Rashmi Mayur has not yet overcome the shock of facing death on the 18th story of a high-rise in Bombay, as the repercussions of the earthquake in Bhug Gujarat made themselves felt 400 km from its epicenter. That day, January 26, 2001 (Independence Day in India) the earthquake claimed 9,000 villages and 65,000 lives. It left 160,000 injured, and 1.5 million refugees, among whom were 13,000 orphans. Mayur went out there. "Everything had been turned to dust. There was no rescue system, there were no connections, no phone, no Internet." As it turns out, it was not only the earthquake itself that caused the deaths of all these people. The losses of human life took place over six long days of agony, due for a large part to the inability to get help, because whole areas were cut off from the rest of the country, and due also to the lack of preparation or practical first-aid measures.

"The most vulnerable victims of disaster are children, whom one should take care of first, and who are key in any type of education and preparation," Mayur says. "I saw children in Gujarat dying of dehydration and malnutrition, especially those who lost their parents." When Mayur was on site, a small child fell off a chair before his feet, and died a few hours later: he had only had one cup of water the whole day, and got so overheated that his body stopped functioning. At the time of our interview, Mayur had already gathered donations to start building the first "Hope for the Children Home". Each home is designed based on ecological principles, and is intended to provide education in ecology and ecovillage principles, cooperative farming, as well as ecological disaster preparation for 100 orphans. Rashmi Mayur is actively seeking more funds for children's homes and ecological reconstruction. "You see, with ecological systems such as those used in ecovillages, we can both solve problems and prepare for disasters," he says.

Water Management
Water management is an example of this. In India, each house could have a water harvesting system gathering water from the roof, and enabling every household to keep water from the monsoon rains for the dry season, storing it in a container in the ground. In Mozambique, the problem of water management is a very different one, which can also be solved ecologically: they have large dams, and these explode with the pressure of floods. Mayur advocates smaller dams, and an ecological waterways system, combined with a tree-planting program – he has consulted with Mozambique's government about this solution.

Housing
"In terms of housing, if we rebuild homes with unfired compressed earth blocks, they will be cooler in the heat,

and retain heat in cold weather. These houses will also be earthquake-resistant, according to ecological building principles, as they dissipate the S-waves which cause the physical damage," Rashmi advises. A parabolic design is one way to make buildings earthquake-resistant. Experiments with this type of design by ecological builders have been very successful. The great advantage of compressed earth blocks is that the building material, earth, is right there, and building blocks can be produced on site with a mobile compressing machine.

Sanitary Waste Treatment
Another problem, which can best be solved ecologically in refugee camps, is the processing of human waste to avoid pollution and disease. When many people – refugees – are gathered in one place with no amenities whatsoever, one of the first things to do is to build compost toilets which separate urine from solid human wastes, turning each component into a safe and beneficial fertilizer, and allowing areas with low water supply to save water for other uses. In a compost toilet system, solid wastes start composting very quickly, without odor or health hazards. Ecological waste treatment in general is a sanitary way of disposing of potentially hazardous waste in confined and dense human settlements.

Social Aspects
"One thing you should remember as well, is that all ecological resettlement after natural disasters is essentially the resettlement of the human heart," Mayur says. "We are dealing with people. Human beings, who have lost everything. If we rebuild areas purely technologically, we end up with concrete highrises (as in Japan, after the earthquake in Kobe) where people get lonely, depressed and weak. What they really need to become strong is community. Relocation of the human heart has to happen artistically, with poetry, and in community," Mayur says. "This is what ecovillages offer. The central social aspect of ecovillages offers people a new home, where they can find community. We human beings need friendship, being together with a common purpose."

For refugees in areas at high risk of natural catastrophes, the practical purpose is to prepare against disaster in the future. The effort starts in community: "We set up a village committee which manages the rebuilding and preparation. I insist that such a committee be composed of at least 50% women," Mayur says. "There can be no disaster reconstruction ecovillages without women, and also children, for that matter." At the time of our interview, Rashmi Mayur was building an ecological Information, Communication and Education (ICE) center connecting the village of Malviana in Gujarat by phone and Internet to sources of information and help. The center was to inform and educate people about ecological reconstruction and preparation, with the ecovillage principle in mind. He said that the next step was to rebuild houses with compressed earth blocks, and install independent alternative energy systems: solar energy for electricity (light, radio for communications), heating and drying (e.g. grain harvested after the rainy season), biogas for cooking, and ecological agriculture using recycled wastes from compost toilets as fertilizer. All the while, Mayur is aware that people need training in the usage of these sys-

PLAN FOR CHILDREN'S CENTRES IN GUJARAT
NOT TO SCALE

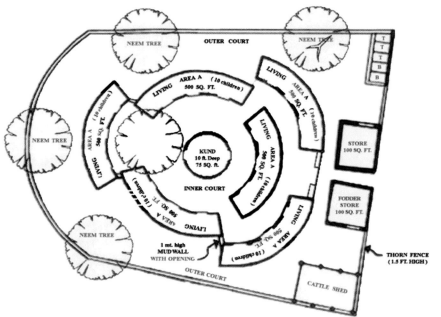

BUILT UP AREA (SQ. FT.)

Sr. No.	SPACE	AREA	NOS.	TOTAL
1.	LIVING AREA FOR CHILDREN	500	5	2500.00
2.	KITCHEN	500	1	500.00
3.	COMMON TOILET	156	1	156.00
4.	STORE	100	2	200.00
5.	MANAGER'S RM.	75	1	75.00
	TOTAL BUILT-UP AREA			3431.00 SQ. FT.

(BESIDES APPROX 2000 SQ. FT. OCCUPIED BY OPEN INNER COURTYARD BUILT ON A RAISED PLATFORM)

"The effort starts in community," says Rashmi Mayur. Here, he addresses a village committee in Saphale village. Photos: IISF

"There can be no disaster reconstruction without women, and also children, for that matter," says Rashmi Mayur. **Left**: *women collecting rainwater from a borewell installed by IISF as part of the ecovillage project in Chintupada, Palghar.*

tems. "I also want training for the children, at the children's homes. They have to plant trees, learn about ecological agriculture, learn to rebuild and prepare for the future," says Mayur, who has issued a booklet (sponsored by the Chamber of Commerce in Bombay) about ecological disaster training.

"To rebuild and prepare for the future, we can't choose the technical way," says Mayur. "Artificial solutions are inappropriate. By integrating the human heart, the natural environment and ecological techniques for self-sufficiency, ecovillages not only remedy immediate practical problems, but harness people against disaster. That is why I coined the term 'Disaster Reconstruction Ecovillages', where people can relocate in community, and meet all of their basic needs while preparing for the future."

iisfb@giasbm01.vsnl.net.in

Auroville's Building Center   avbc-earthunit@auroville.org.in

The Auroville Building Center (above, center) is an Asian resource center in earth architecture and construction, which aims to accelerate the dissemination of technical and scientific know-how in the field. The center has developed a wide range of equipment for building with earth, ranging from compressed earth bloacks (CEB), quality control devices for block making, to hand tools and rammed earth equipment. The Auram press 3000 (above, far left) has become renowned as one of the best presses available worldwide. The center has researched and developed a building system based on reinforced masonry with compressed stabilized earth blocks (hollow interlocking) for disaster-resistant constructions. This technology has been approved by the government of Gujarat as a suitable construction method for the rehabilitation of the zones affected by the 2001 earthquake (above, right, an earthquake-resistant minimum emergency house in Istanbul, Turkey, built in 8 days).

Ecovillages and Cohousings as Planning Paradigms

Integral Societies: From Cohousings to Ecovillages

by Hildur Jackson

My Story

In February 1968 I had my first child (in the same week Auroville was inaugurated), and in April 1969 my second. Sitting with a new law degree and two bouncing baby boys, I asked myself whether there were only two equally impossible choices for women: to have a full career giving over your children to strangers (why then have children?), or to stay at home in a deserted suburb and become totally dependent on my husband (knowing the official divorce rates)? There had to be a third way. I started studying cultural sociology in 1968, to look for different solutions. And I tried to get a group together that would create a better way of organizing our local living situation. Then I persuaded some friends and my husband, who was more than busy building up his business, to be a part of this adventure. This is how we became the founders of one of the first three cohousings in Denmark.

How the cohousing movement started

In 1968, an article in a major Danish newspaper, entitled "Children need 100 Parents", expressed the need for children to be brought up in a larger "family". The nuclear family, where two parents take entire responsibility for child rearing, was not satisfactory. It rang a bell for three groups of Danes – among which was our housing group. Before long, three projects, which would come to be known as "cohousings", were on their way in Denmark. The word cohousing was coined by Kathryn McCamant and Charles Durett in their book, *Cohousing*, after visiting Denmark in 1983 to bring the idea to the USA. Ten years later, there were 150 cohousings in Denmark, a country with five million inhabitants. There are now 55 cohousings in the US, with three times that on their way. They were all built by groups of people who created a joint process and defined how they wanted to live. Subgroups carried out research and took on various tasks – such as designing a community house, getting permissions, finding financing and organizing the process. They never had any support from the government. If you want to know how people want to live, look at cohousings. They show many similarities: One thing they all have in common is that no cars are allowed in the settlements. Some were built around a community house, some in clusters, and others along a connecting road (sometimes with a glass covering). Often they are built around play areas for children. The houses themselves are typically one or one and a half floors high and 100 to 150 m² in size, often with the kitchen as part of the dining area. The community houses are large enough to seat everybody for meals and celebrations. Creating social interaction and a healthy and fun environment for children and grown-ups through a community house with shared meals and common facilities were clearly major goals of the pioneers. All community houses have special facilities for children, young ones as well as teenagers. Vegetable gardens, chickens and animals are often part of the design. Lawns for playing football and other ballgames are common. More recent cohousings often use alternative energy sources. All the first cohousings were based on private ownership. Later, the possibility presented itself to get some public funding for cooperative structures. They are a success story, which can be replicated. Ole Svensson, a senior researcher at the Danish Insitute for Building Research, who lives in the Sættedammen cohousing (see opposite page), says: "The only drawback is that you are having such a good time that you may forget to stay in contact with old friends." Ole maintains that in Denmark all later settlements have been strongly influenced by cohousings in that a community house with shared facilities is a must for most new residential neighborhoods.

The primary cohousing resource in English is the very comprehensive American book: *Cohousing, A Contemporary Approach to Housing Ourselves*.

The Swedish/Dutch experience

The idea of cohousings quickly spread to Sweden, as they are always alert to new ideas. One typical difference stands out. In Sweden cohousings were initiated by builders and planners (top-down), and were not an expression of peoples' own initiative. Whether the group bonding happened later, I do not know. Also, the Swedish cohousings often took shape in high buildings and towns.

The spread of cohousings to the USA, Japan/Asia

Australian architect Graham Meltzer said in a lecture on cohousings at a 2001 International Communities meeting (Zegg ecovillage in Germany), that the cohousing movement now has spread to Japan and Asia.

The Ecovillage movement

Throughout the 80s I worked with the Nordic Alternative Campaign initiated by Erik Damman in Norway. One hundred grass roots movements (environmental, peace, women's groups) cooperated for 10 years with the best of the scientific community in creating a vision

Sættedammen, Denmark

Sættedammen is Denmark's oldest, and therefore the world's oldest cohousing (in modern terms). It was founded in 1972. There are 27 houses, a community house with sauna, kitchen, dining room, pool room, "pillow room" (where kids can jump about freely), and a washroom. The center of the settlement is a much used community area with a lawn, playgrounds and picnic tables.

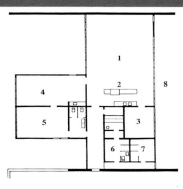

The kitchen in the community house (see plan, right), is used several times a week for community dinners, and can be reserved by individual members for celebrations and other activities.

Left: Gunnar plays a bit of violin for the little ones on his way back from rehearsing with the Folk music group in the community house. Bottom left: No one misses the carnival, and everyone dresses up (or down).

Bottom right: Folk dance at Sættedammen's yearly celebration which gathers all the residents for a day of games, theater, good food and fun.

The community house, 1:300 in red on the main plan
1. Dining and living room, 2. Kitchen, 3. Playroom,
4. TV-room, 5. Billiards room, 6. Bath and sauna,
7. Laundromat, 8. Outdoor terasse.

where global, social and ecological problems could be solved in one single vision. We held Nordic seminars on all possible topics from "Economy as if people mattered" to "Ecology all the way round", and "Cooperation between The North and a corresponding number of African countries", at the ecovillage of Svanholm. My conclusion after seven years was, that we had all the necessary knowledge to create a sustainable, socially well-functioning and spiritually satisfying society consisting of communities and that we just had to implement these ecovillages. I had then lived 20 wonderful years in our cohousing, seen 12 children grow up there, and wanted to develop the idea further. From creating a social solution for raising children, I now grew into wanting to be part of a more comprehensive experiment, which, if all people lived that way, would create a sustainable Earth. This was not possible within the boundaries of our existing cohousing. We spent some years finding a suitable place, where all the elements of an ecovillage could be implemented: a permaculture design with food production and earth restoration, job creation on the spot, education, daily meditations in a group. Robert and Diane Gilman (In Context Institute) from Seattle moved with us to Thy, Denmark, where we invited some key people to the first network meeting about "ecovillages", which took place in September 1991. Gaia Trust invited people from the best sustainable communities around the world that we knew of, projects which had an integrated approach and were tolerant, for example regarding spiritual paths. Two years later, we held a second meeting in Thy. In 1993 we invited people for the creation of a Danish network (LØS), which now has its office in Hertha ecovillage (Denmark), has two secretaries, and issues a quarterly magazine. In 1995, we supported the Findhorn conference on "Ecovillages, Sustainable Communities for the 21st Century", and after the meeting this group decided to launch GEN formally at the UN Habitat conference in Istanbul in 1996.

Ecovillages/Cohousing

The difference between ecovillages and cohousings is a question of how far or deep the transformation of lifestyle is, and not a matter of suburb versus countryside. If you intend to give up commuting and live and work in one place, then ecovillages are the way to go. The need to reduce the CO_2 release in the atmosphere calls for the structural change that ecovillages represent. Localizing one's daily life by merging private and work lives, as well as a large percentage of self sufficiency, calls for less transportation. Cohousings take one step in the right direction by creating a good social environment. If you want to make ecological and social practices and/or spirituality an important part of your life, an ecovillage is the way to go. For planners and as a planning paradigm, cohousings certainly seem like an easier model to implement at first. What planners need to remember is that without people being a part of the process of defining the cohousing, the social bonding will not happen. So they need to work together with the future residential group. But why not become a full member of the startup group as a planner, and be part of creating an ecovillage? The example of Munksøgaard shows how popular the ecovillage concept is, and how possible it is to realize: people are waiting in line to move in (see p. 162).

Special Groups: Senior Cohousings and Integration of the Differently Abled

In the near future, all the societies of the West will face an age spread where the percentage of elderly people relative to younger groups is skewed. The welfare state will have problems providing pensions, services and care for everyone. This has led to the creation of multiple senior cohousings in several countries. We also see projects integrating the differently abled. A Danish municipality has recently adopted the model of Hertha's reversed integration of mentally handicapped youth for their own projects. They could see how much better it was to integrate ordinary citizens with these youngsters. Other examples of integration projects are the Camphill villages. For elderly people, greater integration may also be desirable (i.e. with other age groups).

Building firms and "Do It Yourself" Builders: Creating a Social Structure

Most cohousings were built by traditional developers whereas most ecovillages to date are the result of people creating their own community. Certainly ecological building calls for a different kind of construction with careful handling of soil and materials, different machines, sometimes more labor-intensive processes etc. Increasing numbers of new firms will probably start up with all the necessary knowledge and a willingness to work with self-builders. We hope that local and national authorities will welcome this positive development, and support these endeavors as fully as they support industrialized, environmentally damaging building practices. In Denmark, the parliament has just granted DKK 80 million to ecological building.

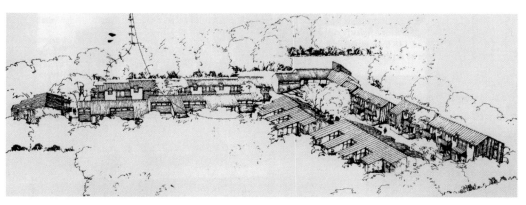

Trudeslund Cohousing in Denmark has 33 homes located on 18,000 m² of land. Buildings occupy 22 percent of the grounds. The land was purchased in 1978/79, and construction began in 1980. Residents started moving in 1981. Architects: Tegnestuen Vandkunsten. Drawing from the Danish book: Cohousings (Bofællesskaber) © Trudeslund Tegnestuen Vandkunsten.

How Can Local Planners Support Ecovillages?

Ecovillages Can Help Solve Social and Planning Issues

Excerpts from a report by David Kanaley, Australia

David Kanaley is the Director of Environmental Planning Services at Byron Shire Council in Australia. In 1999, he went to Europe on a scholarship and visited ecovillages, to see which ideas could be used by local municipal councils in Australia for the creation of more sustainable settlements in public planning. In Fall 1999 he visited ten projects: Torri Superiore and Damanhur (Italy), Lebensgarten (Germany), Hjortshøj and Eco 99 (Denmark), Hooipolder and EVA Lanxmere (The Netherlands), Findhorn (Scotland), Tweed Valley Ecovillage and Hockerton Housing Project (UK). He came back with solid arguments for local governments to include ecovillages as planning paradigms, and identified areas where local authorities could support this type of development.

David Kanaley advocates new housing concepts based on ecovillage models, finding that they "provide for better application of sustainable design principles, together with a clearer understanding of the relationship between humans and nature. The European experience also suggests that ecovillages provide for more sustainable communities through better social interaction and the enabling of employment opportunities."

Kanaley's major point is that "Ecovillages need local government support and guidance if they are to succeed." This implies that: "Local Governments need to seek specific opportunities for ecovillage development. This could include identifying suitable areas through the preparation of rural or town settlement strategies. It could also include identifying old industrial buildings, convents and monasteries with a view to enabling their conversion to ecovillages. In some circumstances, Local Government may even be able to provide land at a below market rate to enable an ecovillage to be developed. It could also encourage joint partnerships with government housing providers for ecovillage developments with affordable social housing components."

David Kanaley's main findings about ecovillages are listed below, accompanied by a description of ways in which local authorities can best support and benefit from

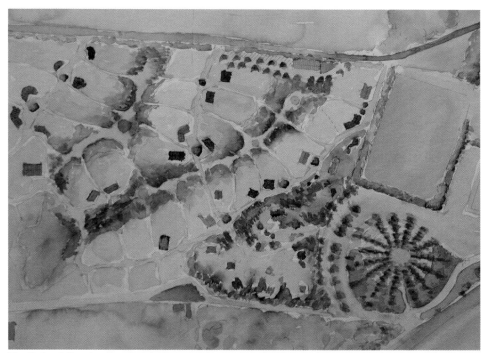

The Friland (free land) project in Denmark has gathered widespread support. Twelve natural houses are planned. They must be loan-free (the basic concept being a debt-free lifestyle). A national TV station has taken Friland under its wings, and plans to follow the building process over the next three years. Ecological builder Steen Møller is the initiator. Photo: courtesy Steen Møller. www.dr.dk/friland

the creation of ecovillages (comments related to governments' role in this are written in italics).

Ecovillages recognize community

"In each ecovillage there is a documented and conscious effort at developing community, and a sense of belonging," Kanaley writes.

The local government should therefore ensure that there is a core group of people established "up front", who intend to establish an ecovillage. Kanaley finds that successful ecovillages are not developer-led. The houses, land packages and management plans are all created with involvement from at least a core group of intended residents. This means that local government may need to initiate a public meeting to establish a core group, which will then proceed to develop an ecovillage proposal with landowners and professional people.

Ecovillages apply new technologies

All new projects must be based on the application of innovative renewable energy technologies and the reuse of treated sewage and gray water. The level of application of sustainable technologies in food production and in business enterprises varies. Permaculture, based on Bill Mollison's design principles, is fairly common in the ecovillages, which Kanaley visited.

Kanaley proposes that governments establish targets, such as a 20% self-sufficiency rate for energy, and a 100% level of re-use for treated water and gray water.

The size of ecovillages varies

David Kanaley has seen ecovillages ranging from a five-house project to a model like Damanhur, with 400 full-time residents (and 350 more loosely attached). At Damanhur people live in several dozen houses, which form four communities, which again make up the federation of Damanhur.

Note: At the Findhorn meeting in 1995, when it came to defining what an ecovillage is, there was a unanimous agreement that an ecovillage should be between 50 and 500 persons with exceptions counting up to 2000 (traditional villages).

Local government needs to be responsive to a range of ecovillage sizes. No one size is perfect. The issue is to create good communication and decision-making structures. The size will reflect a range of variables such as cultural background, socialization and communication skills. It will also need to be responsive to site characteristics.

Ecovillages provide for employment on site

Local governments should encourage on-site employment opportunities, and not see ecovillages as res-

Svanholm (DK) provides employment on-site. Photo: Svanholm

idential areas only. They could ensure access to internet and intranet and office space in each house. Ecovillages could be asked by authorities to identify their concept plans for locally based green industries.

Ecovillages need to be planned

Each ecovillage needs the following in its planning:
Layout of houses and other shared facilities, pedestrian system, car parking areas, community food production/ agricultural areas, work space and Earth restoration/ wilderness areas
A total water cycle management and recycling plan
A plan for renewable energy according to targets of self-sufficiency
A plan or guidelines for eco-houses
A landscape plan utilizing native plants and if desired fruits, nut trees and herbs.

Local governments need to be clear about their expectations in this direction.

Ecovillages need to be car-free

This is a general trait of ecovillages.

For local Government this entails the need to establish access points for emergencies and for garbage collection. Easy public transportation is also an issue.

Ecovillages need a social contract or social management plan

This plan details:
The vision and objectives of the ecovillage
The ultimate size of the ecovillage
How to join the ecovillage, including a trial period
How to leave an ecovillage, perhaps first granting other residents an option to buy or a limited right of refusal to an intended buyer of a house
An internal decision-making and conflict-resolution system
A range of other matters which concern the functioning of the ecovillage and development of "community" within the village.

Local governments need to ensure that the plan is adequate and in the least covers the above points.

In his report, David Kanaley further explains how ecovillages in Denmark and the Netherlands consist of a blend of privately owned houses and socially supported buildings, which creates a good social mix. He underlines the need for residents to be able to choose new inhabitants contrary to usual practices in social housing.

See also David Kanaley's video: "The Future of Paradise, the European Ecovillage Experience." The video features ecovillages in Italy, Germany, Denmark, Holland and the UK.

Available at: Byron Shire Council, PO Box 219, Mullumbimby, NSW Australia 2482
Phone: +61-2 66267000 Fax: +61-2 66843018

Munksøgaard, Denmark

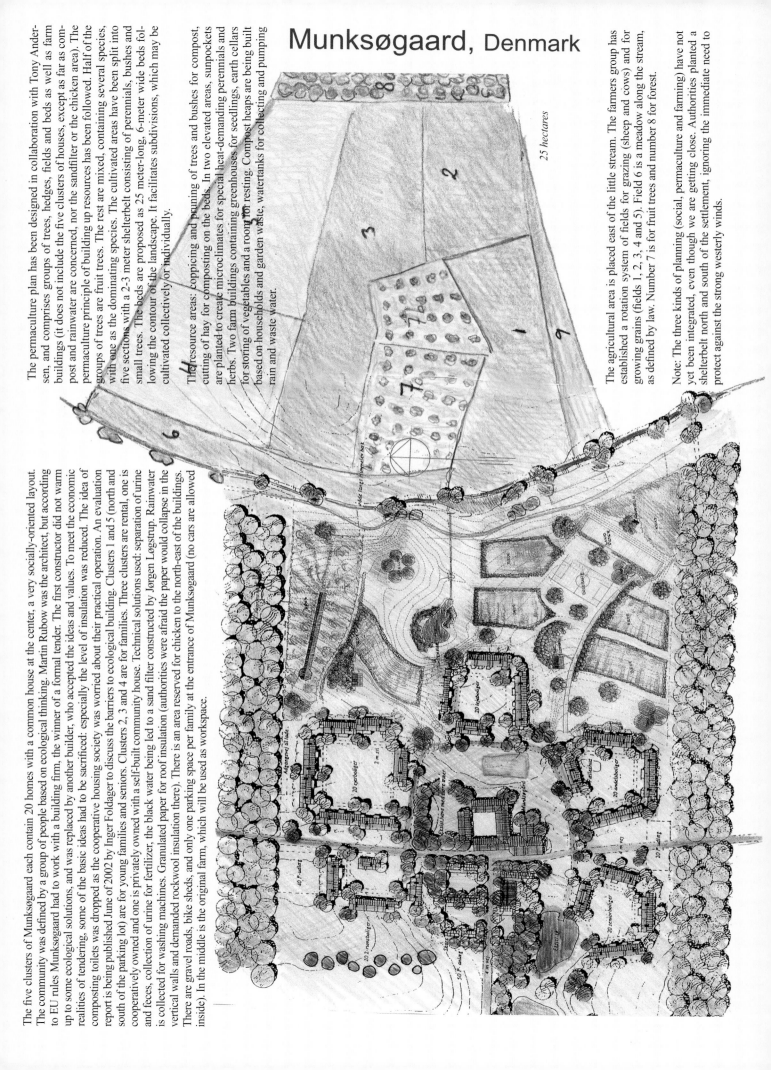

25 hectares

The permaculture plan has been designed in collaboration with Tony Andersen, and comprises groups of trees, hedges, fields and beds as well as farm buildings (it does not include the five clusters of houses, except as far as compost and rainwater are concerned, nor the sandfilter or the chicken area). The permaculture principle of building up resources has been followed. Half of the groups of trees are fruit trees. The rest are mixed, containing several species, with one as the dominating species. The cultivated areas have been split into five sections with a 2-3 meter shelterbelt consisting of perennials, bushes and small trees. The beds are proposed as 25 meter-long, 6-meter wide beds following the contour of the landscape. It facilitates subdivisions, which may be cultivated collectively or individually.

The resource areas: coppicing and pruning of trees and bushes for compost, cutting of hay for composting on the beds. In two elevated areas, sunpockets are planted to create microclimates for special heat-demanding perennials and herbs. Two farm buildings containing greenhouses for seedlings, earth cellars for storing of vegetables and a room for resting. Compost heaps are being built based on households and garden waste, watertanks for collecting and pumping rain and waste water.

The five clusters of Munksøgaard each contain 20 homes with a common house at the center, a very socially-oriented layout. The community was defined by a group of people based on ecological thinking. Martin Rubow was the architect, but according to EU rules Munksøgaard had to work with a building firm, the winner of a formal tender. The first constructor did not warm up to some ecological solutions, and was replaced by another builder, who accepted the ideas and values. To meet the economic realities of tendering, some of the basic ideas had to be sacrificed: especially the level of insulation was reduced. The idea of composting toilets was dropped as the cooperative housing society was worried about their practical operation. An evaluation report is being published June of 2002 by Inger Foldager to discuss the barriers to ecological building. Clusters 1 and 5 (north and south of the parking lot) are for young families and seniors. Clusters 2, 3 and 4 are for families. Three clusters are rental, one is cooperatively owned and one is privately owned with a self-built community house. Technical solutions used: separation of urine and feces, collection of urine for fertilizer, the black water being led to a sand filter constructed by Jørgen Løgstrup. Rainwater is collected for washing machines. Granulated paper for roof insulation (authorities were afraid the paper would collapse in the vertical walls and demanded rockwool insulation there). There is an area reserved for chicken to the north-east of the buildings.

There are gravel roads, bike sheds, and only one parking space per family at the entrance of Munksøgaard (no cars are allowed inside). In the middle is the original farm, which will be used as workspace.

The agricultural area is placed east of the little stream. The farmers group has established a rotation system of fields for grazing (sheep and cows) and for growing grains (fields 1, 2, 3, 4 and 5). Field 6 is a meadow along the stream, as defined by law. Number 7 is for fruit trees and number 8 for forest.

Note: The three kinds of planning (social, permaculture and farming) have not yet been integrated, even though we are getting close. Authorities planted a shelterbelt north and south of the settlement, ignoring the immediate need to protect against the strong westerly winds.

The Advent of the Mainstream Ecovillage

Munksøgaard in Denmark

Interview with Mikkel Strange by Karen Svensson and Hildur Jackson

Mikkel Strange is a member of the core group that developed Munksøgaard Ecovillage in Denmark (see design page 162). He has recently graduated in geology, and lives at Munksøgaard with his wife and two children. He is also on the board of LØS, the Danish Association of Ecovillages.

Introduction:

Munksøgaard, the latest Danish ecovillage, is situated next to RUC, the University Center of Roskilde (a city of 45,000 people three km away) and the railway station of Trekroner, with a direct train connection to Copenhagen (35 km) and the airport. Its 5 clusters, each of 20 dwellings, have been built around an old farm. The houses, built of wood, have two floors and the facades are painted in different colors for each cluster. One cluster is for young people, and another is for older people, both providing rentals through a non-profit housing association. The three remaining clusters are family housing: one is for private owners, one is a private co-op and one is rental. All clusters have a community house. East of the settlement, the surrounding fields slope down towards a stream and rise again towards the horizon. This is where Munksøgaard has animals grazing, and is starting to grow vegetables and grains. Residents first moved in in 2001, and now the grass is up, more than 100 new trees have been planted and you feel welcome when you walk in (cars are parked outside). Two years ago, before building the ecovillage, Munksøgaard won the first prize in a Danish competition for the best sustainable settlement for the 21st century (organized by LØS – the Danish Association of Ecovillages – and supported by five ministries in partnership with Gaia Trust). Munksøgaard's buildings have a homogenous look, but when you look closely you can detect differences between, for example, the youth cluster and the privately owned houses. The ecovillage represents all layers of Danish society and all age groups. The day people moved in, there was already a long waiting list of about 500 people, enough for two more such projects. This says something about the wide appeal of the concept in Danish society.

Mikkel Strange:

"We worked hard for five and a half years toward the creation of Munksøgaard as a small-scale model of a future sustainable society. The planning process started in March 1995, and soon we agreed on the following vision:

'We want to build a community of 100 dwellings. Some must be for young people, some must be for senior citizens, some must be for people who can afford to own their house, some must be for people who can afford to pay part of their house and others must be for people who can only afford to rent their house. The houses should be made of the best and healthiest materials and we should in every aspect strive for 'the most sustainable solutions'.

After a long search for the right land, we decided to build around an old four-winged farm, Munksøgaard, which lent its name to the community. We started a negotiation process with a non-profit housing associa-

Below: Planning division of the Danish Ministry of the Environment, on a one-day visit-cum-meeting at Munksøgaard. Foreground, from left, Suzanna Maxen of the Landsby 2000 ecovillage project, and chair of the Danish Association of Ecovillages, and Bent Pedersen, one of the heads of the planning division.

Above: Top left: Children playing with sand in front of their homes. No cars are allowed inside the ecovillage. Top right: Mikkel Strange (center) shows around Rashmi Mayur from IISF in India, and Sergio Lub from Friendly Favors in the USA. Above left: Torben (left) and Line (on the bike) of the Danish Association of Ecovillages (LØS) put in their few hours' worth of work during a LØS week end in April. Above right: a colorful sign was made of the grounds, for the entrance, after an ambulance was having difficulties finding the home of one of the residents. All photos: H. Jackson.

tion (which builds and owns houses for rent), and asked them to support the building the 60 rental dwellings. Later, we had to cancel these negotiations and start a new process with another non-profit housing association. The reason for this was mainly that they were not as impatient as we were to start building, and we felt that they did not really believe in the ecological solutions we wanted, like compost toilets and walls of clay. Thus we had to stop the co-operation to save the project. The second company was more willing to take some chances, which was absolutely necessary. In the striving towards 'future solutions' it is very often not possible to provide as much documentation for the quality of natural, alternative materials and solutions as for today's mainstream building practices. Therefore the technical solutions – e.g. how the wastewater is treated – are decided upon not only on a basis of documentation, but also on human intuition and most of all, on experience from other ecovillages. Because of this it is absolutely necessary that your partners really believe in the project.

Q: How did Munksøgaard establish a precedent for integrating the ecovillage concept into mainstream thinking?

Mikkel: Munksøgaard is an alternative theatre using mainstream actors. From the start, we chose to go for a traditional architecture with a homogenous look, where greenhouses, bay windows and color provided the necessary variation. Sizes of apartments and houses vary: they range between 30 m² (for a single room) and 110 m². I myself have a 78m² apartment for my wife and me and two children. In our case, the community facilities reduce the requirements for individual space. We spend a lot of time outside the home, but we have our own apartment. Our project can be used as a more generic model of sustainable living regarding buildings and community: people from housing associations and from other municipalities, as well as from the government (lately a division of the Ministry of the Environment) come to visit us when they are thinking about planning new zones. People are very interested in our idea of mixing different clusters.

We built with a mainstream developer, and a mainstream non-profit housing association. A very interesting aspect is the fact that our partners in the project have trusted our knowledge and intuition on ecological matters. They have both been interested in using this project to learn from, and to gather knowledge about possible solutions for a future sustainable society. I believe that a reason for this could be, that we have tried very hard to see things from their point of view, and help as much as we could during the whole process.

Joan Jackson playing with her sons, Christoffer and Benjamin. In the background, one of the rental clusters.

We cooperated with the municipality. By building Munksøgaard, we were helping the local government to build up the area of Trekroner. Our ecological project fitted in with local planning stipulations, which expressed an interest in creating a "green" zone. The mayor was very positive, and his enthusiasm trickled down through the organization. We received special treatment: we got the land a bit under the market price, and local government showed flexibility in interpreting rules. They helped us farm out some of the land, and individual officials gave us their private phone numbers in case we needed to call them in the evenings! Local government officials became our allies, and they kept their positive attitude: the neighboring land is now in the process of being sold on a similar basis, with a priority given to "green" housing. So we paved the way for others who want to increase flexibility in interpreting laws in favor of sustainable solutions, and identified areas where more tolerance or new rules are needed. We have recently been awarded a grant to report on the existing difficulties in establishing sustainable settlements, and to identify the laws which need changing and the areas in which increased flexibility is needed to allow for a more sustainable form of development.

Munksøgaard represents mainstream society in its makeup. There is respect for people's different focus: some want more privacy than others, some want community before all. Generally, we are more a cohousing than a commu-

nity. In the youth cluster, you see people try out landscaping options together in the garden. Around the private homes, there are small perfectly groomed garden plots with individual looks. Differences are interesting and pleasant. Our makeup mirrors the freedom of decision also found in mainstream society. We don't place too many demands on each other. We don't raise eyebrows at each other, but we offer possibilities, for example sharing cars or eating together in the community room.

Q: What ecological solutions did you implement?

Mikkel: We had to drop our dream of having composting toilets, due to particular regulations. We had to settle for toilets with urine separation. We are treating our household-wastewater locally, discharging the cleaned water into a neighboring brook. We are gathering rainwater, and using it for washing in the community houses. This enables us to use very little groundwater, and much less washing powder for the laundry. We have a local heating system, based on a combination of wood chips (combustion) and solar panels (water). The solar panels provide us with 50% of the energy used for water heating. Our houses are built out of wood, with inner walls made of clay stone (unburned bricks). We have three cars, two Fiats and a Berlingo, which are co-owned by 40 members of the community. We are hoping to keep our use of electricity, heating and water down at a very low level, compared to traditional houses, but this has yet to be proved. We do not believe that all our solutions necessarily are the solutions for a future sustainable society, but we have tried to take a step forward in every single aspect. The paints we used outdoors are based on linseed oil, and inside we use natural indoor paints. Our water treatment system can't tolerate non-organic elements, so there's no discussion there. For food consumption, people sometimes disagree. Our shopping group for communal meals agrees on 100% organic foods. Some other groups disagree based on availability and price, and the discussions are interesting.

Q: What do you count as your successes, and what did you not realize?

Mikkel: The fact that we managed to build rental, co-owned and privately-owned houses in the same project is very rare, although it seems the idea is spreading fast. We have a lot of laws and regulations in Denmark. Co-ops can only be made by special permission from the government and the number of permissions a year is very limited. Local heating and wastewater systems are not allowed close to the cities, because they compete with the public heating and wastewater systems. Putting up a toilet requires a water and discharge permission, which in principle cannot be given to a separating toilet. I could continue the list, but I guess this should suffice to show the amount of rules you have to deal with, when building ecologically in Denmark. So the mere fact that we got as far as we did is a success.

I also think our community spirit is a success. There are a lot of possibilities for community without any pressure. There are work groups where people can use their special talents, and ideas are being picked up and carried out extremely fast, which is thoroughly satisfying. We have celebrations, such as Sankt Hans on the longest day of the year, big screen evenings for the Melody Grand Prix and football matches. When people have problems, there is no sensationalizing; we support the people when they show a need for it, without prying. We're there to offer a shoulder or a hand when it's needed. Community acceptance creates self-acceptance.

Q: Is it right to say that your project is a social-ecological project? Do you have a cultural or a cultural or spiritual aspect included?

Mikkel: I would not say that we have a spiritual dimension. We are building a culture with our own traditions and habits and the spiritual aspect is not that distant, but it is not here yet. People here are very active and free when it comes to social or ecological initiatives, and we have a lot of new ideas and projects starting all the time. But when it comes to spiritual matters, people get so shy …

Q: Would you do it all over again if you knew beforehand how difficult it would be?

Mikkel: Of course I would do it all over again, and I am certain this goes for everybody out here. I love this place, because so many people get inspiration from our success. I find it very inspiring to live in a place where ideas can become initiatives in a flash, because people know that they can make a difference. I become proud when people are praising this place and the people here, for carrying Denmark a small step closer to true sustainability. It's also a great place for children, it's safe and it gives them a life close to nature.

Q: How much personal time did people spend on the creation of Munksøgaard?

Mikkel: The main creators have used 37 hours a week or more for four to five years. It's usually the same people who have all the details and the contacts, and who handle the economic aspect. This availability has helped us set the two-year timescale we worked to. Two years turned into five years, but we'd never have done it this fast if we hadn't pushed for two years. It did stress some people though.

Q: How do you see your future at Munksøgaard?

Mikkel: I am at a stage in my life where I'm not interested in being able to say exactly where I'll be in ten years. But I love hearing the people in the "older" cluster say that this is where they're going to be for the rest of their lives. It gives us a sense of stability. It's a gift.

mikkelstrange@hotmail.com

Below: Jytte Abildstrøm, Danish actress and environmental activist, turned this wagon into a children's theater. She lives in the senior housing cluster at Munksøgaard, and runs the Jytte Abildstrøm theater in Copenhagen.

Right: working in community: guests and residents build a playground for the children.

All photos pp. 160-163: Hildur Jackson.

The Social Benefits of Ecovillages

The Spirit of Community:
Creating the Optimal Learning Environment

by Rolf Jackson

Rolf Jackson initiated the Gaia Consciousness Institute (Denmark), and works with knowledge management. He also runs Oberion, an IT company, which developed Internet systems for GEN.

Introduction

Ecovillages are unique places where new cultures and lifestyles are evolving in a framework that fosters personal growth and a sense of connectedness. The ecovillage movement undoubtedly has some essential contributions to make to the future of mankind, and in this article I will try to look at these from the perspective of knowledge creation and cultural evolution.

Releasing the Human Genius

Business, universities and governments have all realized that the ability to create and manage knowledge is what will characterize tomorrow's winners. Those who can learn faster and put this knowledge into productive use will have a decisive edge over the competition.

In the realm of knowledge creation, it has been established that the whole is greater than the sum of the parts. Based on several years' research in the dynamics of organizations from a spiritual perspective, I have found that to achieve wholeness one must find the key to unlock the human heart, which in turn helps release the human potential for genius.

Ecovillages are pioneers of an integrative culture, which is able to create whole persons. Their philosophy is based on balancing all the natural realms (nature, human and spirit) and manifesting this balance in the daily rhythm. The awareness and culture that result from this approach are able to foster a connectedness to the greater whole.

This is important, because unlocking one's inner potential involves connecting to the source of creativity, which is essentially spirit. Many communities have shown that they can establish the right frameworks for this: the spirit of community facilitates the kind of growth in people that can release the human genius. And this genius is of essential importance to the mainstream, lending weight to the vision of communities as a new key institution in the future (alongside with business, universities and government).

The optimal knowledge culture

During our research on knowledge creation, and working from a theoretical perspective, we have identified cultural dynamics that optimize the learning potential in a group. We have named this the optimal knowledge culture, and a summary of our findings is shown in fig. 1.

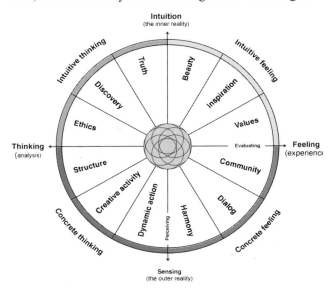

Figure 1: The optimal knowledge culture in relation to learning. The model is based on Jung's concepts. Source: Own research.

Our research has brought with it a realization that communities, especially those with a spiritual focus, have an ability to facilitate transformation in people, unmatched anywhere else; and that this transformation creates a culture which can optimize knowledge development, by releasing the genius in people.

When looking at the aspects which make the community spirit a relevant factor in creating an optimal knowledge culture, I have been able to discern two key elements: one is that the culture in communities embodies many of the aspects of the optimal knowledge culture (described in fig. 1), and therefore allows the true learning potential to unfold. The optimal knowledge culture is in many respects close to what we see in the more mature communities (such as Auroville, Damanhur and Findhorn), substantiating our findings. The other is the existential dimension of communities: community members have, on a deep existential level, committed themselves to each other and to serve the community in a spirit of caring and sharing. This fundamental commitment is an enabler for existential learning processes, which is not found to such a degree in other contexts.

So to sum this up, the community magic for enabling learning processes arises from a combination of a deep commitment to each other, to care for and serve the needs of others (other people, other beings and one's surroundings), and the manifestation of a creative context embodying the optimal knowledge culture.

Gaining Support

One of the hurdles for ecovillages and other communities to overcome before being able to share their knowledge with the world at large, is the need to communicate effectively about the benefits of integrating some of the ecovillages' community know-how in other parts of society. One aspect of this is placing the emphasis on how ecovillages provide a possible solution for current social crises through their community attitude. The other is to attract attention to the way in which ecovillages embody many of the elements of the optimal knowledge culture. At this stage many politicians and other leaders have been seen to misunderstand the idea of ecovillages as cozy, perfect and self-sufficient settlements. This has caused some to judge that the ecovillage solution would not deal with the general problems of society (at least within the foreseeable future).

Greater focus on the essence of community as a piece of valuable knowledge embedded in the ecovillage concept, and communication about this to a larger audience, would address possible misconceptions. There will be ever wider support for the ecovillage vision when ecovillages are seen not only as islands of sustainability, but also as dynamic centers of innovation which create tools, technologies and know-how that help address the systemic problems in society which are essentially due to a fragmented way of thinking perpetuated by the educational system in place. Awareness of the benefits of educational exchange with ecovillages is growing in many places around the world, but the community spirit aspect can be more consistently emphasized alongside the ecological know-how of ecovillages (which is being taught more and more widely in cooperation with universities).

Focusing on the living spirit

Ecovillages and cultural-spiritual communities hold an important key to the future: the ability to facilitate existential learning, in a way which cannot easily be duplicated in other contexts, and the potential to help solve many of society's dis-eases through a spirit of community.

Many ecovillages have developed useful and functional tools for creating and maintaining this spirit. These tools can be applied with success elsewhere. Societal entities (including families, schools, organizations etc.) would benefit greatly from adopting the principles of community spirit gleaned through the experiences and research of ecovillages over the years. For this reason, communities can become a central element in the future societal culture. They can inspire others by their inherent attitude of care and community, and the magic which they spin in social and learning environments.

rolf@oberion.com

The spirit of community at work at Findhorn, Scotland. Photo: ©Findhorn Visuals

Creating Partnerships

The Findhorn Foundation:
Cooperation with the United Nations

by May East

May East lives at Findhorn (Scotland), and is in charge of Findhorn's ecovillage education program. She also works for the International University in Brazil and represents Findhorn and GEN at the UN. Cooperation with National and International organizations is an important part of expanding the ecovillage concept as a planning paradigm. In this article, May East explains how Findhorn tackles this task.

Building alliances for a sustainable future

On December 8, 1997 the Findhorn Foundation was approved for association with the United Nations Department of Public Information. This recognition was a culmination of a series of official collaborations between the United Nations and the Findhorn Foundation. It was also sign of a great maturity of our community, which has been promoting principles of sustainable development as put forward by the major UN conferences of the last decade, including the environmental aspect of the Rio Earth Summit, the human settlements aspect of Istanbul, and the women's aspect of Beijing, thus providing a contemporary and evolving model of sustainable living. This association is a commitment on the part of the Findhorn Foundation "to disseminate information and raise public awareness about the purposes and activities and achievements of the United Nations and issues of global concern", related to sustainability, environment, peace, shelter and a new world order.

Non-governmental organizations eligible for association with UN must share the ideals of the United Nations Charter, operate on a not-for-profit basis, and demonstrate an interest in United Nations issues. In addition, they must have a proven ability to reach large or specialized audiences with well-developed information programs.

Our involvement with the United Nations occurs at a time when the global agenda has never been so varied, so critical and so complex. It is demanding of the international community of NGOs new approaches, new visions and new commitments of higher will. Whatever the field of service – human rights, humanitarian relief, sustainable development, international law, disarmament, poverty eradication, peace education – NGO's influence over the world scenario is incontestable. Nongovernmental organizations are creating new coalitions around emerging issues and are equipping themselves more and more for a new global era of transcultural diplomacy.

The United Nations is also undergoing an unprecedented transformation. It is reforming its structures, manage-ment and priorities in a drive towards greater coherence, agility and unity.

The cooperation between the United Nations and the NGO community can provide a bridge for communication between the people of the world and policy makers at the national and global levels. This cooperation has the potential to be a major vehicle for human evolution as it supports the process of putting current issues into a context of global interdependence.

The recognition of the Findhorn Foundation as an NGO gives wider exposure to us and allows the work of the Foundation to be made visible to a broader spectrum of people and organizations that under normal circumstances would not have the opportunity to know what we are doing. By becoming part of the global NGO community we are able to efficiently collaborate with like-minded organizations, weaving new alliances, while nourishing old and current ones. It is a great privilege and responsibility to be part of the larger action network, which supports the process of implementing the principles of the United Nations on Earth.

www.findhorn.org

The Findhorn Foundation specializes in high-quality training and information programs. Photo: Findhorn Visuals/May East.

The Findhorn Foundation chose this artistic representation as a symbol for their International conference on Earth Restoration education in April, 2002. It was placed on an outside wall as a welcome for participants. Photo: Hildur Jackson.

Idebanken, Norway

The Alternative Future project was started in 1981 in Scandinavia as a coalition of 100 grass roots movements (peace, women, ecological solidarity movements), with the purpose of creating a vision to solve the global, the social and the ecological problems in today's world. In 1987, Idebanken (The Bank of Ideas) was initiated as part of this project. Today the Bank of Ideas has a staff of ten plus three volunteers, and a turnover of 6.2 million NOK (check abbreviation) of which 3,5 million are granted by the Ministry of the Environment.

"The purpose of the Bank of Ideas is to support social change, whereby social goals, environment and resources are prioritized over material and economic considerations."

This has led to 3 main strategies:
To describe practical examples which promote sustainability, global solidarity, democracy or quality of life. Communication happens through the Internet, own publications and media, lectures, seminars and study tours, and via the library and information center of the Bank of Ideas.

To contribute to "new dialogues about the future". This implies placing long-term challenges and possibilities for change on the agenda, contributing to dialogue across groups and sectors, and using new tools that facilitate a democratic, creative and focused dialogue.

To make positive visions (future visions) known, create a debate around them, and contribute to new visions.

The Bank of ideas works with municipalities, the private sector and NGOs. Since 1994, the Local Agenda 21 has been the most important focus.

The daily leader of the Bank of Ideas is Kai Arman. Mads Nakkerud is responsible for seminars, Future Workshops, publications and information activities.

Idebanken@idebanken.no
www.idebanken.no

Ecovillage Networks

Making the Best Use of GEN's Network

by Lucilla Borio

Networks are a good support tool for people who are trying to establish ecovillages and communities across the world. In this chapter we bring you two concrete examples of how networks function and how they can be used by members.

Introduction

GEN – the Global Ecovillage Network is organized in three main regional secretariats based in Australia (GENOA) for Oceania and Asia, in the United States (Ecovillage Network of the Americas and GEN-Americas) for North and South America, and in Italy (GEN-Europe) for Europe, Africa and the Middle East. We also have two smaller sub-regional nodes in Sri Lanka (for South Asia) and in Turkey (for the Middle East). The Ecovillage Network of the Americas is organized in nine ECOs (Ecovillage Contact Offices), in Canada, Western US, Eastern US, Meso-America, Caribbean, Northern South America, Brazil, Southern South America, and the traveling ecovillage "La Carabana". GEN-Europe is formed by 15 national networks and many member ecovillages.

Each of the main regional offices has also specific tasks in international co-ordination: GEN-Europe supervises on the communications sector, GENOA co-ordinates the realization of trans-regional programs, GEN-Americas oversees structure development and fundraising. The GEN International Board is formed by 2 elected representatives from each region as voting members, plus other non-voting members or other people with specific functions, like website and newsletter co-ordination. It meets every 9 -12 months in different parts of the world. Given the huge distance that separates ecovillages from each other, we are exploring video conferences as a possibility for the future, even though face-to-face, heart to heart meetings have a different quality and cannot be replaced by technological means.

GEN's four musketeers, from left: Hamish Stewart (International Secretary until 1998), Albert Bates (ENA International), Max Lindegger and Declan Kennedy (chair of GEN for the first important years). Photo: GEN.

Each region has an autonomous governing body which rules over its budgets and activities; the GEN-Europe Council has five members and meets twice a year.

Internal communication is based mostly on email mailing lists, of which about 35 exist today. The "governing lists" (like the International Board and Regional Councils) have a decision-making policy that enables the members to know when and how a decision is made, and strengthens transparency within the structure.

The internet is a basic tool for our network, and the www.gaia.org website lists several hundred pages about ecovillage living across the globe. The GEN structure has since the beginning been largely financed by Gaia Trust, a Danish Charitable Foundation, and is presently developing an independent fundraising policy to support the growth of the organization. GEN-Europe has recently received a substantial grant from the Environmental Department General of the European Union.

How best to use the network

We advise all interested people to contact the regional office nearest them to get first-hand information about current initiatives. Our staff can send printed material and redirect searches to the appropriate office or ecovillage. Through the website one can find many addresses and descriptions (with photos) of ecovillages and networks in all continents, as well as a resource list which features articles and references on the most relevant topics related to sustainability (permaculture, alternative technology, ecological building, community dynamics etc.). We offer free space to ecovillages to publish their pages along with information on their courses, events and initiatives: the GEN content managers receive a constant flow of information which is transferred into the website to make it lively and attractive. National networks have also the possibility of setting up their own mailing lists in their language. However, we are well aware of the fact that few people from the southern hemisphere have access to this tool, so we invest a fair amount of time and resources in publications. GEN-Europe´s newsletter, for instance, is published via seven magazines in different European countries, and reaches over about 30.000 people in seven languages.

Through the secretariats one can keep track of when and where the networks meet, and can attend courses. This provides an immediate variety of benefits: to learn from direct experience and avoid the pitfalls which others have been through; exchange "favors", i.e. work with others who are good at doing things; it has a strengthening effect and gives you the reassuring feeling that you are not alone; it encourages exchange of visits among ecovillages and with newcomers. For instance, the last GEN-Europe assembly in Poland was combined with a Facilitation and Consensus course held by Bea Briggs of Ecovillage Huehuecoyotl in Mexico, and followed by a majestic ecovillage festival, which featured theatre plays, concerts and workshops, with the release of a music CD.

The European *Ecovillage Travels* program connects member ecovillages with ecotourists, and will offer organized tours to reduce overheads for ecovillages while facilitating the experience for individual guests. It offers visitors the chance to see a few of the many aspects of our network, becoming part of our "work in progress".

Newsletters, magazines and printed material in general are a fundamental communications tool, a physical proof of existence and validity of our vision and mission. They spread information to the wider public and facilitate interconnection among activists. Unlike the newspapers available at the average news- stand, we aim at circulating information which positively affects people's perception, producing at the same time useful material to hand out to authorities, local communities, potential partners and donors willing to support the cause of sustainable living on the planet.

A clear message we receive from our member ecovillages is that belonging to a larger network enhances their credibility. In fact, GEN is accredited by the UN as a consultative member of the ECOSOC (Economic and Social Commission), and this adds a different weight to our actions worldwide. The regional secretariats represent their national networks and individual ecovillages, and speak on their behalf at many conferences and conventions, presenting videos and slide shows. National networks like the Danish LØS and the English EVNUK have contacted officials on behalf of their members to lobby in favor of the application of Agenda 21 and advocate for more support to sustainable human settlements. As a member of GEN, you have representatives who speak on your behalf in special meetings like the State of the World Forum and other important occasions.

Another positive effect of belonging to an organization like GEN is that it can connect you with other networks on a global scale, making you a part of a larger group. It can extend to the wide "Cultural Creatives" movement, which possibly includes several million people; it can be a bridge to the LETS systems, the Global Clearinghouse created by Bernard Lietaer, and the Friendly Favors alternative economics system (see article page 76). It also has connections with the anti-globalization movement, where it can offer a positive alternative to today's socio-economic challenges and represent a different pattern of development.

info@gen-europe.org

The Global Ecovillage Network was started at the 1995 conference on sustainable communities at Findhorn, Scotland, with this core group of members. **In the picture, first row from left:** *John Talbot (Findhorn), Max Lindegger (Crystal Waters), Declan Kennedy (Lebensgarten), Albert Bates (The Farm), Vladen Liavdanska (Sortevala, Russia).* **Second row:** *Patric Gibben (The Farm), Hamish Stewart (Gaia Trust), Robert Gilman (In Context Institute), Stephan Wik (Findhorn), Ross Jackson (Gaia Trust), Judy Buhler (Findhorn), Marily Mehlman (Sweden), Diane Gilman (In Context Magazine), Jillian Conrad, Linda Joseph and Kailash (EarthArt).* **Third row:** *Andrea Barsos (Gyurufu), David Bienn (Russia), Bela Borsos (Gyurufu), Kai Hansen (Hjortshøj), Hildur Jackson (Fjordvang), Alexander Mehlman (Sweden), Robert Tap (Crystal Waters). Photo: GEN.*

The Ecovillage Network of the Americas - ENA

by Linda Joseph

The Ecovillage Network of the Americas covers North, South and Meso-America, and the Carribbean. Linda Joseph is ENA's President. She lives and works at EarthArt ecovillage in Colorado, USA.

The mission of the Ecovillage Network of the Americas (ENA) is: "To engage the peoples of the Americas in a common effort to join the global transformation towards an ecologically, economically, and culturally sustainable future."

Everyone involved in ENA – many volunteers from throughout North, Central and South America – are united in this mission, though we come from diverse cultures, societies, climates, economies, spiritualities and personal experiences, and we speak different languages. This diversity is also reflected in the Global Ecovillage Network's other regions – GEN Europe and GEN Oceania & Asia, perhaps even more so. Communications, the lifeblood of our work, is also one of our greatest challenges!

The ecovillage networks exist to support communications between ecovillages, interested individuals, related organizations, institutions and agencies, so that those working toward a sustainable world can do so more quickly and effectively together. By enhancing the flow of information, ideas, questions, and solutions we are building the network's capacity as an effective clearinghouse for ecovillage and sustainable living resources.

When ENA convened its first Council of the Americas in 1999, with two representatives from each of ENA's nine regions plus the GEN Secretary for the Americas – nineteen Council seats altogether – we came face to face with this challenge. We had a tool at that first meeting which was a potent force in unfettered communication – a grant for simultaneous interpreters and rental equipment, which enabled everyone present to express themselves in their own language and style. Our translation kit consisted of 20 or more headsets and wireless receivers and two wireless microphone headsets for the interpreters. With everyone able to listen in their native language, the psychosocial barriers of our differences were minimized, which resulted in an extraordinary opportunity to build understanding and trust, allowing us to focus constructively on our common work. ENA is seeking funds to purchase (or receive a donation of) interpretation equipment, so that at our working meetings, we can always have the benefit of direct and clear communications.

Above: ENA members in Columbia, bathing in the Gulf (2000). Photo: Kailash.

Another tool which has supported both our solidarity and effective communications is consensus decision-making and facilitation. By learning these skills ourselves, and by having neutral, professional consensus facilita-

Below: EarthArt ecovillage in Colorado, Linda Joseph's home and the location of the ENA Central Office. Photo: Albert Bates.

tors for our decision-making meetings, we have cultivated an environment of inclusiveness and cooperation. This allows us to meet, exchange ideas and make organizational decisions efficiently and in an equal and aligned way.

Communications between annual meetings is a different challenge. Current translation programs are inadequate for deep and meaningful discussions on email. We are reliant upon a small group of translation volunteers so our most important business is accessible in the main languages in the Americas – English, Spanish, Portuguese and French. ENA is publishing its biannual Electronic Newsletter, and its biannual newspaper, *Ecovillages*, in the four major languages of our hemisphere.

Information management systems are key to communications. Besides the Ecovillage Directories, Resource database and Calendars of Events that GEN offers on the Web (www.gaia.org) each region of GEN uses various listserves, databases and publications to spread the word about ecovillage living, and to assist Councils, volunteers and project committees in communicating. For example, ENA is establishing listserves for volunteer workers in each of the nine Americas regions, and has Council and committee lists for taking care of business.

The ecovillage networks continue to pioneer and build this framework for communications, so that information on how to live sustainably can flow faster and more easily, and our movement can blossom throughout even more cultures and contexts.

linda@ecovillage.org

Top: ENA members in Columbia, at the home of Claudio Madaune of the Reserva Integral Sasardi. Far right, standing, Albert Bates and third from right, standing, Linda Joseph.

Middle row left: Claudio Madaune and his partner Luisa, middle, with local women in Colombia. Middle row top right: Street theater performed by a member of La Caravana, the traveling section of the Huehuecoyotl ecovillage (Mexico). Middle row bottom right: ENA members at EarthArt ecovillage in Colorado, 1999. Photo: courtesy Albert Bates. Right: "Hydro group", ENA members working on a water project. Photos: ENA.

EcoVillage @ Ithaca
An Envisioning Plan

EcoVillage at Ithaca
NY, USA

The Ecovillage at Ithaca (EVI) in New York State (USA) was started in 1991. It covers 176 acres of land, of which 80% is intended to be left open for bio-diversity and recreation. EVI is one of the most mainstream initiatives we know of in the USA, with multiple cohousing neighborhoods in the making. The first cohousing, "Frog", with 30 homes, creates a happy community life for its residents (20% of whom are of Hispanic, African and Asian origins). The second, "Song", is being built now, with 12 houses already in use. It will be finished by the end of 2002--including some strawbale constructions, compost toilets, and photovoltaics. The third neighborhood is planned for 2003-4. A ten-acre organic farm runs a Community Supported Agriculture scheme, and has 150 subscribers (the EVI newsletter recently said that no more subscriptions can be taken this year). They feed 1000 people each week. They also have a five-acre berry farm. A non-profit organization is now also creating new projects and occupations on the spot. There is a sustainability education center placed at the heart of the village, which cooperates with Cornell University (20.000 students) and Ithaca College (8.000 students). The center also cooperates with EcoYoff in Senegal, via Cornell University. The EVI newsletter circulates information about the project. EVI has received a $ 112,000 grant for 6 homes in a low income group development.

Left: The envisioning plan for the 176-acre Ithaca site calls for 100-150 houses, with 80% of the land left as open space. Housing is built in clusters such as the first cohousing neighborhood by architect Jerold Weisburd (below left and right).

Top row, right; man with child on his back, making his way toward the common house at the end of the pedestrian street. Photo: Laura Beck. Above left: West Haven Farm, with Jen and John Bokær-Smith, the farmers, who sell their extra produce at the Ithaca Farmers Market. Photo: Mary Webber. Above Center: Cornell Rural Sociology graduate class in environmental Management (students from seven countries who came to EVI for two class sessions). The students learned about Community Supported Agriculture by visiting West Haven Farm, and helping out there. Photo: Liz Walker. Above right: Students from Hobart-Smith College working on the farm. Below left: Annual community Maypole dance at EVI. Photo: Nancy Brown. Below center: Water fun in the EVI pond on a summer day. Photo: Courtesy EVI. Below right: "Guys baking pies". This is a much-loved annual celebration in which neighborhood men and boys pick wild blackberries from the land, and then bake pies. The whole neighborhood is then invited to eat the "fruits of the land". Photo: Jared Jones.

Why Ecovillages and Localization?

Epilogue

by Helena Norberg-Hodge

As the effects of economic policies that ignore the needs of people and the planet become glaringly apparent, rebuilding community and local economies becomes more and more urgent. Today's global economy is mostly made up of speculative investors and giant transnational corporations which, by their very nature, have to generate maximum profits in as short a time as possible. In an era of absentee ownership and 'foreign direct investment', there is little room for social, ecological, or spiritual values. The result is rising social and environmental breakdown.

However even though business and government leaders continue to push their outdated economic models on the world, resistance is growing by leaps and bounds. New coalitions are bringing together labor unions, environmentalists and farmers from the developed and developing worlds alike. This growing resistance is further strengthened by thousands of grassroots initiatives that are reweaving the fabric of community, restoring ecosystems and rebuilding local economies, of which ecovillages are some of the most holistic and therefore most important. These smaller-scale communities nurture more intimate relations among people and ensure that everyone is seen, heard and recognized – providing a sense of individual identity that is lacking in the anonymity and isolation of mass society. When people live in smaller-scale social and economic units, where mutual support is necessary, the human capacity for caring and kindness is enhanced. As a consequence the individual – including very importantly the children as well as the aged – experience the joys of a more loving environment.

Ecovillages also encourage a sense of connection and responsibility to the natural world, which goes far beyond a reduction in the use of natural resources. They give the world community an altogether new development vision with different economic underpinnings, energy use, social structures and values from those of industrial society. Ecovillages provide models for living close to the land and in community with one another – a vision that is inspiring for the increasing numbers of people who long to live in a way that is spiritually rewarding, as well as ecologically sustainable.

Right: Helena Norberg-Hodge (foreground, left) attends a women's meeting in Ladakh, where she actively supports the preservation of local culture through her work with ISEC, the International Society for Ecology and Culture, for twenty years.

Resources

Books are listed in 15 sections, following the sustainability circle (see page 4). We also list:
Videos
Magazines
Internet portals
Ecovillages (GEN offices)
Building and energy centers

Books and Catalogues:

We recommend that our readers get hold of local book catalogues as our ability to find and evaluate the overwhelming amount of books covering the 15 dimensions of this publication is limited. We have restricted ourselves to English language books.

Catalogues

Natural House Catalogue
by David Pearson
Part One features 100 pages covering waterpower to worm bins, air ionisers to Feng Shui. A US source book for architects, builders and designers. Illustrated throughout.
www gaiabooks.org

Earth Repair Catalogue No 6. Dec 2001, 47 pages. Published by Permanent Publications. Permaculture, gardening, composting, wildlife in gardens, wild plants, mushrooms, fruit trees, berries, chickens, hedges, seed saving, building, alternative energy, water treatment, crafts, human scale economy, community, conflict resolution, kids, and much more.
Get a free copy:
orders@permaculture.co.uk
www. Permaculture.co.uk.

CAT, Centre for Alternative Technology, Wales, UK. Approximately 50 in-house publications. www.cat.org.uk. mail.order@cat.org.uk

Earthscan Catalogue
New books on cities and communities. www.earthscan.co.uk. earthinfo@earthscan.co.uk

Green Books
Mail order catalogue including many ecobuilding books. Distribute Chelsea Green books in the UK and Europe.
www.greenbooks.co.uk

Jade Mountain Catalogue.
Building a Sustainable World. 256 pages, 8000 products, price: £9. Alternative energy Products. Energy Efficient Appliances. Conservation and Ecology Products. Water pumping, storage and purification, lighting, heating and cooling.
www.jademountain.com
info@jademountain.com

Fellowship for Intentional Communities (FIC), USA. 134 titles www.store.ic.org

Amazon.com
www.amazon.com

Chelsea Green
A wide range of books on sustainable living.
www.chelseagreen.com

Books

Ecological

Permaculture, Ecovillage Design

Stormy Weather: 101 Solutions to Global Climate Change. Guy Dauncey and Patrick Mazza. Distributed in the UK by Jon Carpenter Books. English and Italian. carpenter@oxfree.com
www.earthfuture.com

Bamberton
www.earthfuture.com/bamberton

After The Crash
The Emergence of the Rainbow Economy, by Guy Dauncey, Green Print, 1989

Permaculture, A Designer's Manual, Bill Mollison, 1988.
www. permaculture.co.uk

Earth Users' Guide to Permaculture. Rosemary Morrow, 1993
Ecovillages and Sustainable Communities
In Context Institute, 1991.
www.incontext.org

Ecovillages and Sustainable Communities
Findhorn Press, 1995

Designing Sustainable Communities: Learning from Village Homes, Judy and Michael Corbett. Island Press, USA, 2000.

Designing Ecological Settlements, by Margrit and Declan Kennedy. Dietrich Reimer Verlag, Berlin, 1997.

Icons of Garden Design
Caroline Holmes, Prestel, UK 2001

Creating Sustainable Cities
Herbert Girardet. Green Books/ Schumacher Society, 1999

Eco-cities, Building Cities in Balance with Nature. Richard Register and Hazel Henderson, 2001

Saving the Environment
Ted Trainer, 1998.
ISBN 0 86840 648 1

Places of the Soul
Architecture and Environmental Design as A Healing Art, Christopher Day, 1993. Thorsons, London.

From Eco-cities to Living Machines
John Todd and Nancy Todd.

The Nature of Design: Ecology, Culture and Human Intention. David Orr, 2002
www.oberlin.edu/newsservice

Ecological Building, Renewable Energy and Local Watercare

Earth to Spirit, In Search of Natural Architecture, David Pearson. Gaia Books 1994/2000

The Gaia Natural House Book: Creating a Healthy and Ecologically Sound Home David Pearson, Gaia Books 2000.
www gaiabooks.co.uk.

New Organic Architecture, The Breaking Wave. David Pearson. Gaia Books Ltd.UK

Rudolf Steiner's Building Impulse and Organic Architecture, Peter van der Ree. Indigo, 1999

Recollection and Change
Ecological Architecture. Kirsten Klein, Inger Klingenberg, 1995.

Third International Eco-Cities Conference Report. From the conference at Yoff, Senegal, in January 1996. Edited by Joan Bokear, Chris Canfield, and Richard Register

EcoCity Builders,
5427 Telegraph Ave., W2, Oakland, CA 94609.

Energy Efficient Building, The Best of Fine Housebuilding. 29 articles from the American Homebuilding Magazine covering a wide range of subjects. A must for builders.
www.permaculture.co.uk

New Independent Home. People and Houses that Harvest the Sun, the Wind and Water. Michael Potts.
www.permaculture.co. uk

Simply Build Green. A technical guide to the ecological houses at Findhorn. John Talbott 1995. Findhorn Press

Adobe and Rammed Earth Buildings
Paul Graham McHenry, Jr., 1989 University of Arizona Press,

The Adobe Story, Paul Graham McHenry, Jr., University of New Mexico Press, 1998

The Alternative Building Sourcebook, Steve Chapell, Fox Maple Press, 1998

Alternative Construction, edited by Lynne Elizabeth and Cassandra Adams, John Wiley and Sons, 2000

Serious Straw Bale: A Home Construction Guide. Building in humid climates.Paul Lacinski and Michael Bergeron Chelsea Green, 2000

The Art of Natural Building
edited by Joseph Kennedy
New Society

The Beauty of Straw Bale Homes Athena and Bill Steen, Chelsea Green, 2000

Buildings of Earth and Straw
Bruce King, P.E., Ecological Design Press, 1996

Build It With Bales
Matts Myhrman and S.O. MacDonald, second edition, 1997

The Natural House
Daniel Chiras
Distr. Chelsea Green, 2000

The Rammed Earth House
David Easton,
Distr. Chelsea Green, 1996

Straw Bale Building
Chris Magwood, Peter Mack, New Society Publishers, 2000

The Straw Bale House
Athena and Bill Steen, David Bainbridge. Chelsea Green, 1994

Ceramic Houses, Nader Khalili, Harper and Row, 1986

The Earth Builders' Encyclopedia Joseph Tibbets, Southwest Solar Adobe School, 1989

Talking Cedars
www.earthfuture.com

Ferrocement Water Tanks: A cheap method for long lasting construction.S.B. Watts.
www.permaculture.org.uk

Renewable Energy

Solare Weltwirtschaft
(A Solar World Economy, 1999) by Hermann Scheer, translated into Chinese, Spanish, Danish and French, and an English version is under way.

Anwalt der Sonne (Hermann Scheer, Advocate for the Sun, Hermann Scheer, 1998): A compilation of writings on Hermann Scheer. Published in 1998.

Solar Cookers International
sci@igc.org
www.solarcooking.org

The Humanure Handbook #2
Joseph Jenkins.
Chelsea Green

Lifting the Lid: An Ecological Approach to toilet Systems. Peter Harper and Louise Halestrap. CAT

A Chinese Biogas Manual
Translated from Chinese by Michael Crook.
www.permaculture.org.uk

Sewage Solutions: Answering the Call of Nature. Grant, Moodie and Weedon. A guide to the many solutions to household black and grey waste, decomposition methods and installation CAT

Power Plants: An Introduction to Biofuels. For anyone seeking alt. fuels in the home, on the farm, in transport and industry.

Solar Electricity: A Practical Guide to Designing and Installing Small Photovoltaic Systems, Simon Roberts

Energy Without End
Friends of the Earth. On modern renewable energy systems.
www.cat.org.uk/shopping

Local Watercare

From Eco-Cities to Living Machines Principles of Ecological Design.
J. and N. Todd.
The book sets out the emerging precepts of biological design and then shows how they can be incorporated into the redesign of communities.

Living Water
Victor Schauberger's work with energy transformation of the spiral forces of water and air Olof Alexandersson

Local Organic Food Production, Consumption and Recirculation

The Complete Book of Self-sufficiency, John Seymour.
www permaculture.co.uk

One Straw Revolution, and: **The Natural Way of farming** Masanobu Fukuoka
www.permaculture.co.uk

From the Ground Up:
Rethinking Industrial Agriculture. Peter Goering, Helena Norberg-Hodge, and John Page. Zed Books /ISEC

Bringing the Food Economy Home. The social, ecological and economic benefits of local food production.
www.isec.org.uk

Keeping Food Fresh
Terre Vivante
with Eliot Coleman
Chelsea Green

The Organic Baby and Toddler Cookbook
Daphne Lambert and Tanyia Maxted-Frost. Green Books.

The Organic Baby Book: How to plan and raise a healthy child.Tanyia Maxted-Frost. Green Books

Wilderness, Biodiversity and Earth Restoration

The Restoration of Land: Ecology and Reclamation of Derelict and Degraded Land.
UCA Press 1980

The Ages of Gaia: A Planetary Healer. Gaia Publications 1991

Earthday Guide to Planet Repair Dennis Hayes, 2000.
www.islandpress.org

Restoring the Earth: How Americans are working to renew our damaged environment.
John J. Berger.
Random House, 1985.

Restoring the Earth: Visionary Solutions from the Bioneers. Kenny Ausuber
Published by Chelsea Green

Green Businesses, Lifecycle Analyses

The Ecology of Commerce:
A Declaration of Sustainablity. Paul Hawken, 1993

Small is Beautiful, Big is Subsidised. Steven Gorelick, Helena Norberg-Hodge et al.

Social

Building Community Decision-Making Conflict Resolution

Eurotopia: Directory of Intentional Communities and Ecovillages in Europe
www.eurotopia.de

Ecovillages and Communities in Australia and New Zealand. Global Ecovillage Network Oceania/Asia inc. (GENOA) www oceania.ecovillages.org

Directory of Ecovillages in Europe Barbro Grindheim and Declan Kennedy
www.gen-europe.org

Communities Directory
600 North American and 100 international communities.
FIC (Fellowship of Intentional Communities) www.ic.org

Diggers and Dreamers
Guide to Communal Living Jonathan How et al., 2002
www.permaculture.co.uk

Creating Sustainable Cities
Herbert Girardet,
Green Books

Cohousing: A Contemporary Approach to Housing Ourselves Cathryn McCamant
and Charles Durett.
www.permaculture.co.uk

Cohousing: Ecovillages and Sustainable Communities Chris and Kelly Scott Hansson. www.cohousingresources.com

And we are doing it! Building an Ecovillage Future.
J.T. Ross Jackson, 2000
www.ross-jackson.com

Shared Visions, Shared Lives: Communal Living Around the Globe, by Bill Metcalf Findhorn Press, 1996

Village Wisdom, Future Cities
Richard Register and Brady Peeks. Material from third ecocity conference in Yoff, Senegal, 1996

Calling the Circle
The First and Future Culture. Christina Baldwin.
Swan Raven, 1994

The Different Drum:
The Creation of True Community, the First Step to world Peace, by Scott Peck
Arrow Books, 1987

Builders of the Dawn:
Community Lifestyles in a Changing World.
Corinne Mc Laughlin and Gordon Davidson
Ten Speed Press, 1986

Cities of Light, Donald Walters. Ananda Community, Assisi

Great Meetings: How to Facilitate Like a Pro
Dee Kelsey and Pam Plumb www. ic.org

Creating Harmony: Conflict Resolution in Communities edited by Hildur Jackson Permanent Publications/Gaia Trust

Sitting in the Fire:
Large group transformation using conflict and diversity. Arnold Mindell.
Lao Tse Press, 1998

Facilitator's Guide to Participatory Decision-Making Sam Kaner el al.
New Society, 1996.

Introduction to Consensus
Beatrice Briggs, available from the author, also in Spanish briggsbea@aol.co.

On Conflict and Consensus
C T. Butler and Amy Rothstein (spiral bound, 1987)
www.consensus.net

Building United Judgement:
A Handbook for Consensus Michael Avery et al.
Reprinted by FCI, 1999
www.ic.org

A Manual for Group Facilitators
Brian Auvine et al.
FIC, 1999 www.ic.org

The Skilled Facilitator
Practical Wisdom for Developing Effectice Groups Robert Schwarz
www.josseybass.com

Non-violent Communication
Marshall Rosenberg, 1998 Puddle Dancer Press

Zukunftwerkstatten
about Robert Jungk
Hofman und Campe.

Creating Community Everywhere:
Schaffer and Aunudsen, Jeremy Tarcher/ Pedigree Books, 1993

The Book of Games for the Whole family
Putnam Group

The Book of Games and Warm-Ups for Group Leaders
Gale Centre Publications

*Healthy Lifestyle
Preventive Medicine
Complementary Medicine*

Medical Marriage:
Partnerships between Orthodox and Complementary Medicine
Cornelia Featherstone, 1997

Energy Foods
Kirsten Hartvig, Nic Rawley 2000

Emotional Intelligence:
Why It Can Matter More than IQ
Daniel Goleman

Dark Night, Early Dawn:
Steps to a Deep Ecology of Mind
Christopher M. Bache

Gesundheit!
Patch Adams, 1998
Vermont Healing Press

Perfect Health: The Complete Mind and Body Guide
Deepak Chopra, 1990

Health and Community
Mike Money (ed)
Green Books, 1993

*Education
Communication
Transportation*

Sustainable Education:
Steven Sterling
Green Books
Schumacher Briefing

Tomorrow's Children:
A Blueprint for Partnership Education in the 21st Century,
Riane Eisler, 2000

Nizioni:
The Higher Self in Education
Chris Griscom.

**Sri Aurobindo
and Mother on Education**
www.auroville.org

Natural Learners
Christine Gable, 2002.

Pedagogy of the Earth
Carlos Hernandez
and Rashmi Mayur, 1999.

Earth In Mind:
On Education, Environment and the Human Prospect
David W. Orr, 1994

Divorce Your Car
Katie Alvord
New Society Publishers

*Modernizing Welfare
Balance Male/female*

The Gendered Atom
Genderless science
Theodor Roszak
Conari Press/Green Books

Cultural Creatives
Paul Ray and Ruth Sherry Anderson, 2000
Harmony Books

The Reinvention of Work:
A new vision of livelihood for our time, Matthew Fox, 1994

*Localization
Complementary
Currencies*

The Future of Money and the Mystery of Money
Bernard Lietaer.

Natural Capitalism:
The Next Industrial Revolution.
Paul Hawken, Amory Lovins and Hunter Lovins

Beyond Globalisation:
Shaping a Sustainable Economy
Hazel Henderson

The Post-Corporate World
David Korten, 1998

The Case against the Global Economy, Jerry Mander & Edward Goldsmith (eds), 1996

Shaping Globalisation: Civil Society, Cultural Power, and Threefolding, Nicanor Perlas

The Ecology of Money
Richard Douthwaite
Green Books

Short Circuit: Strengthening Local Economics for Security in an Unstable World
Richard Douthwaite, 1996
Lilliput Press/Green Books

Localization:
A Global Manifesto
Colin Hines, 2000

Interest and Inflation-Free Money
Margrit Kennedy, 1995

Our Ecological Footprint
Mathis Wackernagel and William Rees
www.permaculture.co.uk

Small is Beautiful: Economics as if the Earth Really Mattered
EF Schumacher,1989, Harper and Row, NY, USA.

Eco-Economy: Building an Economy for the Earth. Lester Brown, Earthscan, 2001 +44 1903 828503

Spiritual/Cultural

*Creativity
Personal Development*

Cultural Creatives:
How 50 million People Are Changing the World.
Paul Ray, Sherry Ruth Andersen.

The Life We Are Given
Integral transformative practice
M. Murphy, George Leonard
www.itp-life.com

What Really Matters
Searching for Wisdom in America, Tony Schwartz

The Adventure of Self Exploration, Vol. I-IV
Stanislav Grof, 1987-2002

Essential Spirituality
Roger Walsh

Integral Psychology
Ken Wilber
www.shambhala.org

Toward a Transpersonal Ecology
Warwick Fox, Green Books

The Seven Spiritual Laws of Success
Deepak Chopra, 1995

Manifestation, The Inner Art
David Spangler

Flight into Freedom
Eileen Caddy
Findhorn Press, 1988

Choices of Love
Dorothy Maclean
Lindisfarne Books, 1998

*Spirituality
Oneness with Nature*

Science and Spirituality:
A Quantum Integration
Amit and Maggie Goswami.

Gaia - The Next Big Idea,
Mary Midgley
Demos, 2001

Thinking Like a Mountain
Towards a Council of All Beings. John Seed et al., 1988.

The Power of Now
Eckhart Tolle, 1997
Hodder and Stoughton

Religious Feminism and the Future of the Planet
Rita Gross, Rosemary R. Ruether
Continuum, USA

Mother Earth Spirituality:
Native American Paths to Healing Ourselves and our World
McGaa (Ed), Eagle Man
Harper, 1990

All the Marvellous Earth
Krishamurti
www.permaculture.co.uk

Sahaj Marg
Litterature
www.srcm.org

Religions of the World and Ecology
John Grim, Mary E. Tucker, 1994

The Heart of the Buddha's Teaching:
Transforming Suffering into Peace, Joy and Liberation
Thich Nhat Hahn, 1999
www.amazon.com.

How to Practice:
The Way to a Meaningful Life
The Dalai Lama, 2001

The Magus of Strovolos and **Hommage to the Sun** and **Fire in the Heart**. Three books about a Christian Mystic in Cyprus, Stylianos Atteshlis by Kyriakos Markides, 1984-1991. Arkana, The Penguin Group

The Esoteric Teachings
The Stoa Series
Stylianos Atteshlis1987,1992

*Celebrating Life
Cultures and
Natural Cycles*

Ancient Futures:
Learning from Ladakh
Helena Norberg-Hodge
Sierra Club Books, 1991

The World and the Wild,
David Rothenberg and Marta Ulvaeus
University of AZ Press, 2001.

The Book of Elders: The Life Stories and Wisdom of Great American Indians.
Harper, 1994

Festivals in the New Age,
David Spangler. Findhorn Foundation, 1975

Of Water and the Spirit:
Ritual, Magic and Initiation in the Life of an African Shaman.
Malidoma Some, Arkana, 1994

Eco-geography
Andreas Suchanke.
Floris Books, 2001

The Great Work
Thomas Berry, 2001

The Dream of the Earth
Thomas Berry, 1990

Earth in Mind and **Ecological Literacy**
David Orr

*Holistic Worldview
Science and Philosophy*

Ethics for the New Millennium
The Dalai Lama

Zoence, A Science of Life
Peter Dawkins, UK.

A Pattern Language
by C. Alexander et al.
Oxford University Press, 1977

The Web of Life: A synthesis of mind and matter and **The Hidden Connections:**
A Science for Sustainable Living
Fritjof Capra

New Metaphysical Foundations of Modern Science
Willis Harman with Jane Clarc

Genetic Engineering:
Dream or Nightmare
Mae-wan Ho

Margins of Reality
Robert Jahn with Brenda Dunne

Order Out of Chaos
Ilya Prigogine, Isabelle Stengers

The Conscious Universe
Dean Radin

New Science of Life
Rupert Sheldrake

Sustainable Settlements
Barton, Davis, Guise
University of the West
of England
The Local Government
Management Board, 1995

Global Healing:
Essays and Interviews on
Structural Violence, Social
Development and Spiritual
Transformation.
Sulak Sivaraksa, 1999

The Participatory Mind:
A New Theory of Knowledge
and of the Universe
Henryk Skolimowski, 1995

Passion of the Western Mind
Richard Tarnas, 1991

Sex, Ecology, Spirituality
and **A Theory of Everything**
Ken Wilber, 2002
www.Shambhala.org

Kindred Visions
Ken Wilber et al.
Shambhala Press, 2002

Spiral Dynamics:
Mastering Values, Leadership
and Change
Don Edward Beck
Christopher C. Cowan
Blackwell Publishers, 1996

This I believe
E.F.Schumacher
Green Books

The Way:
An Ecological Worldview
Edward Goldsmith
Green Books, 1992

The Fabric of the World:
Towards a Philosophy
of Environment
Maurice Ash
Green Books

**Thomas Merton
and Thich Nhat Hanh**
(from Plum Village, France)
Engaged Spirituality in an Age
of Globalization
Robert King
Continuum Publications, 2001

Kali Yuga Odyssey:
A Spiritual Journey
J.T.Ross Jackson
www.ross-jackson.org

*Localization
Bioregional Politics
Resisting Globalization*

**When Corporations
Rule the World**
David Korten
Earthscan Publications, 1995

Biopiracy:
The Plunder of Nature and
Knowledge
Vandana Shiva
Green books, 1998

Stolen Harvest:
The Hijacking of the Global
Food Supply,
Vandana Shiva, 2000

Staying Alive:
Women, Ecology
and Development.
Zed Books

**The Violence of
the Green Revolution**
Zed Books

The Weight of the World:
Social Suffering
in Contemporary Society
Pierre Bordieu et al.
Polity Press, 1999, 2002

Globalization:
The Human Consequences
Bygmunt Bauman
Polity Press 1998,1999, 2000

The Co-creators Handbook:
Birthing a Co-creative Culture
Connect@globalfamily.net

And We Are Doing It
Personal story of Gaia Trust and
the Global Ecovillage Network
J.T. Ross Jackson, 2000
Robert D. Reed Publishers
www.ross-jackson.com

Mahatma Gandhi:
An Apostle of Applied
Human Ecology
T.N. Khoshoo, 1995
Tata Energy Research Institute

**Ecology into Economics
Won't Go**:
or Life is not a Concept
Stuart McBurney
Green Books, 1998

Quality of Life Indicators
Calvert-Henderson

The Breakdown of Nations
Leopold Kohr with new Fore-
words by Neal Ascherson and
Richard Body
Green Books

Books from Ecovillages

Ancient Futures:
Learning From Ladakh
Helena Norberg-Hodge
Sierra Club Books, 1991
www.isec.org.uk

Is It Utopia Yet?
Twin Oaks Community
Kat Kinkade

Damanhur:
The Real Dream
Jeff Merrifield
www.damanhur.org

The Kingdom Within (Findhorn)
Alex Walker
Findhorn Press, 1994

Voices from the Farm
Rupert Fike

Sarvodaya, Sri Lanka
Collected Works, Vol. I-VI
A.T. Ariyaratne
www.sarvodaya.org.

The Auroville Adventure:
On environmental work, village
action, spirituality,
economy and education
www.auroville.org

Gaviotas:
A Village to Reinvent the World.
Alan Weismann.

Living Lightly: Travels
in Post-Consumer Society
Walter and Dorothy Schwarz.
Jon Carpenter Books

Sustainable Communities
Lessons from
Aspiring Ecovillages
Malcolm Hollick
Christine Conelly
Praxis Education.

Videos and CDs

Ecovillages in Europe (CD)
A commitment to our Future
Agnieszka Komoch
Eduard Gonzales
www.gen-europe.org

**Ecovillages
The Dream of the Dreamers**
Documentary on the 2001
ecovillage meeting in Poland
Michel Tarkowski
www.gen-europe.org

Progress? A New Millennium
Peter Engberg
peter@transformedie.dk

Local Futures:
Beyond the Global Economy
Helena Norberg-Hodge
www.isec.org.uk

The Gaia Theory
James Lovelock
www.permaculture.co.uk

The Forest Gardener:
A tribute to Robert Hart
www.permaculture.co.uk

Farming with Nature:
A case of succesful
temperate permaculture
www.permaculture.co.uk

The Future of Paradise:
The European Ecovillage
Experience
David Kanaley
Byron Shire Council
Ph: +61 2 66267000

Auroville (Interactive CD)
Encyclopedia on Auroville
and Integral Yoga
www.aviusa.org

More videos about ecovillages:
Crystal Waters, Lebensgarten,
Manitou Foundation, Findhorn,
Damanhur, Auroville.
www.gaia.org

Magazines

Communities Magazine
Journal of Cooperative Living
www.ic.org

Permaculture Magazine
Solutions for Sustainable Living
www.permaculture.co.uk

Resurgence
www.resurgence.org

Positive News/Living Lightly
www.positivenews.org.uk

Yes! Journal of Positive Futures
www.yesmagazine.org

The Permaculture Activist
North America's Journal of
Design and Sustainable Culture.
pcactiv@meralab.unc.edu

**Sustainable Energy News
Inforse** (International Network
for Sustainable Energy)
www.inforse.org

The Last Straw
www.strawhomes.com

Ecology and Farming
(The International Federation
of Organic Agriculture
Movements)
www.ifoam.org

Home Power: The hands-on
Journal of home-made Power
www.homepower.com

Global Village News
Newsletter for The Social
Venture Network (a network
of socially responsible
businesses in Europe)
www.svneurope.com

Internet Portals

Ecovillages:
www.gaia.org

Ecovillages in Russia:
apress.ru/pages/chernykh

The Cohousing Network
www.cohousing.org

Fellowship for Intentional
Communities (FIC). The
fellowship includes ecovillages,
cohousing, residential land
trusts, communes, co-ops, and
other related projects
www.ic.org

The Earth Charter
www.earthcharterusa.org

www.webiosphere.org

Centre for Human Ecology
www.che.ac.uk

Idebanken
Bank of Ideas, Norway
www.idebanken.no

Jubilee USA Network
www.2000usa.org

The Interfaith Center for Corporate Responsibility
www.iccr.org

Wuppertal Institute for Climate and Energy
www.wupperinst.org

Eurosolar
www.eurosolar.org

Worldwatch Institute:
www.worldwatch.org
In Context Institute:
www.incontext.org

Integral Institute initiated by Ken Wilber: Integral media, medicine, business, ecology, education, art, politics, psychology, spirituality
www.shambala.com
announcements:
www.shambhala.org

The Bridge
Japanese Newsletter
www.thebridge21.org

The Union of Concerned Scientists
www.ucsusa.org

The International Journal of Sustainability in Higher Education
www.ulsf.org/ publications_ijshe.html

FuelCells
www.fuelcells.org

Rural Advancement Foundation International (RAFI)
www.rafi.org

New US-based developments
www.horizons-ecovillage.com
www.thequarries.com
www.ecotopia.com/ecovillage

OmPlace
Free services for the 'conscious living' community worldwide
www.omplace.com

Ecosustainable Hub
Resources and tools related to environment and sustainability
www.ecosustainable.com.au

EcoLINKvillage
Ecovillages and alternative living resources. Available in Spanish and Portuguese.
www.ecolinkvillage.net

The Simple Living Network
www.nfnc.org

Other links:

www.sustainableabc.com

www.permaearth.org

www.attra.org

www.i4at.org/library.html

www.thesustainablevillage.com

www.thefarm.org/ permaculture/pclinks.html

www.envirolink.netforchange.com

Global Ecovillage Network (GEN)

Offices

GEN Europe/Africa
Lucilla Borio
Via Torri Superiore 5,
18039 Ventimiglia, Italy
info@gen-europe.org
www.gen-europe.org

GEN Oceania/Asia
Max Lindegger
59 Crystal Waters, Maleny,
Queensland 4552, Australia
lindegger@gen-oceania.org
oceania.ecovillages.org

Ecovillage Network of the Americas (ENA)
ENA International,
Albert Bates
The Farm/Ecovillage Training Center
PO Box 90, Summertown,
38483-0090, TN, USA.
ecovillage@thefarm.org
www.thefarm.org

ENA Central Office
Linda Joseph
64001 County Road DD, Moffat,
CO 81143, USA
ena@ecovillage.org
www.ecovillage.org

GEN South Asia
V. Ariyaratne
Sarvodaya Peace Movement
Damsak Mandira, 98 Rawatawatt Road, Moratuwa, Sri Lanka
gensa@sri.lanka.net
www.sarvodaya.org

Note additionally, there are subregional network nodes and national network offices all over the world. To contact the GEN office nearest to you, see www.gaia.org, or contact your regional secretariat.

Natural Building Resource Centers

USA

Natural Building Ressources
The Black Range Lodge
Star Route, Box 119
Kingston, NM 88042
Ph: + 1 (505) 895-5652
blackrange@zianet.com
www.strawbalecentral.com

California Earth Art and Architecture Institute
(Cal-Earth)
10376 Shangri La Avenue
Hesperia, CA 92345
Ph/Fax (706) 244-0614/244-2201
calearth@aol.com
www.calearth.org

Cob Cottage Company
P.O. Box 123
Cottage Grove
OR 97424
Ph: (514) 942-2005
www.deatech.com/cobcottage

DAWN/Out On Bale By Mail
6570 W. Illinois St.
Tucson, AZ 85735
dawnaz@earthlink.net
www.greenbuilder.com/dawn

Development Center for Appropriate Technology
P.O. Box 27513
Tucson, AZ 85726-7513
Ph/Fax (520) 624-6628/ 798-3701
info@dcat.net
www.dcat.net

Earth Building Foundation, Inc.
Earth Architecture Center Intl.
5928 Guadalupe Trail NW
Albuquerque, NM 87107-5430
Ph: +1 (505) 345-2613
mchenry@unm.edu
www.earthbuilding.com

Econest Building Company
P.O. Box 864, Tesuque, NM 87574
Ph: (505) 984-2928/989-1813
bakerlaporte@earthlink.net
www.econests.com

Ecovillage Training Center
The Farm
P.O. Box 90
Summertown TN 38483-0090
Ph/Fax: (615) 964-4324/2200
ecovillage@thefarm.org
www.thefarm.org/etc

Fox Maple School of Traditional Building
P.O. Box 249
West Brownfield, ME 04010
Ph (207) 935-3720
Fax: (207) 935-4575
foxmaple@foxmaple.com
www.foxmaple.com

Institute for Solar Living
P.O. Box 836,13771 S. Hway 101
Hopland, CA 95449
Ph/Fax: (707)744-2017/1682
isl@rgisl.org
www.solarliving.org

Solar Energy International
P.O. Box 715
Carbondale, CO 81623
Ph/Fax: (970) 963-8855/8866
sei@solarenergy.org
www.solarenergy.org

Southwest Solaradobe School
P.O. Box 153, Bosque, NM 87006
Ph/Fax: (505) 861-1255/1304
www.adobebuilder.com

Ecological Building Network
209 Caledonia Street
Sausalito, CA. 94965-1926
Ph: (415) 331-7630
Fax: (415) 332-4072
ecobruce@aol.com
www.ecobuildnetwork.org

International

Association for Environment Conscious Building (AECB)
P.O. Box 32
SA44 5 ZA
Llandysul, Wales, UK
Ph/Fax + 44 (0)1559-370908
buildgreen@aol.com
www.aecb.net

CAT
Centre for Alternative Technology
Machynlleth, Powys
SY20 9AZ, Wales, UK
Ph: +44 (0)1654 705950
Fax: +44 (0) 1654 702782
info@cat.org.uk
www.cat.org.uk

BASIN (Building Advisory Service and Information Network)
www.gtz.de/basin

BASIN Selected partners:

CRATerre
Maison Levrat
Rue du Lac B.P. 53
F-38092 Villefontaine, France
Ph/Fax +33-474-954391/6421
craterre@club-internet.fr
www.craterre.archi.fr

EcoSur
Apdo 107, Jinotepe, Nicaragua
Ph/Fax: +505-4223325
ecosur@ifxnw.com.ni
www.ecosur.org

German Appropriate Technology Exchange (GATE)
Deutsche Gesellschaft für Technische Zusammenarbeit (GTZ)
P.O. Box 5180
D-65726 Eschborn, Germany
Ph/Fax +49-6196-793084/7352
gate-basin@gtz.de
www.gtz.de/gate

Intermediate Technology Development Group
The Schumacher Centre for Technology and Development
Bourton Hall, Bourton on Dunsmore
Warwickshire CV23 9QZ, UK
Ph/Fax +44-1788-661100/1101
itdg@itdg.org.uk
www.itdg.org

Renewable Energy Centers

From the first European Conference for energy Centers, Folkecenter, Denmark, September 24-30, 2001

LEV, LandesEnergieVerein Steiermark
Ulz Gerhard
Burggasse 9/II, A-8010 Graz, Austria
Tel: + 43 316 877 3389
ulz@lev.at

CAT (see "International")

IFED
Federal Agricultural Research Centre (FAL)
N. El Bassam
Bundesallee 50, D-38116 Braunschweig, Germany
Ph: + 49 531 596 2310
nasir.bassam@fal.de

Little Earth (De Kleine Aarde)
Frank Zanderink
P.O. BOX 151, 5280 AD Boxtel,
Klaverblad 1, Netherlands
Ph/Fax + 31 4 11684921/3407
info@dekleineaarde.nl
f.zanderink@dekleineaarde.nl

Artefact
Werner Kiwitt
Bremsbergallee 35
D - 24960 Glücksburg, Germany
Ph: +49 463 161 160/631
artefact@pin-net.de
info@artefact.de

Energy 21
Jackie Carpenter
Tamarisk, Bishop's Walk
Whiteshill, GL6 6BW Stroud
Ph: +44 1453 752 277
info@energy21.org.uk

Ecopower cvba, renewable
energy cooperative
Dirk Knapen
Oude straat 145
B - 2610 Wilrijk
Antwerpen, Belgium
Tel: +32 228 217 31
dirk.knapen@ecopower.be
dirk.knapen@bblv.be

Green Action Zagreb
The Energy Group
Toni Vidan
P.O. BOX 952
10001 Zagreb
Croatia
Tel: +385 1 481 3096/3097
zelena-akcija@zg.tel.hr

Re Energy Wendland
Christian Lutz
Dieter Schaarschmidt
Landstr. 6
29462 Güstritz
Germany
Tel: +49 5843 444
wendland-wind@t-online.de

**Sunflower Farm Ecological
Technology Centre**
Krzysztop Wietrnzny
Stryszow K/Krakowa
34-146 Stryszow
Poland
Ph: + 48 33 879 78 16
krzysztof@sunflowerfarm.com.pl

Ecosite de Meze
Christopher Thornton
27 impasse de Charges
38300 Bourgoin Jallieu
France
Ph: +33 474 930 793
or: +33 608 049 594
M: +33 608 049 594
thornton@thornton.fr

Ecoserveis
Josep Puig
Via Laietana 15, 3er, 4a
08003 Barcelona
Spain
Tel: +34 933 193 586,
or: + 34 934 272 449
ecoserv@eic.ictnet.es
peppuig@eic.ictnet.es
gctpfnn@mx3.redestb.es
contact person
EUROSOLAR Spain
Eduard Toda 98, 1,2
E-08031 Barcelona

**The National Energy
Foundation**
Gareth Ellis
Davy Avenue,
Milton Keynes MK45 5EA
UK
Tel: +44 1908 665 555
gareth@greenenergy.org.uk

**Samsø Energy and
Environment Office**
Birgit Bjornvig
Issehoved 41
8305 Samsø
Denmark

**Economic Institute of the
Belarus National Sciences
Academy**
Pavel Stroev Valerevich
office 1207
Surganova str. 1-2
220072 Minsk
Belarus
Ph: + 375 17 284 18 59
nopoul@pisem.net

Solarinitiative MVc.V.
Brigitte and Ditmar Schmidt
Haus Nr. 9, D-23966 Triwalk
Germany
Ph: +49 3841 78 04 09
solar.simv@t-online.de

Institute EKODA
Alenka Burja
Glinskova ploscad 18
SLO - 1113 Ljubljana
Slovenia
Tel: +386 1 566 14 77
Mobile: +386 41 943 358
alenka.burja@guest.arnes.si,
aburja@yhaoo.com

OVE Europe
The Danish Organization
for Renewable Energy
Gunnar Boye Olesen
Gl. Kirkevej 56
8530 Hjortshøj
Denmark
Tel: + 45 862 270 00
ove@inforse.dk

**Georgian Energy Brigade/FoE
Georgia**, Lasha Chkhetia
182, David Agmashenebeli Ave,
Green House, Mushtaidi Park
380012 Tiblisi
Georgia
Tel: + 995 32 35 19 14/47 51
Fax: + 995 32 35 19 14/00 16 85
energy@greens.org.ge
lasha_chkhetia@hotmail.com

**Albanian Ecological Club -
International Friends of Nature**
Ali Eltari
Rr. Todi Shkurti
P. 13 Sh. 4
Ap. 32, Tirana
Albania
Tel: + 355 4 373 148
eco-club@san.com.al

**Open joint-stock company
ARTES**
Vassily Vessart
Kavalergardskaya ul. 8
office No. 5
193015 St Petersburg
Russia
Ph: +7 812 275-5013/2604
artes@ctinet.ru
vessart@odusz.elektra.ru

Lithuanian Energy Institute
Vladislovas Katinas
Breslaujos 3
LT - 3035 Kaunas
Lithuania
Ph: + 370 7 401 841
Fax+ 370 7 351 271
dange@isag.lei.lt

**Association for Utilisation of
Renewable Energy**
Jan Motlik
The Czech Republic
Ph: + 420 2 210 82 631
motlik@csvts.cz

Czech Environmental Institute
Miroslav Safarik
The Czech Republic
Ph: + 420 2 671 22 267
safarik@ceu.cz

**St Petersburg State
Technical University**
Victor Elistratov
Vladimir Breusov
Polytechnicheskaya 29
195251 St Petersburg
Russia
Ph: + 812 552 77 71
elistrat@cef.spbstu.ru

**Bay Energy Services &
Great Lakes Renewable
Resource
Institute**
Martin Hamilton
3500 N. Putnam Rd., Suttons
Bay, MI 49682
USA
Ph: +1 231 271 4860
mhamilton@bignet.net

Mali-Folkecenter
Tom Burrell
Ousmane Ouattara
B.P. E4211 Bamako
Republic of Mali
Ph: +223 20 06 17/18
mali.folkecenter@afribone.net.ml,
tb@afribone.net.ml

**Renewable Energy Centre
Appolonia**
Wisdom Ahiataku - Togobo
Senior Programme Officer
Ministry of Energy
Private Mail bag
Ministries Post Office
Accra
Ghana
Ph: + 233 21 667 151-3
M: +233 208 139 326
wisdom@netafrique.com,
wtogobo@hotmail.com

**Asia-Pacific Biogas Research
and Training Center (BRTC)**
Zhao Yufeng, Deputy Director
Wu Libin
Director of the Department for
International Exchange
No.13, 4th Section,
People s South Street
Chengdu
610041, Sichuan
P.R.China
Ph/Fax: 0086-28-5252659
or 0086-28-5230695/5230735
wulibin_cbs@sina.com,

Centre for Rural Technology
P.O.Box 3628
Kathmandu, Nepal
India
Ph: 977 1 260 165/256 819
Fax: 977 1 257 922
crt@wlink.com.np

Ganesh Ram Shrestha
ganesh@infoclub.com.np

Rajeev Bahadur Munankami
munankami@wlink.com.np

**Egyptian Wind Energy
Association**
Galal Osman, President
Electrical Eng. Dept., Fac. of
Eng., Mansoura University
P.O. Box 6, Mansoura
A.R.E., Egypt
Ph/Fax: +20 50 320319/322291
mohosman@yahoo.com

Monmar Eng. Co. LTD
Chadraa Batbayar
P.O. BOX 70
Ghinggis Avenue 3
UB - 13 Ulaanbaatar
Mongolia
Ph: +976 951 528 18
Fax: +976 11 342 692
monmar@magicnet.mn

**Association for Development
of the West Region of
Mongolia**
Demberel Terbish
210620 A Ulaanbaatar
Mongolia
Ph/Fax: +976 11 310 937
terbis@mail.parl.gov.mn

Tata Energy Research Institute
Krishna Raghavan
Habitat Place, Lodi Road
110003 New Delhi
India
Ph: +91 11 468 2100/2111
raghavan@teri.res.in

University of Aden
Hussain Al-Towaie
P.O.Box 7141
Almansoora Aden
Yemen
Ph/Fax: 00 967 2 344 510
altowaie@gmx.de

CREATA - IPB
Kamaruddin Abdullah
Indonesia
Ph/Fax: + 62 251 621 886/7
kdin@Bogor.wasantara.net.id

Claude Turmes
MEP, EP
Bureau ASP 08G114
Rue Wiertz
B - 1047 Brussels
Belgium
Ph: + 32 2 28 472 46
cturmes@europarl.eu.int

Folkecenter in Thy,
Kammergaardsvej 16
7760 Sdr Ydby, Thy
Denmark
Jane Kruse
Preben Maegaard, dir.
Information and Training
Ph: + 45 97 95 66 00
jk@folkecenter.dk

Children are our future.

Let us help them become whole human beings, and create a lifestyle which offers them a loving community in a safe environment …

© Peter Engberg

Welcome to the Future ...